Asylum-Seeking **Trauma**

Asylum-Seeking **Trauma**

A Journey Without a Destination

Roben Pfumai Mutwira

Photo: IFCR. www.ifcr.org and ourworld-yourmove.org

Library of Congress Control Number: 2012909515
ISBN: Hardcover   978-1-4771-1879-5
                 Softcover   978-1-4771-1878-8
                 Ebook   978-1-4771-1880-1

This book was printed in the United States of America.

To order additional copies of this book, contact:
Xlibris Corporation
0-800-644-6988
www.xlibrispublishing.co.uk
Orders@xlibrispublishing.co.uk
304002

CONTENTS

'Choose asylum and you lose your property, femininity, dignity, profession, maturity, and life: You become a nobody everywhere.'

Roben Pfumai Mutwira

INTRODUCTION

The experience of the pain of watching a relative being tortured to death; abandoning a dying child, parent, or friend because the alternative can only be your own death; the experience of seeing mutilated bodies of people you used to live with; and watching your homes and what was your village reduced to ashes—all these experiences is unlikely to be adequately reported by people who are not emotionally involved. The people who can tell the whole story are people who experienced this suffering, this pain. Unfortunately, these people often do not have the resources; often do not have a sympathetic audience; and often do not have communication skills, education, or even the correct language. Often these people do not have the time because they are struggling to get basic commodities. They are in the forest looking for places where there are human settlements, because if wounded their wounds may have become septic or because they have contracted malaria; they are trying to avoid bandit groups that will kill them for their little possessions; they may be in the Sahara Desert looking for cover from the merciless sun and boiling sands; or struggling to prove to people in the societies they have chosen to seek asylum that they are victims and not criminals as often assumed. They may be learning the hard way that people do not usually accommodate the foreigners. Even priests who bring food to them as the destitute do not take them into their homes—no. They leave them under the bridges, in collapsing buildings, and under subways. So once you, as an a asylum seeker, leave what is left of what was your home, you know it is the beginning of an endless suffering, of a journey without a destination, and that you are likely never to see your home again. You may be bitten by poisonous snakes; killed by that creeping crocodile; be shot by that child bandit; starved to death in the desert; killed for your faith; drowned in that endless expansion of seawater, be detained and assaulted by what you thought were the civilised people who would save you; and deported back to where you started. But asylum seekers are not choosers. They receive what societies of this world offer them. Their biggest problem is to prove to everyone that they are genuine victims and not criminals.

I am a Zimbabwean asylum seeker who became a destitute in the United Kingdom and was forced to sleep rough for more than thirty days, partly because I did not know where to get help and partly because the help I needed would not be found easily. By the standards of destitution in World over, thirty days is nothing. People have been destitute for years in Europe and elsewhere. But those few days were some of the most frightening in my entire life, not because I would be attacked and killed but because I did not have a clue as to how to solve the problem of destitution. I did not know exactly where I was. I did not know where to go. I did not know how to go because I did not have much money. So I decided to budget and survive on the little money I had. I lived on a small tin of spaghetti and a small packet of biscuits each day. I bathed in the river, which I think was on a farm. During the day, I went around the shops at a local village, collecting newspapers, not for reading but to use as my blankets at night. I was very warm under the trees because newspapers that are wet on top are heavy and warm inside. If I had known where to get my next meal and where to go in winter, I would have felt better. As lecturers and teachers, we were regarded by the Zimbabwe government as the people that taught students and rural people to support opposition parties; that wrote anti-government articles in the papers; and that planned to replace ZANUPF governing party with the MDC. We were therefore in serious danger of being silenced through existing violent means. While my government used a variety of the well documented repressive tools to silence the opposition, their most effective method was common assault. They raided homes at night and took victims to what they called 'bases' and where victims were brought back dead or with serious injuries. If my application for asylum had failed and I was deported, I would probably have gone back to this type of treatment.

Similar forms of torture are now practised in many sub-Saharan African dictatorships. People suffer immeasurable pain for their views, for democracy, which I found to be taken for granted in many countries in Europe. Innocent people have had their limbs chopped off. People have been burned in their houses. There have been mass killings and many have just been driven off their homes. While the war Sierra Leone ended decades ago, there are still post-war conflicts that force people to seek asylum elsewhere. These conflicts often become quite pronounced at election times. There is a lot of post-election victimisation which will meet the requirements of the 1951 UN Refugee Convention. Countries in Africa and Europe approached by people from Sierra Leone should interview these asylum seekers with the understanding of this very disturbing background. In the Great Lakes region, the civil war or indeed regional war involving parts of the Democratic Republic of the Congo, Rwanda, Burundi, parts of Uganda, and parts of southern Sudan was of ethnic rivalry, the attempt by one ethnic group to try to exterminate another and vice versa. Gangs of, say, Hutu soldiers, police, civil servants, and men and women who feel that life would be better without their Tutsi countrymen armed themselves with machetes, spears, knives, and other weapons to kill every Tutsi. They carried out a scorched earth eradication scheme. The Tutsi replied with their own eradication murder scheme. The victims are ordinary people without political agendas. People ran away with only their lives. Genocide swept across countries and the region, and large numbers of mass murders followed. There is a story of a little boy who spent the day herding cattle only to return home to find everyone killed and the home burned down. The boy could be one of the unaccompanied minors that have reached many countries in Europe looking for asylum. Some of these children travel long journeys to claim asylum as unaccompanied children. We will see these children detained and deported;

instead of being sent to school, they are sent to death through deportations.In Somalia, civil wars were caused by shortages of food. The world has seen Somalis that have turned into pirates and labelled all Somali nationals as pirates; the truth is that those that have turned into pirates are a small minority. Majority have become refugees because there are bandits that attack them to steal their little food. These people qualify to be protected under the UN 1951 Refugee Convention.

So each region of the sub-Saharan African subcontinent is experiencing some form of violence, and there is no place asylum seekers can go to except out of the region. Most Zimbabweans have moved south into South Africa. Somalis have moved into Kenya, Tanzania, Eritrea, and many parts of Africa; people of the Great Lakes have also moved into the Kenya, Tanzania, Zambia, Angola, and South Africa. Refugees that chose to seek asylum in neighbouring African countries found themselves caught up in violence similar to or even worse than that they faced at home. But they had one big advantage—they had moved to other countries. They obviously faced many problems, but they managed in some cases to resettle elsewhere.

However, there has been a large number of Africans who, perhaps because of colonial influence, thought they would find sanctuary in Europe. These are the people that made me write this book. Their suffering has not received the 'brutal' press analyses we read of African tragedies, mainly because to do so would indirectly expose the negative side of Western civilisation. But their suffering has been real and lasting. If they did not lose their life in the Sahara Desert, they lost their dignity, their profession, their identity, or their lives in North Africa, in the Mediterranean, or in Europe itself. Those that dared walk across the desert were usually ill-informed youths. Most of them died before they reached any desert settlement.Attempts to cross using organised and paid tranport often carried more water containers than passenger. The average asylum seeker could not afford such transport. Those that did often had to offer their labour to be exploited and abused before they could manage a seat on top of these lorries.

Majority of asylum seekers were guided by local transporters along the outskirts of the deserts but many of these people lost their lives in the Sahara from dehydration, exhaustion, and hunger. Many were cheated by criminals that claimed to know how to take people across the Sahara. There is a full section on the problems of crossing the Sahara in the book.

Majority of those that reach North Africa tell stories of unparalleled form of discrimination, ill-treatment, and imprisonment. Captured persons are detained, often assaulted, and deported back to the south or just into the desert.

But there are those that manage to live in the forests, under bridges, in abandoned places, and so on. There are those that even manage to work and save money to hire boats to cross the Mediterranean Ocean. Majority can only afford to hire makeshift boats and choose to cross the ocean in dangerous, crowded boats which can only be used by people who are ignorant of how rough the sea can become, and without any form of radio communication, they can get lost and die in the sea. In fact, many makeshift boats have been seen floating with dead bodies in the sea. Many ships capsize when sea waves rock the tiny overloaded makeshift structures or small fishing boats meant for fishing along the sea coast.

Many have been turned away by joint Italian and Libyan forces, and some have been rescued hanging on to capsized vehicles. All the southern European states have put in place mechanisms to monitor their seas for stranded ships. Europe has also set up the organisation Frontex to rescue drowning people and bring them to the coast and arrange to take them back to Africa.

Europe is different from Africa in that they have asylum legislation to operate on. While treatment of asylum seekers has been bad and sometimes worse than in some parts of Africa, Europe often records its actions. Many asylum seekers that reach southern Europe are captured, detained, and either deported without further processing, or processed before deportation, or processed for asylum. The places they are detained are generally overcrowded and untidy and unsuitable for human habitation. Any detention centre in southern Europe that does not fit this description is an exception. Most detention centres are prisons, former army barracks, and storage rooms at airports, abandoned homes, and similar places no longer used in the current state structures.

The book details detention systems and lengths of detention in each country. But there are those that choose not to claim asylum in the coast countries, because to do so would force them to remain in these countries as their asylum homes. They chose to live in subways, under bridges, abandoned buildings, and even in caves until they found ways to raise money to travel to countries they wished to claim asylum. They often have no money and survive on donations or help from charities or churches.

Life is particularly difficult in cold seasons. In countries where there are helpful voluntary organisations, they are provided with food and sometimes even provided with temporary accommodation. But there are countries where asylum seekers that have not yet claimed have had to build temporary accommodation using available resources.

Few are lucky to get asylum in countries of their choice. But most asylum seekers wait for an average period of five years.

This book is therefore about helping people, from African politicians to European governments, that the life of an asylum seeker is very difficult. It is a life of dedication, self-determination, and struggle. When an asylum seeker approaches you, please appreciate what he could have gone through. While your word *yes* or *no* could be easy to say, it would affect the life of a person who may have been suffering in different places in the world to reach your office. Your *no* may mean the end of his life or may mean the person has to go through the many years of suffering again.

CHAPTER 1

Sub-Saharan Africa—the Home of Private Armies

When the European countries receive asylum seekers, it is important to bear in mind that the sub-Saharan Africans are not coming from first world states with democratic governments, modern economic systems, and developed social structures. Many of them are coming from villages regularly raided and taxed by rival bandit groups based in the neighbourhood; by self-styled police units that serve the state by day and are bandit leaders at night; and by state armies that often force the villagers to provide free labour at private mines, on their farms, and elsewhere. Politicians also hire these armies or militias to force people to attend political gatherings and to vote for them. Reprisals for disobedience are usually brutal, characterised by assaults and murders. The state often has no machinery to follow up cases of violence in rural area, and often they secretly approve of it. There are several reasons why sub-Saharan security systems are in a state of decay and why many families are displaced and are seeking refuge in other parts of the subcontinent and the diaspora. At the end of the colonial system, newly elected African leaders were made to inherit unbearable IMF and World Bank loans for economic decisions made by their former colonisers, and that had little benefit to the non-urban majority population. They were asked to continue the colonial system and become the new colonisers.

African politicians, therefore, rejected monetary systems directly controlled by American, British, French, IMF and World Bank, and other UN economic structures and opened doors to new as well as informal alternatives. The result was that the sub-Saharan transnational organisations acquired significant power resources. Transnational corporations such as former South African corporation, Lonrho (London/Rhodesia) and Bridgestone, that chose work with the post colonial leaders, became political players in sub-Saharan African economies as they were turned into mediators between rivals informal traders and became providers of the link between Europe and sub-Saharan Africa. Many new regional multinational companies followed their example. Over thirty locally based multinationals emerged, some of which are Equity Bank in Kenya, operating in Kenya, southern Sudan, Uganda, Rwanda, and Tanzania; Atlantic group in Ivory Coast, a broad conglomerate with operations ranging from agribusiness to insurance in nine countries and in France; SEACOM based in Mauritius—it lays submarine and terrestrial fibre optic cable to supply communications bandwidth across much of African continent, especially East Africa; United Bank of Africa—it has branches in seventeen sub-Saharan countries; AICO Africa Limited based in Zimbabwe—involved in integrated agribusiness. It started in 2003 and distributed seed mostly Zambia and Malawi for expansion into Tanzania, Kenya Ethiopia, and other countries in the region; Gulf Energy in Kenya is involved in trade, distribution, and retail of petroleum-based products. It has expanded into Rwanda, Tanzania, Uganda, and Zambia; Imara Holdings Limited in Botswana—provide financial services specialising in corporate finance, assets management, and securities trading; and many others. All these had to cooperate with the state structures in order to survive. Through these institutions, the sub-Saharan politicians channelled misappropriated personal wealth to the international banks. They bought private and personal properties in Europe using state resources. The result is that throughout the region, national institutions have virtually disappeared: There are no proper roads, bridges, schools, and hospitals in most of the countries, but everywhere politicians have become extremely rich and irresponsible. The few paragraphs below analyse how security systems of the sub-Saharan region have become chaotic, how security systems have been turned into violent structures serving the political elite, and why millions of people have had to seek refuge in other parts of the world.

One of the most profound effects of the end of the Cold War has been the reduction of the US government involvement in African affairs. The United States during the Cold War had moulded the African political landscape, not necessarily in a favourable way as can be seen from the aid they offered Sudan, Zaire, Kenya, Somalia, Ethiopia, and Liberia. Africa suddenly lost strategic significance to both United States and Russia. Throughout the Cold War, buildup continued to be financed by countries of the north even though sub-Saharan Africa could not pay for them, and much of the debt was written off. The end of the Cold War suddenly changed all that. *Today, military spending in sub-Saharan Africa accounts for less than one per cent of global military expenditure and continues to fall* (Clapham, ibid., p. 195). Only Angola, South Africa, and Nigeria have been importers of reasonable quantities of arms in the post-Cold War sub-Saharan Africa. Globally, manpower absorbed in military activities has been declining. But sub-Saharan Africa failed to follow this trend and increased the number and names of armies in the 1990s. In the sub-Saharan context, the exact number of soldiers in a country is not even known by the commanders. Not only are the variable statistics notoriously unreliable, but more importantly, the delineation of what should be considered as armed forces is ambiguous, as many countries have seen a proliferation of a variety of armed formation in recent years. Presidential guards are often better paid and equipped than the army, navy, or air force. *Sometimes, it is also unclear whether state formations have been appropriated for private interests or whether private formations have come to substitute government functions. In any case the functions of the military in sub-Saharan Africa do not reflect the clear separation between internal and external security which is normally represented by the police and the military separately.* (Peter Lock: Africa, military downsizing and growth in the security industry: Strategic Analysis: Vol. 22, No. 9, 1998; p. 15). Logistical capacities of the national armed forces often do not cover the entire national territory, and operational equipment seldom amounts to more than small arms and the most basic infantry equipment. The Stockholm International Peace Research Institute (SIPRI) claims that between 1993 and 1997, only 144 tanks, 352 armoured vehicles, eight combat aircraft, eleven helicopters, 54 pieces of artillery, and fourteen transport aircraft or helicopters at most were imported by countries engaged in conflicts in the region. All the imported systems were relatively unsophisticated, and most were second hand. According to SIPRI, however, these imported weapon systems did not play a significant role in the conflicts (Lock, ibid.). Police forces are in equally disastrous condition.

One development which has been a major source of instability and violence is the attempts being made by some politicians to redraw the boundaries of states along ethnic lines. Somalia, Central African Republic, Sudan, Eritrea, Uganda, Nigeria, and Democratic Republic of the Congo, to name just a few, are awash with ethnic rivalries. Ethnic groups in Eritrea and southern Sudan have managed to secede from Ethiopia and Sudan, respectively. This was achieved at a heavy loss of human life and destruction of property. Many innocent people from these areas are still struggling to get a place to stay. Some of them have reached Europe and are among the refugee communities there. Like in the colonial days, the control of resources has become the key to the demarcation of political power. One of the main factors for the emergence of southern Sudan besides religion was the control of the pastures and the minerals. The Biafra section of Nigeria wants to secede from the rest of the country for the same reasons. But there are other reasons. The violence in the Lakes region of Central Africa is tribal. The Hutu or Tutsi rivalry has cost the region millions of lives. Unfortunately, because of the availability of rare minerals in the region, criminal elements have financed the ethnic rivalries in order to force villagers to mine and export minerals for them. They used the most extreme forms of violence—rape, torture, abduction of school children, and forced prostitution. The local elite are the absolute arbiter and main beneficiaries. They control not only the armed bandits, informal miners, and traders but also communications with the external traders. The incumbent elite have masterminded the new corruption rooted in the logic of economic and political liberalisation, reflecting the activity of rapacious local elite, no longer subject to the domestic and international constraints of the Cold War era, and increasingly pervaded by criminal or Mafioso forces. Under pressure of adjustment, the incumbent elite often abandon their social obligations and concentrate on safeguarding their economic fiefdoms, while duly paying lip service, the imposed state or financial regime. As more and more core functions of the state are passed on to the financial regime, we end up with the creation of shadow states. In a number of sub-Saharan countries, the state is slowly being merged into a web of informal business associations instituted by the rulers who have little interest in carrying out the traditional functions of the state and who do not recognise or respect boundaries while enriching themselves through trade. The failure of the formal state as a normative authority made the informal settlement the norm, arbitrariness the rule, corruption a political philosophy, and shrewd double-dealing the only means of existence.

The elite networks maintain their leverage at the price of relying increasingly on violent coercion, while the cannibalisation of all public goods becomes the rule. Rent-seeking continues to expand alongside the growth of illegal activities and an influx of dirty money. Violence, as a mode of economic regulation, penetrates an increasing number of economic spheres and thus prepares the ground for an escalation of armed conflict and anarchy.

The ensuing structure of economic, financial, and political power increasingly deprives the formal state of the means with which to carry out even its minimum functions. The extensive community of public servants which expanded under the patrimonial state is now being denied and relieved of its income. The state fails to pay salaries regularly, if it does at all. Rampant inflation, often caused by criminal fiscal manipulation such as bringing printed money into circulation on behalf of kleptocratic leaders, has devalued public salaries to such an extent that office holders must either extort illegal fees for their services or moonlight in the private sector or the informal economy. The elite, both in the state and the informal structures, abandon withdraw allegiance and abandon their former power base without remorse (Lock op. cit. p 20).

The police and the military are not spared from this absolute weakening of the state and the resulting privatisation of its functions. In all but name, all armed agents of the state in most countries can be described as demobilisation in slow motion. The rules on which the market economy is based are no longer enforced. On the contrary, the public security forces either sell their services to an oligarchic group or live on some form of extortion themselves. In response to the resulting general insecurity, all social sectors take up their defence against criminality. This privatisation of security polarises society, because security is converted into a commodity. It can either be purchased in the regular economy from a private security company, in a grey area by buying off state agents, in the informal sector by militarisation, or in the criminal sector by paying a racketeer. Once violence has begun to regulate economic transactions, the search becomes a major occupation, as it is a functional precondition to the successful conclusion of any transaction. An escalation in private security providers is the logical consequence, which eventually takes on the dimension an internal arms race, encompassing mainly small arms. The productivity of the economy, including the criminal and informal sectors, rapidly contracts further because of cumulative transaction costs related to security.

It is a small step from such a condition in a society to the breakdown of armed conflicts, from a criminalised economy to a war economy. In both cases, security is the major concern and violence a principal means to achieve mainly economic objectives. While demobilisation is typically associated with the end of armed conflicts, it is argued here that many weakened states are faced with the de facto demobilisation of their armed agents even without an open-armed conflict coming to an end. In the process, security personnel, both military and police alike, transform themselves into private instruments of violence, offering their services to the highest bidder either as moonlighters or full-time, notwithstanding the criminal character of the services required. Alternatively, they enter into the world of pillage, looting, and extortion (Lock, ibid., p. 20).

The key interest of this book is the plight of the refugees who are victims of this whole political and economic confusion. Refugees get caught up in five types of violence. There is violence between the refugees and the sending states. We have seen that the sub-Saharan states are generally urban centred, too weak to defend their borders, and often do not have the resources to do so. So sending states often follow the refugees in their refugee camps for taxes, labour, and other benefits. Often they end up with the most destructive results. Rwandan Hutu raids into the Democratic Republic of the Congo, after the Rwandan genocide had disastrous results. Somali rebel groups entered Kenya to punish refugees that entered the refugee camps there, and the result was that the Kenyan army entered southern Somalia in a fully fledged war. The entry of refugees into a neighbouring state can result in conflict between the refugees themselves and the receiving state. When 3,000,000 Zimbabwean refugees entered South Africa in the year 2000, there was chaos and the breakdown of systems as Zimbabwean refugees became destitute on the streets of the main towns and they flooded the employment agencies for jobs. Then the Palestinian refugees in Jordan in 1988 nearly catalysed a civil war. Refugee groups may have ethnic of factional infighting, which, in turn, draws the receiving state into the conflict. Various Burundian Hutu groups in Tanzania suffered such spill over violence in 1972. The arrival of refugees may spark internal conflict within the receiving state, possibly by creating an unstable ethnic balance. The best example is the Kosovo-Albanian refugees who fled Macedonia-aggravated tension between ethnic Albanians and Serbs in Macedonia in the late 1990s. Interstate wars or unilateral intervention may target refugee groups. The 1998 Rwandan intervention in the DRC, for instance, aimed at removing Hutu refugee groups in the eastern DRC.

Besides governments that have become dysfunctional, there are some that have become so irresponsible that they have employed tactics of terrorism in the brutal crackdown against opposition members in Zimbabwe. President Omar al-Basher of Sudan has become the first sitting head of state to be indicted by the International Criminal Court for crimes against humanity. In Senegal, riots erupted in the streets to protest against President Abdoulaye Wade's attempt to change the constitution in an effort to be elected another term in office. Refugees have had to escape from state orchestrated terrorism and to travel to foreign countries for asylum. But most of the rural regions of sub-Saharan Africa are controlled by terrorist groups that have a wide range of objectives. Below are a few examples of terrorist groups that have made life impossible for the ordinary living people and have forced them into exile.

Uganda

Uganda has two main rebel groups that have forced thousands of Ugandans to go into exile: the Allied Democratic Forces and the Lord's Resistance Army. These are two 'religious' but politically motivated groups that have caused at least 10 000 deaths in their respective military regions. They have fought against state forces and among themselves. They have caused millions of displacements, resulting in the creation of several IDP communities and forcing many to seek asylum beyond their borders. Like other bandit groups in the Great Lakes area, they have taken advantage of the military weaknesses of the host countries to diffuse across multiple borders namely Democratic Republic of the Congo, South Sudan, Uganda and Central African Republic.

(i) The Allied Democratic Forces

They are a rebel group formed in the 1990s, comprising of self-identified 'religious crusades' from the Muslim Tabligh sect, opposing the government. They were based in western Uganda and moved frequently into the DRC. Attacks are varied from the use of brute force and assaults to kidnappings and hostage taking of youths who would be forced to assist the Allied Democratic Forces. They made two notable abductions in 1998: One involved the kidnapping of thirty students from the Mitandi Seventh Day Adventist College in Kasese, and the other involved the abduction of more than 100 schoolchildren from the Hoima District. In another brutal display of terror, the Allied Democratic Forces killed eighty students of the Kichwamba Technical College in the Kabarole District. They locked the dormitories and set them on fire. Between 1997 and 2001, the Allied Democratic Forces' violent campaigns were centred around Kampala. Here they detonated forty-eight explosive devices, which killed forty-eight people and injured an estimated 200 others.

(ii) The Lord's Resistance Army

The movement dates back to 1987. In the last twenty-five years, it has carried out atrocities directed at civilians in the northern region of Uganda. Operating as an ideologically apocalyptic Christian group opposing central government, its modus operandi has been to use violence or the threat of violence to intimidate and instil fear in the Ugandan people, and more specifically the Acholi tribe. Although its objectives are not always clear, the decades of indiscriminate violence with political undertones have made this group one of the more well-known rebel groups using terrorism as a method in their campaigns. Recently, this rebel group has begun operating the borders of the DRC and Sudan, showing that the leadership may not be contemplating fighting a war to take over any government. They just want to trade informally, accumulate personal wealth, and persecute people they abuse as labourers, soldiers, and spies. Meanwhile, they have followed families they previously displaced and robbed and tortured them, forcing them to seek asylum further afield.

The bandit movement continues to take advantage of the structural weakness of its host environment to diffuse across multiple borders, namely the Democratic Republic of the Congo, southern Sudan, and the Central African Republic.

Overall, the Allied Democratic Forces and the Lord's Resistance Army are examples of two non-state, religious, and politically motivated groups that have caused at least 10,000 deaths in their respective military campaigns and millions of displacements, resulting in creation of several IDP communities and forcing others to seek asylum outside the region.

Sudan

Darfur area: There are over fourteen armed bandits in the area alone. This is why Sudanese from this area are applying for refugee status in many parts of the world.

(i) Justice and Equality Movement

It is an exclusively Zaghawa tribe movement with a few combatants, perhaps 3,000 men. But it is the only movement with a lot of money. Although the Zaghawa make up only 2 per cent of the population of Darfur, Justice and Equality Movement has links with the National Popular Congress Party, a split wing of the ruling Nation Congress Party. The leader of the National Popular Congress Party, Hassan al-Turabi, took most of the money from the National Congress Party when it split, and now he finances the Justice and Equality Movement.

Other Sudanese Militia Groups: There are twelve to fourteen movements, which start with Sudan Liberation Movement. They then add the name of their tribal names, for example, Massalit, Meidob, Tunjier, or Dajo, to distinguish themselves from each other. These various Sudan Liberation Movements together can command between 12,000 and 15,000 men, but they are all financially broke. They, therefore, depend on either looting from the poor villagers or outside support from Libyans,

Chadians, and Eritreans. Overall, they are very poor, armed, and dangerous.

Chad

There are more than seven armed bandit movements in Chad.

(i) Union des Forces pour la Démocratie et le Développement

This is the main terrorist group that has between 2,000 and 3,000 men. It is mostly Gorane movement. The Gorane are northern tribes and are part of the Borkou or Ennedi or Tibesti group of tribes bordering Libya. In 2006, they signed a 'peace deal' in Tripoli, together with a number of other groups, but they did not insist very much on the implementation, because they preferred violence, which remained their only source of livelihood.

(ii) The Rally des Forces pour le Changement (RFC)

This is almost a family movement coming from the Kobe Zaghawa clan and the Bidayat people, who are closely related. The RFC enjoys plenty of support from Khartoum, which is trying to achieve two things by supporting the RFC: (a) overthrow President Idriss Déby who supports anti-Khartoum Darfur guerrillas; (b) undercut the ethnic base of Zaghawa ethnic base of the Justice and Equality Movement by creating a pro-Zaghawa armed group, which can then be used against the anti-Khartoum Zaghawa. The RFC commands about 3,000 men.

(iii) The Front Uni pour le Changement (FUC)

FUC is based on the small Tama tribe in eastern Chad. It joined the government in March 1998, and Mohammed Nour Abdelkirim became the minister of defence. But he refused to have his men disarmed, and in October, they began to be involved in dissident attacks on government forces, even as their leader remained as minister of defence, creating an ambiguous situation. So

Derby sacked him in November. His men have now joined the anti-government violent activities, which characterise the nation.

(iv) Front Populaire pour la Renaissance Nationale

This is a small force of only about 800 men. They are led by a former Chadian Army Colonel, Adam Yakub. Although small, they have attacked the Chadian army position with some success.

(v) The Convention Nationale Tchadienne (CNT)

The CNT was one of the organisations which signed the peace agreement in Tripoli. Although its leadership had respected the agreement the subordinates did not and fighting broke out between the parent movements. There is constant infighting within the 1,000 plus body of bandits.

(vi) Mouvement Populaire pour la Renaissance et le Développement

It is an ethnically mixed movement with a Gorane leadership and a southern rank-and-file. It has about 500 men. They started fighting in late 2007.

(vii) The UFDD-Fondamentale

It is a split movement from several others. It has only about 500 men. It signed the October 2006 agreement but away in late December 2007.

In January 2008, a number of these organisations joined forces to try and remove President Déby with the support of Khartoum but failed even though they managed to enter the capital N'Djamena. All the Chadian groups are given almost all their support by Khartoum.

Central African Republic (CAR)

There are no properly organised guerrilla groups in CAR. Bandit operations in the north (around Birao) have been carried out by loose collectives of Sara groups, which used to support Former President Ange-Félix Patassé (overthrown by General François Bozizé in a coup in 2003). These men, who are vaguely politicised bandits, exist only inasmuch as they get money from Khartoum. Khartoum's idea was to re-overthrow the Bozizé regime and bring back their friend, Patassé. This plan did not work because the French (who have intervened in many former francophone disputes in favour of their business associates) sent about 600 men who stopped the ill-equipped rebels that did not even have a serious base.

CAR guerrillas are mostly self-financed through acts of banditry. From time to time, they receive very limited support from Khartoum.

Somalia

There are two main guerrilla movements in Somalia: Alliance for the Re-Liberation of Somalia, supported by Eritrea; and Shabab al-Islami, supported by al-Qaeda.

(i) Alliance for the Re-Liberation of Somalia (ARS)

Somali Islamists, loyal to the transitional federal government, walked past bullet-riddled buildings during a patrol in northern Mogadishu on 26 May 2009. (Reuters/Ismail Taxta)

The ARS is generally subservient to Eritrea. It was founded at a conference there in September 2007 and is based in Asmara. It replaced the Union of Islamic Courts which stopped operations in December 2006. The court-based militias are numerous, and although now a part of the ARS, they have, in fact, never merged. Each has maintained its military commanders, weaponry, and power base. 90 per cent of these court-based militias are in

Mogadishu town proper, the whole movement having very little base outside the capital.

(ii)Shabab al-Islami (Islamic Youth)

While ARS is supported by Eritrea, al-Shabab is supported by al-Qaeda. It is not possible to know how many men are in these two groups. But because of the suffering they have caused to Somalis and their neighbours, the whole region is now involved in trying to control their brutality. Ethiopia has sent about 25,000 soldiers to Somalia; Uganda has sent some 1,600 men. Unfortunately, the Uganda troops do not keep much peace in the country. They just remain holed up in their barracks, go for short trips outside, and hope they do not get shot. Their commander, General Katumba Wamala, in fact, brokered a pact of non-belligerence with al-Shabab, which was only broken in January 2007 when Shabab attacked the Ugandan base. The Burundi armed forces have sent a few hundred men within the AMISOM framework, as the Ugandans have not been equally useful. Only the Ethiopians and the Transitional Federal Government (TFG), which has between 7,000 and 8,000 men, do most of the fighting. Most of the forces are from the Majerteen from Puntland who have been mobilised personally by the Somali President. From the middle of 2011, the TFG received support from Kenya which drove Shabab from the rest of southern Somalia and parts of Mogadishu.

Eritrea

There is no big anti-Isaias, that is, anti—Eritrean government organisation. Rather, the Ethiopians have managed to create a kind of 'federation' composed of fourteen different opposition movements, which included Eritrean Islamic Reform Movement and Eritrean Democratic Alliance. But the federation is of extremely dubious efficiency. There is a third organisation called the Eritrean Revolutionary Democratic Front, which is a big-sounding name for a small fighting commando. In fact, the movement is more of a political organisation rather than a military one.

All Eritrean rebel movements are financed by Ethiopia. In recent years, some organisations have managed to get some funding from overseas, mainly the United States.

Ethiopia

There are two main rebel movements and a couple of small ones.

(i) The Oromo Liberation Front (OLF)

This used to be a very powerful rebel movement with a force of some 14,000 men at its height in 1991. Today it has become much smaller, with about 5,000 men. Although its strength is getting lost around the country, it has, however, maintained a semi-permanent strength among the Wollega in the west, among the Lutheran communities where the Mekane Yesus Church remains suspect of pro-OLF tendencies, and among the southern Sidamo community by the Kenyan border. OLF forces often cross into Kenya when on the run, and there are instances when the Ethiopian forces have pursued them into the Kenyan territory. The organisation can be said to be in financial crisis, but there are times when it receives support from the United States, Germany, and Canada. The movement has solid support from Eritrea.

(ii) The Ogaden national Liberation Front (ONLF)

The movement has its support among the southern Ogaden clans like the Aulihan, the Mohamed Zubeyr, and the Rer Ugas and some northern Ogaden clans and non-Ogaden clans living in Ogaden. At its strongest point, the rebel movement can raise the support of about 8,000 combatants. Its main support comes from Eritrea, but it is receiving support from the United Kingdom, Sweden, and Germany.

(iii) Smaller groups

The Ethiopian Popular Patriotic Front is based in Amhara and operated around Gondar. It has a force of between 5,000 and 6,000 men and mainly supported by Eritrea.

The Tigrean National Alliance for Democracy has a force of about 400 men mainly from Asmara.

There are also the Ugugumo and Ajar Revolutionary Democratic Front.

Sierra Leone

(i) The Revolutionary United Front

The rebel movement was active throughout the 1990s. The objective of this movement was to overthrow the government. Its membership and financial support came from both Sierra Leone and Liberia. The organisation's activities included violent attacks on the communities in order to induce widespread fear and submission. Its decade-long policy of youth abduction to build its ranks and attacks that involved cutting off hands, arms, and legs of civilians and government troops resulted in thousands of child soldiers and amputees by 2002.

Zimbabwe

Although Zimbabwe has not had anti-government guerrilla movements in the country, most of the violence was orchestrated by the ZANU-PF ruling party, which was made up of former liberation war guerrillas who created a dictatorship of the ruling party. Like other sub-Saharan states, its military strength gradually collapsed, and military personnel became strong persons in different parts of the country. But because their leader Robert Mugabe allowed them to independently accumulate personal wealth as long as they did it in the name of ZANU-PF, different violent organisations emerged under the umbrella name ZANU-PF. The major names were Zimbabwe National Army (ZNA), Zimbabwe Republic Police (ZRP), Zimbabwe Prison Service (ZPS), The Presidential Guard (PG), Central Intelligence Association (CIA), Central Intelligence Organisation (CIO), and the War Veterans Association (WVA). All these organisations are headed by the elite, who are almost all former army commanders. There are heads of almost all major commercial institutions, be it in agribusiness, mining, manufacturing, or industry. These use youths recruited in different parts of the country as members of the WVA. The youths work either under operation names for the youth movement or for the particular scheme. For example, where they are used to force people to vote for a particular ZANU-PF candidate, they are formed into a movement, like the Green Bombers, Youth Brigades, or Chipangano. They are to force people to move away from a land the elite have identified for their project; then they give the project a name rather than the youth, for example, Operation Gukurahundi (used to kill opposition members in Matabeleland; 20,000 people were slaughtered) and Operation Murambatsvina, which forced tens of thousands of persons of foreign origin out of the country. These people, who had been the backbone of the farm labour but had been forced into towns when Mugabe took the white-owned farms, were driven out of the country because they had become members of the opposition parties. These youths forced people to gather regularly for ZANU-PF party. The culture of fear became intense at election times. The youths were used to capture opposition candidates and torture and kill some of them. When the workers formed a workers' party, the Movement for Democratic Change, in 1999 and the party became very popular, ZANU-PF turned the country into a war zone, abducting leaders of the MDC and murdering them, beating up villagers for attending MDC rallies, and causing all forms of mayhem. As a result of their violence, over *3,000,000* people took refuge in South Africa. Over a million others sought refuge in the United Kingdom, United States, Canada, and Australia. Smaller numbers moved into the other neighbouring countries.

The Great Lakes Region

The story of sub-Saharan African refugees would be incomplete if we left out the violence, the murders, the genocide, the rape, the human suffering which took place in the Great Lakes region between 1985 and 2005. This is the first of the two regional wars that impacted seriously on the lives of rural poor and resulted in mass emigration and refugee problems in Central Africa and the diaspora. Thousands of asylum seekers struggling to get status in the United Kingdom today escaped from the Rwandan genocide, DRC banditry, and gang rapes and tortures that took place in these parts of the world. People were locked in houses and burned alive. We interviewed a woman who jumped into a burning house to save her daughter. When she came out covered in a flame, people poured water on her to save her. She survived but lost the body skin. Now people do not want her in the village because she is said to be a ghost.

For much of the post-independence period in Rwanda, Uganda, Burundi, and southern Sudan, there was Hutu or Tutsi ethnic rivalry based on the fact that although the Tutsis were in the minority, they were the traditional rulers in the region. This was reversed when a Hutu president was elected and died in a plane crash which was said to have been downed by the Tutsi militants. There followed a civil war which turned into ethnic cleansing. The Hutus tried to clear Rwanda of the Tutsis. In just 100 days, over 800,000 Tutsis were slaughtered in a genocide unprecedented in Africa. Two million Tutsis fled mainly into the DRC. In Burundi, 150,000 Hutus fled from what was regarded as a Tutsi region. Most of them moved also into the DRC. With outside help, a Tutsi-led government was formed in Rwanda, and this resulted. A militia group of Hutus, the Interahamwe, fled also into the DRC in 1996. The Interahamwe were said to have participated in the genocide. Mobutu Sese Seko, who was the president of the DRC which he had named Zaire but had little control of the country outside the main towns, tried to force the Rwandans and the Burundian Tutsis out of Zaire. The DRC Tutsis, the Banyamulenge, had lived in the northern parts of the DRC for 200 years. But the Tutsi groups sought assistance from the newly elected Tutsi government of Rwanda. Rwanda and Burundi helped form a movement led by Laurent-Désiré Kabila, which fought a protracted war that forced Mobutu to leave the country. Then Kabila removed the Tutsi personnel from his command and expelled them. This resulted in a regional war involving armies from Rwanda, Burundi, Uganda, Sudan, Central African Republic, Congo, Angola, Namibia, and Zimbabwe and entered the DRC. The country was split into four regions of warring groups. Kabila's army controlled the area coloured yellow on the map with the help of soldiers and weapons brought in from France, South Africa, and China. There were no DRC government forces in the rest of the country. The three main military groups were the Mouvement de Liberation du Congo (MLC), led by Jean-Pierre Bemba, dominated by the Congolese from the equatorial region, and fought with the help of the Ugandan forces in the areas coloured pink and blue areas on the map below. In the blue area, they were supported by about thirteen militia groups: ex-FAZ, RCD-N, RCD-K, ML, FLC, UNDF, FRPI, Hema militia, UPR, NALU, ADF, LRA, and Lendu militia that were backed by Rwanda forces. In the pink area was the Rassemblement Congolais pour la Democratie-Goma (RCD-Goma) group, led by Ernest Wamba dia Wamba. This was a Tutsi-dominated group assisted by Rwanda.

There were also seven other militia groups: MLC, ALC, FLC, ANC, ex-FAZ, FACO, CAR, and SANDF. The green area was dominated by RCD-Goma. But there were about sixteen militia groups, namely, ex-FAZ, FDRL, ARD, Les Simba, Mai-Mai militia, Banyamulenge, Interahamwe, ALIR, NCDD-FDF, FLOP, les Mongoles, Ngilima, FRP, FLN, and FAB. The yellow area was dominated by the Kabila army, supported by Zimbabwe (ZNA), Angola (FAA), Namibia (NDF), Chad (ANT), UNITA, WNBF, and Cocoye militia. A ceasefire was agreed in 1999, but foreign forces remained in the country until 2003. In fact, in the east of the country, foreign forces went on to form some kind of governing body which remained there until 2010.

In Rwanda alone, over a million people lost their lives. The total number of deaths will never be known. We can estimate it to between three and five million lives lost. Millions of others were displaced. People were injured, children were abducted, and women and children were raped; some were gang-raped. There are numerous documentaries that have been made on the suffering of the people of the Great Lakes. Fewer reports, however, have been made on the process of looking for refuge. Little has been written on how people leave homes hurriedly, with little or no possessions, the basics they are sometimes forced to leave, the forms of transport they use, and where they resettle. Little has been written on how hostile many of the hosts are and the adjustments people have to make. Little is also written of the cost of keeping asylum seekers and of how cooperative asylum seekers become in a foreign country. Hutu fighters who arrived at the Tanzanian border readily surrendered their weapons to the host country officials.

Little is written about the politicians that caused all this suffering. Most literature you read from Africa, in fact, praises the African politicians. African scholars tend to be the mouthpiece of politicians, blaming colonialism for all the errors made in the post-colonial state. But I think African academics must rise above the rhetoric and place the blame where it should be. African problems are not taken seriously by the rest of the world because Africans themselves have not yet accepted that they have irresponsible governments; that the suffering of their people is partly because of their poor administration. This, of course, is not an attempt to exonerate the colonial system. The system was cruel, racist, and brutal, but Africa must learn not to live in the past. There is no justification for failing to notice the suffering of emigrating people as seen in the long queue of women and children trying to leave war zone as seen in the pictures in most papers written of wars in Africa. Women (and children walk many miles under the merciless sun, over treeless mountains, and across sand dunes for safety.

So Africa's greatest problems today are not caused by flooded rivers, earthquakes, or tsunamis but by human beings, mainly politicians so selfish that their subjects have suffered more than victims of floods and volcanic eruptions. Academics that wrote emotionally about slavery and colonialism may have to revise their works after reading what the African politicians have done to their people in the post-colonial African state. African refugees, whose ancestors were forced into Europe as forced labour, now arrive on their own to beg for protection from the African oppressors, and the Europeans now struggle to keep them away. This is the tragedy of the African independent state.

The book will not discuss asylum seeking in Africa, although the majority of displaced African people seek asylum in other African countries. The book will not go into reasons why many African countries have had coup d'états, military governments, and dictators. Many scholars apportion blame to colonialism, cold war strategies, armed races, and corruption. Taking the route of debating these issues require a separate book. My view is African politicians have used all these excuses in order to exploit their own people. They should be replaced by leaders with leaders that love to develop their nations. African people will remain the poorest in the world as long as they fail to replace these disports with democratic persons. The book will look at these people's suffering as it follows the journeys of asylum seeker. So the first and shorter part of the book will be on the routes followed by selected individuals and the problems they faced along the way.

CHAPTER 2

Sub-Saharan Africa's Internally Displaced Persons

According to the *Foreign Policy Magazine* of 3 January 2012, seven of the world's top ten failed states are in Africa: Somalia (1), Chad (2), Sudan (3), Democratic Republic of the Congo (4), Zimbabwe (6), Central African Republic (8), and Ivory Coast (10). From these countries come almost twelve million internally displaced persons (IDPs), nearly half of the world's 27.1 million. An unknown number of persons have been forced out of these countries to be refugees all over the world. The present estimate is three million. This makes Africa the most affected continent, and sub-Saharan Africa the region of the world with the highest number of IDPs. IDPs are not protected by the 1951 UN Refugee Convention and the 1967 Protocol. The region has close to a thousand NGOs, but very little is heard of their work with IDPs. Very little is heard of the work of the African Union (AU) either. Jimmy Kainja said the following of the African Union:

It is absolutely appalling that Africa Union (AU) and its discarded predecessor, the Organisation of African Union (OAU) never bothered to address this issue for their combined forty-six years of existence. The AU finally brought the issue on the agenda last year at a special summit that took place in Kampla, the

Ugandan capital on 23 October 2009. (Untold Stories of Africa's Internally Displaced Persons: 30 November 2010)

Sudan account for more than 40 per cent of Africa's total, with around five million people displaced in various regions. Along with Columbia, it was one of the two countries most affected by internal displacement in the world. The Darfur region alone, with between 1.9 and 2.7 million IDPs, has more IDPs than the two next biggest areas combined, the DRC (1.7 million) and Somalia (1.5 million). IDPs in Sudan, DRC, and Somalia together represented more than 70 per cent of all IDPs in Africa. As the world talks of end of civil wars in Africa, new fresh displacements were reported in CAR, Ivory Coast, Ethiopia, Kenya, Nigeria, Senegal, and Zimbabwe.

Many asylum seekers that have struggled and managed to reach the West from these countries have been denied asylum and, in some cases, deported back to them. The reasons often given are that they do not meet the minimum requirement for refugee status. But the causes of internal displacement are often the very conditions put down in the 1951 Refugee Convention. Below are some of the reasons for displacement in Africa:

1. Conflict between governments and armed groups and inter-ethnic violence. Important examples in 2010 include the CAR, where armed bandits have been the main cause of displacement, and Zimbabwe, where almost all displacements were due to unlawful eviction carried out or conducted by the state.
2. Election violence has been a major factor in independent Africa, because most of the African government are a product of vote-rigging. In 2010, election was a major factor in Ivory Coast's disputed presidential elections in November. They led to violence and displacement. Almost 3,000 people were displaced by November. The United Nations made contingency plans for up to 450,000 in 2011. In Nigeria, clashes between supporters of rival candidates broke out in 2010, months ahead of the presidential and legislative elections scheduled for 2011,

leading to localised short-term displacements. In Sudan, nationwide elections took place in April 2010 after many delays, followed by a referendum on independence in southern Sudan in January 2011. Nationwide violence in newly formed southern Sudan and a border war irrupted between the two Sudan states, leading to internal displacements and to many people entering neighbouring countries for refugee status.

3. Insecurity and violence caused by bandits, which the failed states cannot control, is a major problem. As we have seen above, the Lord's Resistance Army (LRA) continues to cause displacement in a number of countries. The LRA originated in Uganda, but following the signing of the Cessation of Hostilities Agreement between the LRA and the Ugandan government in 2006, it has been more active in neighbouring countries, notably DRC, Sudan, and CAR.

4. Sexual violence, including rape, continues to be a major problem, particularly in eastern DRC.

5. Forced recruitment of children, including internally displaced children, was reported in 2010 in Chad, DRC, and Somalia.

6. Food security in the region and in the IDPs has been a major cause of displacement in the failed states.

7. Lack of access to justice, whether in relation to causes of sexual violence as, for example, in the DRC or in relation to land disputes in the aftermath of conflict, continue to be a major issue for IDPs across the country.

8. Ethnicity: In parts of Central Africa, the Batwa were particularly discriminated against in both Burundi and DRC. They are living in more difficult conditions than the other IDPs. Pastoral groups, such as the Peuhl in CAR, lost the means to supporting themselves and also faced discrimination when forced into sedentary communities.

Camps

IDPs may settle in camps in towns or over a wide stretch of open country. There are numerous factors that determine their forms of settlement. Their forms of occupation are a major factor. For example, pastoral farmers will need open land for pastures; fishermen will need the sea, large river, or lake, and craftsmen will need a suitable place to practice their crafts. But this will also depend on the length of stay they will have in a particular location. This is affected by the availability of the necessary resources, the attitude of the hosting community, security, and other factors such as the weather, seasons, and natural disasters. In desert countries and failed governments such as Somalia and Sudan, IDPs often settle in camps and wait for humanitarian assistance. In countries where the environment can provide alternatives and the host countries are tolerant, IDPs often take up new forms of employment. In Kenya, Somalis are successful traders, but in Sudan, IDPs are gathered in camps. The largest camps in Darfur host many tens of thousands of IDPs. The Afgooye informal camp, near Afgooye in Somalia, hosts close to 500,000 people who fled from Mogadishu, and it is the biggest settlement for the IDPs in the world.

Depending on the country, violent groups enter the settlement communities of IDPs for various reasons. Bandit groups enter to recruit children into their armies for food and to drink and rape women; government groups enter for political support and also for entertainment; and opposition parties also find the IDPs easy recruiting grounds. All these movements often depend on violence to achieve their objectives. This is one reason why IDPs are often moving from one location to another. Sometimes they are forced out of their borders and so become refugees. Some are not welcome in their neighbouring countries. So they keep moving. Some then choose to move north into North Africa, where they are very much ill-treated. Then they cross the sea and find themselves in Europe. Below are sample examples of countries whose people have ended up taking the long and dangerous journeys out of Africa: DRC, Somalia, and Rwanda.

Internally Displaced Persons in the Democratic Republic of the Congo

The DRC has a long and tragic history of predation and pillaging, first under Belgium and then under Mobutu. Mobutu had one of the largest armies in Africa which was not paid but depended on locally organised systems of plunder, extortion, rape, and common violence. Mobutu had so little control of the nation that he was nicknamed the Mayor of Kinshasa.

The recent or current situation is still one of a failed state, intractable armed conflict, poor governance, pervasive poverty, and massive humanitarian suffering, including widespread human rights violations and large-scale population displacement. Over the last fifteen years, including the First and Second Congo Wars (1996-1197) and (1998-2003), respectively, conflict has killed some five million people. At the height of the crisis in early 2003, there were over 400,000 in the Congolese in neighbouring states and over three million internally displaced people. But one of the major problems of the IDP crisis DRC is that reporters are more interested in numbers rather than human suffering. Internally displaced people face suffering equal to and often worse than that suffered by chained slaves during the Atlantic Ocean journey to the United States, but the story is not fully told. The world is told that the IDP population in the Great Lakes region is going down, painting the picture that peace has returned to states like the DRC. But this is far from the truth. While there may no longer be Africa's 'World War' experienced during the Second Congo War, the poorly equipped, poorly trained, and poorly paid armies of Uganda, DRC, and southern Sudan have been carrying out joint missions to try and defeat the bandit movement, LRA. In doing so, they kill villagers suspected to be LRA soldiers, they loot property, and they abuse women and children and move out leaving the villagers exposed to LRA reprisals. Here is a tragic report of the Doctors Without Borders they made in August 2009, a time in when many reporters said, 'Peace is returning to the DRC.'

Joseph (16) and his brother Henry were abducted in January with twenty fellow students during an attack on his village in northern DRC. Joseph's village was just one of those targeted in the relentless series of attacks by the Ugandan rebel group, LRA. Men are lined up. The weak are bayoneted to death. The strong are forced to lie down and beaten into total submission. Women are raped in the open. Homes are looted and then set on fire. The loot is then packed into heavy bags to be carried by survivors to the LRA bases. The offensive by armies of Uganda, DRC, and southern Sudan against LRA is ineffective and exacerbates the situation, sparking more violent reprisal attacks against civilians in the area. 'During these attacks, entire Congolese villages are often looted and burned to the ground. People are hacked to death with machetes and women and children abducted as sexual slaves, forced to carry looted goods, or recruited to fight. "They killed people we passed on the road, right in front of me," Joseph said. "They beat them with sticks, stabbed them with bayonets, and threw their bodies into the river. I was afraid that if I stopped to rest, they would kill me too, so I marched and marched under the weight of that heavy sack. In the morning they gave us 25 lashes each. That was breakfast." In the frenzied panic of fleeing a direct attack, there's often no time to wait for the slowest or oldest, no time to bury the dead. People escape through dense rain forest connecting DRC and southern Sudan. Relentlessly on lookout for rebels, refugees' lives are also at risk from wild animals. Many survive by eating jungle roots and drinking whatever water they can find, only moving forward once they believe the track ahead is clear.' (Congolese Survivors of Attacks Take Refuge in Southern Sudan: Doctors Without Borders: August 2009). Emily Paddon calls the plight of Congolese IDPs 'Conflict within a Conflict'. She wrote thus:

'Formal cessation of hostilities in July 2003 and subsequent elections in 2006, Congolese political space continued and still continues to be defined by those who bear arms and money, and violence plagues much of the country's eastern region. Rather than a simple binary conflict neatly arrayed along a single issue dimension, persistent violence in the DRC is the

result of welters of complex struggles that have local, national and regional dimensions, giving rise to conflict within conflict.' Refugees Studies Centre: Forced Migration Policy Briefing 8: Stabilising the Congo. December 2011)

There are several reasons for this, the main ones being the following:

1. Absence of a functioning state

State institutions in the DRC lack authority and are mired in corruption, leading many Congolese to conclude that the state itself is the criminal. The DRC consistently tanks among the highest countries on the Failed States Index with over 50 per cent of the state budget supplied by the IMF, World Bank, and African Development Bank. The DRC ranked fourth on the 2011 Failed States Index after Somalia (1), Chad (2), and Sudan (3).

2. Weak security

The persistence of weak and venal state institutions is mostly visible in the security sector, where the Congolese national army is largely unpaid and poorly trained. The army has an estimated strength of 120,000 soldiers—a ragtag team of some fifty rebel groups that were incorporated into the alliance with various militias. Keeping alive the spirit of Mobutu, whereby soldiers were not paid and lived off the population, the Congolese army is often the single greatest threat to the Congolese and routinely terrorises civilians, extorting protection money, looting villages, and raping and killing civilians. In the absence of a functioning state and credible security guarantees, force continues to be the principal means of power. From the time of Mobutu (who was nicknamed Mayor of Kinshasa) to the second Kabila, presidential power has never extended far from the capital. From there the presidents have struggled to remain in power through self-preservation and divide-and-conquer techniques. There is always fear of a coup or the fate of the older Kabila who was killed by his own bodyguard. Also despite President Kabila's international posturing, the last five years have demonstrated that the government is more interested in preserving and augmenting its own power than democratic and equitable peace building for the benefit of the country's population.

3. Tension over land, citizenship, and control of space.
4. Externalisation of neighbouring instability

The weakness of the Congolese institutions and the country's porous borders enabled the flow of people and goods, including arms, from around the region, compounding pre-existing tensions. From the influx of over one million refugees into eastern parts of then Zaire following the Rwandan genocide in 1994 to the continued presence of Rwandan army and the advent of new armed groups hostile to the regime in Kigali, much of the violence in eastern Congo has been the exportation of Rwandan political instability on to foreign soil.

IDPs in Somalia

There are several reasons why Somalia is in crisis today. The first, like in many parts of Africa, is the colonial legacy: the fact that colonialism failed to respect political systems and political communities as they existed and went on to create countries based on available resources and politics of Europe. So Somalia had an Italian-controlled south and British-controlled north which were fused into Somalia and has since broken down into Somaliland, Djibouti, and southern Somalia. The second part of the problem is that following the creation of the state of Somalia, the colonial system did not make enough effort to integrate the different ethnic groups to create the concept of human rights and democracy. So of the major post-independence results was failure to create government that respect people's human rights. Without proper government and human rights systems, the next problem became that of clan conflict and fierce competition over the economic and political resources of the post-colonial state. Then in 1974, a major drought struck, and people fought for limited food resources. Then the military defeat in the Ogaden War of 1978. The 1988 armed conflict removed Siad Barre.

Some 400,000 Somalis fled to Ethiopia and Djibouti. The war intensified until 1991 when Barre was overthrown. At the height of the conflict in 1992, some 800,000 Somalis were refugees in neighbouring countries, and two million were internally displaced. By 2002, an estimated 350,000 IDPs remained in Somalia, the result of fifteen years of conflict and the continuing violence in the southern regions of the country.

IDPs in Rwanda

While eastern DRC, Rwanda, Burundi, some parts of Uganda, and Tanzania may have different ethnic communities with localised forms of language, on the whole, political and economic problems of the region have made these people the same. They have greatly intermarried but surprisingly remain very tribalistic in character. Before colonialism, for example, it is estimated that some 500,000 Rwandans and Burundians moved and settled in the neighbouring countries. When political conflicts erupted in Rwanda in the years 1973, 1990, 1996, and 1997-8, large-scale displacements had taken place and refugees found support from the already large resident communities in the neighbouring countries. Burundians fled their country in large numbers in 1972, 1988, and 1993-2001, leading to the formation of Africa's largest group of refugees. The long-term presence of the Rwandan and Burundian refugees has had a decisive effect on the domestic politics of the main host states DRC, Tanzania, Uganda, and, of course, Rwanda and Burundi themselves, which both have hosted large numbers of refugees from each other.

The main groups of people in Rwanda are the Hutus, who make up about 80 per cent of the population; the Tutsi, who are about 18 per cent; and the Twa, who are heavily marginalised by the two and make a very small percentage of less than 2 per cent. During the time of European colonialism, the Belgians came to Rwanda and decided to further the gap between the Hutu and Tutsi. Between 1923 and 1939, the Belgians took the Tutsi to be a special class of Rwandans. They educated them and gave them administrative post in the African sector of the colonial system. They created a special ID card for them. The Catholic Church objected to this, and they, in turn, took Hutus into Catholic institution and gave them church-supported education. The church became very powerful and became one of the mouthpieces of the Hutus and taught them to discriminate against the Tutsis. In 1962, Rwanda gained independence, and the party called the Hutu Emancipation Movement (PARMEHUTU) came to power. The decided on revenge, and 200,000 Tutsi refugees fled to the neighbouring countries. In 1973, a coup by Juvenal Habyarimana undermined Hutu power, but Habyarimana had to depend on Hutu nationalism to remain in power. Refugee Rwandans who tried to return to independent Rwanda were turned away and told they could not return due to overpopulation. Refugees then formed the Rwandese Patriotic Front. In 1993, the Burundi president, Melchior Ndadaye, was assassinated. Ethnic tension heightened because he was a Hutu. Fighting started, and many refugees fled to the neighbouring countries. The United Nations sent some 25,000 officers to keep peace between the Hutus and Tutsis. But on 6 April, President Habyarimana's plane was shot down, and the genocide started that night. The United Nations withdrew its personnel, and no help came from anywhere in Africa, Europe, or the United Nations. In just ten days, between 800,000 and one million people were slaughtered. At first, it was the Tutsi who were victims, because they had the special IDs issued to them in the Belgian days; they Tutsi sympathisers. Eventually, it was the slaughter of your enemy. Rwandans fled in all directions into all neighbouring countries. In the DRC alone, it is suggested that more than 1.2 million Rwandans entered the country in a space of four days. It is estimated that between 28 and 29 April, some 250,000 refugees entered Tanzania. Half a million people went into Sudan, and smaller groups found refuge in Uganda, Malawi, Zambia, Angola, South Africa, Mozambique, and elsewhere. In fact, most countries in sub-Saharan Africa received refugees from Rwanda and Burundi at this time. Fighting continued to take place in Rwanda even after the Rwanda Patriotic Front formed a government. Fighting also continued in the refugee camps in neighbouring countries. In 1996, Tanzania had to close refugee camps because of problems with the Rwandan refugees.

What is, however, critical here is that there were millions of IDPs that formed communities in Rwanda and its neighbours. But the world was shy to assist Africa. One reporter said there were some 500 NGOs operating in Tanzania at the time of the genocide, but none gave help. The Rwandan genocide helps us tell the story that the world is not going to come to Africa until Africans show the world that they can help themselves. There will always be big headlines on African inability to solve its problems, but these are not for Africans but for the consumption of people who believe Africa cannot solve its problems. Many of these Rwandans did not find refuge in neighbouring countries. They continued their search further north; into the desert and across it for the lucky ones; into North Africa and beyond it for the lucky ones; across the sea into Europe; and eventually into the United Kingdom to face the problem of making the British believe they are truly refugees.

CHAPTER 3

Asylum-Seeking Routes Across Africa

Africa has more than a third of the World's population of refuges. No other continent has between seven and ten million displaced persons. There is virtually no safe country in Africa. This chapter will look at the treatment of refugees in the African countries that was said to be safe by Europe and some international organisations. Nearly half the population of Somalia is in either Kenya or Ethiopia, and there are unprecedented levels of internal displacement in the DRC. Nearly four million Zimbabweans, from a nation that used to feed the whole of the subregion, are living destitute lives in South Africa and the neighbouring states. Some three million Sudanese are in Egypt, where they have been pleading with the UNHCR to help them; peoples of the Great Lakes region were killed in gruesome ways for being of a different tribe; they are now scattered in nearly every country of South Africa; and after civil wars that saw people's bodies lie on the streets for weeks because people are scared to go out to bury them, the people of Liberia, Senegal, Sierra Leone, and Nigeria choose to cross the six-hundred-mile desert to North Africa. Why would 75 per cent of these people fail to meet the minimum requirements of the UN refugee status? UN Article 1(A) RC 1951 defines a refugee as *any person who owing to a well-founded fear of persecution for reasons of race, religion, nationality, membership of a particular social group or political opinion, is outside his country of nationality and is unable or owing to such fear, is unwilling to avail himself of the protection of that country; or who, not being a nationality and being outside the country of his former habitual residence . . . is unable or owing to such fear, is unwilling to return to it.* If these people were not running away from 'well-founded fear', they would prefer to go back home than suffer the pain that I will describe below. Majority of countries in sub-Saharan Africa are run by dictators, armies, or governments that do not respect human rights. Most asylum seekers prefer not to tell the whole story of their suffering because they are not guaranteed they will get asylum. If returned to these countries, some of them would surely face the death penalty. Most refugees do not know the UN Refugee Convention. Some are unable to tell their story because they are not English speakers and cannot give the details of their suffering. In some cultures, some stories can't just be told. Even in the English culture, how many women can tell a stranger the details of how they were raped? Yet as we shall see, more than 70 per cent of women in some districts of the DRC were raped or gang-raped in the wars at the beginning of this century. It takes a very brave woman to tell anyone that she was raped! Many young men who were forced to choose between killing their parents and losing their lives cannot tell the world they slaughtered their families in order to save their lives. The majority of people that claim asylum suffered in unbelievable ways as they struggled to escape with their lives from sub-Saharan Africa. Many have some very tragic stories. This chapter will briefly discuss the level of violence in different areas of Africa and follow each area with individual escape stories.

Europe does not know that some of the people they process would have had more than five years of travelling, of suffering, and of pain and loss of close relatives and friends as they struggle to leave this continent. So when Home Office in Europe turn away something like 75 per cent of asylum applicants each year, it is not because all these people are not refugees. It is because Europe is now refusing to accept some of the obligations they signed for in the 1951 Refugee Convention.

Majority of sub-Saharan Africans that reach the United Kingdom, for instance, come from Zimbabwe, Somalia, Eritrea, Nigeria, Sudan, Nigeria, Ivory Coast, and the DRC. These are countries whose records of political violence are well documented. We have already seen that these countries have had civil wars since the 1990s, the most protracted ones being the war in Sierra Leone (1989-2001); Liberia (1999-2003), and Nigeria which has never really seen peace since its independence in 1960. Ivory Coast has had on-and-off civil wars from 1999 to 2011. Recently, war in Ivory Coast made it impossible to bury the dead that remained littered on the streets of the capital for weeks. In Zimbabwe, Robert Mugabe killed more than 20,000 people in Matabeleland between 1982 and 1987 and perhaps many more in yet to be properly documented murders in the rest of the country between year 2000 and 2010. Most immigration from the Democratic Republic of the Congo started after the fall of President Mobutu in 1997, but because of the limited forms of communication in the country and the rise of illegal and informal diamond and Coltan trade, millions of people in the DRC have lost their lives over the years, and the world has ignored these people's pain. The 1990s also saw civil wars in the Great Lakes region states of Uganda, Rwanda, and Burundi. Hein de Haas says that recurrent warfare in Sudan and the Horn of Africa has fuelled migration to Egypt and Libya. The International Catholic Migration Commission agrees that Libya became the North African migration pole after 1973 oil crisis as sub-Saharan Africans worked at the Libyan wells and factories to raise boat fees to cross the Mediterranean Sea. There are countries like Zambia which are not under violent regimes but are major recipients of refugee from the region. All this is well documented. Majority of refugees that reach Europe pass through North African states of Libya, Tunisia, Algeria, Morocco, and Mauritania. Although not properly recorded, sub-Saharan Africans have been grossly ill-treated in these countries. A detailed analysis of how they are treated will show that much of the trauma is based on religion and racism. Refugees have been cheated of their money, thrown into the desert, kept in prisons, raped, enslaved, and killed in the North African countries. But there are two other routes refugees have used from sub-Sahara which are generally not written much about. These are the route taken by people escaping from Zimbabwe to South Africa which is recommended by the European countries as a safe country and those escaping from Sudan and the eastern Horn area who chose to go to Israel, through Egypt and the Arab states across the Red Sea. Very little is recorded on the plight of asylum seekers that take these routes.What is also not written much about is the fact that the refugees that reached Europe and other parts of the World is a tiny percentage of the vast refugee population of sub-Saharan Africa. It is very difficult to travel across Africa because of poor transport, differences in currencies, violence, corruption, and natural disasters. Majority of the people that try to seek refuge outside Africa never reach their destinations. They move from one area of violence into another; they are arrested and imprisoned; they are shot and killed; they die in overcrowded ships that sink as they attempt to cross the oceans; and they die of diseases because host countries refuse to give them medical services. Almost all the countries to which sub-Saharan Africans escape to in order to travel to safe countries are very dangerous countries with hostile communities and unsympathetic governments. There are six escape destinations where most sub-Saharan refugees travel through. There are six escape destinations where most sub-Saharan refugees travel through.

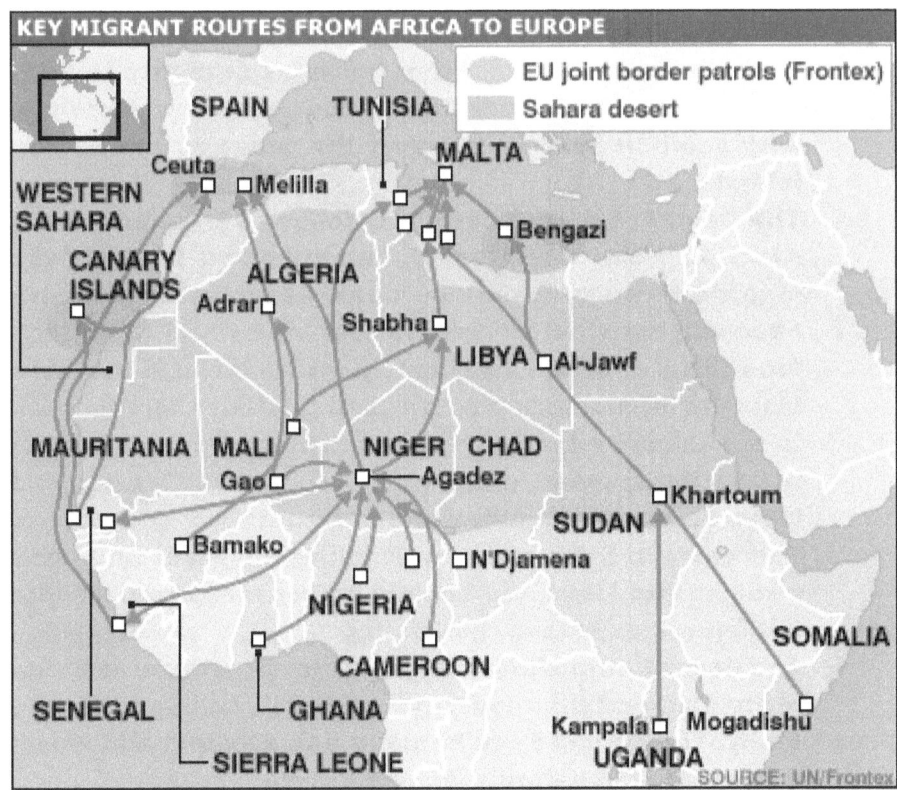

Source: BBC News: 2 July 2007: Key Facts: Africa to Europe Migration

1. **The South African Route:** We will analyse the treatment of Zimbabwean refugees there. One of the problems they have faced is that the South African government has not distinguished them from economic migrants. As a result, efforts to invite international aid to assist them has not been prioritised.

2. **The West African Route:** From Liberia, Sierra Leone, Guinea, Guinea-Bissau, Senegal, the Gambia, Mauritania, and western Sahara, people travelled to the Atlantic coast, where they looked for smuggler boats. They were charged between 1,000 and 1,500 euros for a boat ride from Africa to the Canary Islands.

3. **The West Sahara Route:** It is taken primarily by West Africans originating in the Ivory Coast, Ghana, Burkina Faso, Togo, and Benin. From there they migrate to Mali, Mauritania, western Sahara, and southern Morocco, with some ultimately crossing the ocean to the Canary Islands.

4. **The Central Sahara Route:** It is followed by sub-Saharan Africans from countries of Cameron and Nigeria who migrate through these two countries into Niger before choosing between a numbers of routes. From Niger they face three choices. They may migrate through northern Mauritania, western Sahara, and southern Morocco on to the Canary Islands; through northern Morocco across the Mediterranean into Spain; or through Tunisia and Libya across the Mediterranean into Italy.

5. **The eastern Sahara Route:** It bypasses Niger and head straight into Libya and Tunisia before many board boats to Malta, Lampedusa, and Sicily.

6. **The Horn of Africa Route:** Migrants from the Horn of Africa route also end their journeys on Malta, Lampedusa, and Sicily. They begin from Somalia and Ethiopia and travel through Sudan before reaching Libya.

The South African Route: Zimbabweans Escape Mugabe's Torture

Over three million Zimbabweans have taken refuge in South Africa. They run from politically motivated violence from being punished because you live in a particular village where it is assumed the majority of the people there attended a political rally organised by members of an opposition party. They run from being accused to be opposition members because they belong to a family of a prominent opposition person. They are accused of not belonging to a religious movement in the area, a movement whose leadership is being bribed to make its members vote for the ruling party. They are accused of not being active in a party which is murdering their relatives. They are accused of having an independent mind, of having been to school, and of being teachers and so capable of advising people against the cruel political system. I have talked to tortured victims; they told me that most of them were blindfolded before they were driven to very secret places. Those that die are buried there secretly and no one will ever know. Thanks to the formation of the MDC in that country; we now know that people are tortured in special places inside presidential palaces spread across the country. People are also tortured at secret rural army depots. When I was lecturing at The Belvedere Technical Teachers College, both students and lecturers were forced to do a subject named Political Economy. The reading materials were nothing but indoctrination—initially towards understanding Maoist Communism but later on just to turn academics into political tools. One of the reasons why lecturers throughout the country became targets for 're-education' is that they resisted such indoctrination. People chose to seek asylum in South Africa, but they had to cross the crocodile infested Limpopo River. And South Africa put a razor-sharp fence between the two countries, and at some points electrified the fence. People have had to take the risks such as shown below to enter South Africa (under the razor wire). Black Zimbabwean workers who did not support the ZANU-PF party also lost their land, homes, and jobs. It is not the white people only who lost their land and lives, as is publicised in the local press.

A mother and baby crawl under the barbed wire to cross the border from Zimbabwe into South Africa. Photograph: Themba Hadebe/AP (Source Annie Kelly in Musina: The Observer: 13 June 2010)

But life in South Africa has been far from rosy for refugees there. The Doctors Without Borders report of June 2009 summarises the plight of Zimbabweans in South Africa. It reports that instead of finding the refuges they so desperately need, the Zimbabweans endure intolerable suffering on their journey to and within South Africa. *Violence, sexual abuse, harassment, appalling living conditions, and a serious lack of access to essential healthcare define the desperate lives of thousands of Zimbabweans in South Africa . . . (No Refugee, Access Denied, Medical and humanitarian needs of Zimbabweans. MSF, June 2009)*

The report goes on: *We see thousands of sick, wounded, psychologically scarred and marginalised Zimbabweans in Johannesburg and Musina every month, said Dr Eric Goemaere, Medical Coordinator for MSF in South Africa, They come to us because they have nowhere to turn to. Many of those who reach us have chronic diseases such as HIV and TB and severe violence-related injuries, most often from rape and sexual assault experienced while crossing the border from Zimbabwe, but also in South Africa. (Bianca Tolboom: MSF nurse: Zimbabwean Nightmare of neglect continues in South Africa; Doctors Without Borders/Medecins Sans frontiers (MSF) 2012)*

A separate report I read was on six teenage girls who, after crossing the border on their own, were captured by a group of fifteen men who raped them interchangeably for two weeks. One day, they allowed them to go and use the bush together, and thus they managed to escape. When such people get to hospitals for treatment, they are denied the service. The MSF report continues:

South Africa's constitution guarantees access to health care and other essential services to all who live in the country-including refugees, asylum seekers and migrants-regardless of legal status. But in reality Zimbabwean patients are rejected outright, or are charged exorbitant fees and subjected to long delays, inappropriate treatment, or premature discharge. (Phakamile Magamdela: Zim Illegal immigration denied access health care. MSF 20-06-2009)

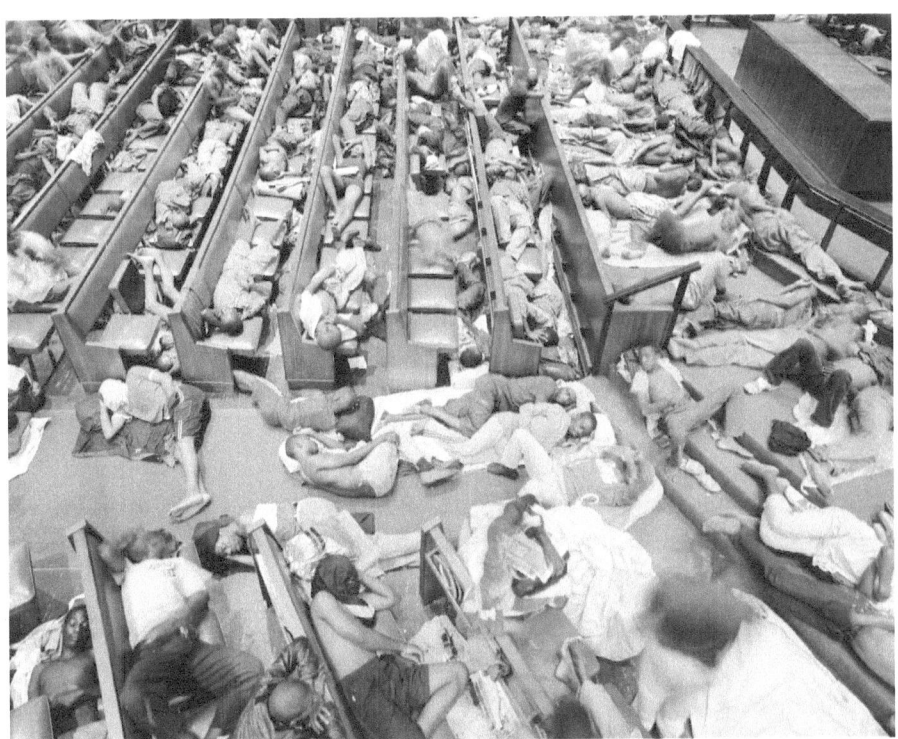

Refugees from Zimbabwe sheltering in the Central Methodist Church on Pritchard Street in the city: 22 March 2009: Photo by David Goldblatt in African Colours: David Goldblatt at Goodman gallery Johannesburg 28-09-2010)

Bianca Tolboom, MSF nurse and project coordinator, said that stories from patients were truly shocking. She went on: *I am talking about pregnant women, unconscious or critically ill patients, even a six year girl who had been raped who* *were all refused the medical care they urgently required. It's deplorable, it's a breach of medical ethics and it's a violation of their rights under the South African constitution.* The MSF report end by summarising the desperation of the Zimbabweans and the dangers into which all of them—men, women, and children—land. *In April, more than half of those treated had survived gang rape and 70 per cent had been raped under threat of a gun, knife, or other weapon. Another worrying trend is the number of unaccompanied children crossing the border alone. They make their way to the Central Methodist Church, a journey of more than 500 Kilometres where as many as 4,000 Zimbabweans shelter each night.* The Zimbabweans in South Africa are desperate to leave that country and have no place to go. Very few have relatives in Europe; very few can raise the air fare, and very few will convince Europeans that they are Zimbabwean refugees that could not find proper refugee facilities in South Africa. Zimbabweans have not received much assistance in other neighbouring countries either. Botswana used to accept Zimbabweans but hardened its policy by insisting that all refugees be detained in the UNHCR camp in the desert.

Before discussing the treatment of refugees in the countries of North Africa, let us look at the dangers refugees face as they cross the Sahara Desert.

CHAPTER 4

The Desert Journeys and North African Hosts

Tens of thousands of refugees met at designated rendezvous places outside towns after raising the required fees to cross the Sahara. Many of them knew the risks, yet they took the trips. If these refugees were not running away from life-threatening dangers, not so many of them would take the trips. Below are some of the dangers faced by the migrants.

(i)   Dehydration: Being told is, of course, different from experience. Some people knew while others did not know health problems that could make it difficult to endure desert heat. Travellers often underestimate the heat problems of the desert. Transporters often discourage people from carrying large amounts of water because this would affect the number of persons they could load onto a vehicle. They are said to have gone to the extent of mixing some the water with petrol to discourage people from taking too much water along the way. So many people died along the way and were buried in the sand. In 2005, Moroccan and Algerian security forces began reporting that they were finding decomposing bodies and dehydrated corpses in the desert. Crossing the desert became especially difficult during this time, because illegal immigrants

entering Algeria and Libya had to pass through Niger's
Air Mountains, circumventing a mountain rebellion,
increased mountain banditry, and North Africa's border
crackdowns.

(ii)   **Unsuitable and dangerous trucks:** Migrants leaving
Agadez, Niger for Libya, or Algeria describe gathering
30 km outside Agadez in the middle of the night to
begin their trips in tarpaulin-covered Toyota 4×4s.
Other migrants entering Libya from Sudan told stories
of groups of twenty-five to forty-five people being
packed into Toyota land cruisers for the ten-day trips.
Sometimes they were transferred at the border into a
new vehicle with Libyan licence plates. These trucks
broke down often, which is extremely dangerous
considering the very limited supplies of food and water
they carried, the extreme heat, absence of shelter, and
problems related to the fact that it is very difficult to
help people stranded in a desert.

(iii)   **Armed bandit attacks:** Armed bandits often knew
when a trip would start and would waylay the vehicles,
attack them, and robe the refugees of their money and
other possessions. A twenty-three-year-old Ghanaian
migrant, identified as Freddy Kasseri, claimed he was
stripped of everything of value when the truck he
was travelling in was stopped by armed interceptors
some 500 km outside Agadez in August 2008. The
interceptors also took five Ghanaian women and five
Nigerian women into the desert.

(iv)   **Abandoned:** A week before the six bodies of decomposed
sub-Saharan migrants were found in the desert near
Adrar, Algerian police came across a group of eighty
sub-Saharans in the same region. They said they had
been abandoned without food or water by traffickers
who were supposed to bring to the coast (Sule, from
Kano, Nigeria; *Reuters 11/9/2011*). Sule escaped the
wars in Kano and decided to enter Europe through
Libya. He had heard the stories of Africans tortured
and executed in Libya on suspicion of fighting as
mercenaries alongside Muammar Gaddafi's forces. He

knew that before even reaching the sea, the gamble meant passing through what may be the most dangerous place in the world for a refugee. ID cards of nationals from Chad, Niger, Mali, Sudan, and other African states had been found on bodies of men whom anti-Gaddafi forces suspected were pro-Gaddafi mercenaries. But Sule decided to take the risk and travelled over 3,000 km of desert country to reach the sea. He joined a group that travelled 700 km to Agadez in Niger. This is a town that used to be popular with tourists that wanted to get a feel of desert life. But from 2007, a string of al-Qaeda-linked kidnappings made it a no-go area. Sule and his group waited for a signal from the guide to start the 3,000 km journey north, across the Air Mountains and the rest of the desert into Libya. When the time came, Sule paid 300,000 CFA francs ($625) for the 3,000 km journey. He was one of the sixty people packed like sardines in a pickup truck. But just outside Agadez, they were stopped by an armed gang of men and had all their belongings stolen from them.

(v) Working one's way to North Africa: There is no way one would walk to North Africa. So the poor would not cross the desert until they had raised the money. So many sold their labour for almost nothing until they had raised the fees. One person who could not raise the transport fees was Morgan from Lagos, Nigeria (*BBC News*, 12 September 2006). Morgan could not raise the large sums of money demanded by the smugglers. So like many in his situation, he chose an even more dangerous approach to leave Nigeria and reach where he would get refuge. He started on 11 January 1998. He worked his way through Niger and into Libya. He was captured and escaped on the way to detention. He then changed course and decided to leave through Morocco. In Algeria, he worked wherever he could, selling goods and working as a barber. On trying to cross into Morocco, he was caught by on various occasions. They beat him very badly, so badly that they dislocated his legs. After recovering, he managed to enter Morocco and travelled until he reached the port. He worked to raise the 300 euros needed for the boat transport to the Canary Islands. After six years running away from the Nigerian problems, he was captured on 7 August 2006 and returned to Nigeria. Morgan could not take the risk of returning home. He immediately set off again using a different route, this time through Togo, Benin, Burkina Faso, Mali, Algeria, and Morocco. In Mali, he and other migrants paid a truck driver to take them into Morocco, but the driver dropped them in the middle of the desert in Algeria. For two days they travelled without food and water. Some collapsed and died, but Morgan and other survivors were rescued by the Algerian police and driven back to Mali. They started again from Mali until they crossed the Canary Island. Another person whose story of wandering across the desert, being used by different exploiters, was a seventeen-year-old boy. Muhammad Silah (aged seventeen) escaped with his parents from the rebels of the Revolutionary United Front to Guinea Conakry, but, unfortunately, both his parents were killed by these rebels. He was taken captive by the bandits who planned to train him to join them. There he met a fourteen-year-old captive, Massar Beng, and the two planned to escape. They managed to reach Gambia. From there they moved to Senegal and Mauritania. There they met other boys, and they decided to go to Darker and then to the coast so as to catch a boat and sail to Tenerife on Canary Islands. Finally, an example of a woman that was cheated, lied to, and struggled through all the difficulties until she reached Europe. Fayza Ahmad from Sudan (*BBC News* 3/7/2007) was one of millions of displaced women in Darfur, Sudan. She was a woman activist in Darfur. She was arrested three times and tortured for her fight for human and women's rights. She decided to leave Sudan with her children when her journalist husband was arrested and then disappeared. She embarked on a journey that would take her two years. From Darfur she fled with her three children to Khartoum to the west of Sudan. From there she went to Chad and then Syria. She did not have a passport then, so she had to buy a false one. She approached someone who told her that she could enter Europe through Ukraine because she would not need a visa. The man disappeared with her tickets, her money, and the false passports. She spent the next six months trying to enter Ukraine without a passport but failed to do so. So she had to travel back to Syria to get another passport. She then managed to enter Ukraine. As a black person, she had very difficult time trying to receive assistance. She was often racially ill-treated. Eventually, she got someone who advised her to go to Moldova. She walked for five hours to cross the border. She was lucky to meet the Sudanese there who helped her reach the United Kingdom. For two years she slept rough with her children. There was no schooling for them. They often went for some time without food. But she struggled on. She is probably one of the people the UK Home Office refused to give asylum because she had travelled through what the United Kingdom regarded as a safe third country.

After the journeys across the desert, those that were lucky arrived in the North African states, and a new set of traumas awaited them. This chapter will look at the countries that received majority of refugees and how they treated them.

Egypt

Sudan is a southern neighbour of Egypt. For centuries, tens of thousands of Sudanese have settled in southern sections of Egypt. In fact, there is a resident population of Sudanese in Egypt, but the Egyptians have always racially discriminated against the Sudanese. The UNHCR estimate that there were between two and three million Sudanese in Egypt in 2007 (Amnesty International: Egypt-Deadly Journey through the Desert. August 2008). There is also thousands of Eritreans and

Ethiopians. But Egypt is one of the worst hosts of sub-Saharan refugees. The refugees have staged several protests in front of the UNHCR offices to process their asylum cases because they say it is very dangerous to live in Egypt, and the UNHCR is not doing enough to help them. There are varying figures on the numbers of cases that have been processed each year, but overall, they are very low. Vivian Salam in Protestors Cry for Help put the number of Sudanese that were given refugee status in 2005 at 14,400 and those that applied for asylum at 10,000 only. Another source says that between 2004 and 2007, some 67,000 Sudanese claimed refugee status in Egypt and only 20,700 were recognised. Of the recognised, the UNHCR had resettled only 14,300 people. Between 1999 and 2003, only 33 per cent of applicants were recognised.

Several sources mention different forms of ill-treatment of refugees in Egypt. These include racial insults, assaults, rape, slavery, shootings, killings for body parts, and deportations.

Racial insults: Egyptians openly abuse sub-Saharan refugees, and the government does nothing to stop it. Asley Bates wrote, *Egyptian civilians have ostracized them with racist names like 'samara' meaning black, 'funga monga' meaning monkey or 'abit' meaning slave (African Refugees in Egypt sit out the protests: 31 January 2011).* David Rosenberg talked to a Sudanese refugee who told her how she was treated in Cairo in these words: *She has lived in Cairo for twelve years, a refugee from war torn Darfur in Sudan. But she says she is regularly the subject of catcalls on the streets. People ask her if her family descends from monkeys and some other African animals. Her skin is the brunt of jokes. Egyptians routinely express surprise that she can read and speak Arabic. (African refugees in Egypt eye exodus: Media Line 25/9/ 2011).* Barbara Harrell-Bond says that there is a big problem of racism in Egypt, but the Egyptians often deny it. Barbara, who is the founder of Africa and Middle East refugee assistance and an expert on refugees globally, told MediaLine: *But I think it's getting more and more difficult to deny it, because more and more people are seeing*

the consequences of the lives refugees lead and the fears that
they live under because of being refugee.

Assaults: Where refugees are found alone or if they walk into
certain parts of town, they are surrounded and assaulted.
Vivian interviewed a woman who said, *The streets are not safe*
for us here. People hit us with stones, this is normal to us.
Finding jobs is difficult. Our children are abused. Our women
are raped. (Vivian Salama op cit).

Slavery: Fred Plutgen and Fedal Fahmy reported that
sub-Saharan Africans are chained, tortured, and enslaved in
Egypt. *Many are enslaved and tortured and women raped by*
the Bedouin tribes of the Sinai if they are unable to come up
with large sums of money the Bedouins try to extort from them
and their families, to smuggle the refugee across the border
into Israel. As a result, many remain imprisoned in camps on
the Sinai Peninsula . . . They are chained and kept in camps in
the open with no bathrooms and little water and treated worse
than animals. (Death in the desert: Tribesmen exploit battle to
reach Israel. November 2011)

Killed: Amnesty International is one of the numerous
organisations that have reported that Egyptians kill refugees for
a number of reasons. There are several that die in prisons each
year because they will have been condemned in the Egyptian
military court for 'attempting to exit unlawfully the Egyptian
eastern border'. In 2008, Amnesty International reported that
some 1,300 civilians had been tried in the military court and
imprisoned. Although sentences are said to be six months,
refugees have died in Egyptian prisons. Majority of the victims,
however, are killed when trying to jump the fence into Israel.
Egypt has reached an arrangement with the Israeli government
to prevent refugees from jumping the fence in return for
financial benefits. Instead of setting up security guards that
capture refugees and take them to the UNHCR which have
offices in Cairo, Egypt chooses to kill the refugees. David
Rosenberg reported that in 2007, some 50 refugees—men,
women, and children—were shot dead at the Israeli border by

Egyptian soldiers. Amnesty International reports that between January and July 2008, some seventeen more people were shot dead, and in fourteen separate incidents, tens of others were injured. Egyptian soldiers drive along the 250-mile-long border and shoot anyone they see near the fence. One source reports how this man with his wife and daughter had almost managed to cross the fence when the baby cried and the man was shot dead. Amnesty International gives names to make the world know that Egyptians are shooting down people without proof of why they are where they are. They wrote, *Mervat Ner Hatover, a thirty-seven-year-old-man, was killed from a shot to the head as she jumped over a barbed wire border fence near El Kutilla region in the Sinai Peninsula on 16 February 2008. Mervat Mer Hatover who was accompanied by her two young daughters, was shot by Egyptian security forces at the border with Israel. Three days later, fifty-year-old Ermeniry Khasheef, a Sudanese national was shot dead near Rafar; another Sudanese, Adam Mohammed Othman, aged twenty-three was killed in the same area on 10 March 2008. On 28 June, a seven year old Sudanese girl and a man were shot dead by Egyptian security forces near Rafah.* Scores of refugee demonstrators are killed and hundreds injured each time refugees go on to the streets asking the world to see how they are being treated and the absence of help from the UNHCR. After the twenty-eight-day sit-in at the UNHCR offices by refugees demanding action from them, the UNHCR did not help them. They called the Egyptian police. Egypt has a 'shoot to kill' against refugees that cause any disturbance to their system. They moved into the UNHCR premises and beat up, killed, and injured many of the demonstrators.

Killed for body parts: There have been in recent European press reports that Egypt is arranging with foreign organisations to kill refugees and sell body parts. *The New Generation Foundation for Human Rights and the Everyone Group, from Italy have presented evidence that bodies of African refugees have been found in the Sinai Desert with organs missing . . . One Bedouin tribal chief did put CNN in touch with a Bedouin who used to be involved in people smuggling and who was close to the original thief scheme . . .*

The doctors dealt directly with the Sawarka family, and they bought the organs starting from $20 000, the source said in a phone interview. He offered further details of the logistics required to keep the organs fresh for the transplant in their new owners' bodies. The doctors come with some sort of mobile fridge where the organs can be stored for six to eight hours and resold in Cairo or elsewhere. (Fred Plutgen and Mohammed Fedal Fahmy op cit).

Non-refoulement: Although Egypt signed both the 1951 Refugee Convention and the 1967 Protocol, it still arrests and deports asylum seekers and refugees. Since the middle of 2007, hundreds of refugees, asylum seekers, and migrants from countries in sub-Saharan Africa—men, women, and children—have risked their lives trying to cross the Egyptian border into Israel. Aided by local smugglers, they arrive at night and are dropped in small groups near the 250 km-long border fence between Egypt and Israel. Egypt shoots to kill people on both sides of the fence. So those that are shot and survive on the Israeli side go to Israeli hospitals. *Many of the wounded arrive at hospitals with serious bullet injuries to the chest, back, thighs of legs. In August 2007, forty-eight people who had managed to cross the border were forcibly returned to Egypt by the Israeli authorities; around 20 of them were then reportedly forcibly returned from Egypt to Sudan. The fate of the others remains unknown.*

Since February 2008, hundreds of Eritreans have entered Egypt through its borders with Sudan or by crossing the Red Sea. Although many had already been recognised as refugees by the UNHCR in Sudan, they have been denied access to UNHCR representatives in Egypt to access their asylum claims there. Up to 1,200 Eritrean nationals were subject to collective expulsion from Egypt to Eritrea between 12 and 19 June 2008. Egypt breaches the principles of non-refoulement.

Alain Morice in Critical Chronology of European Policy (June 2011) said that Egyptian police opened fire on 2,000 Sudanese refugees crowded outside the UNHCR office in Cairo on 30 December 2006. Alain goes on to say following pressure from Egypt on African Union member to renegotiate the non-refoulement condition of the 1951 Refugee Convention. Egypt pushed the ACP (Africa, Caribbean, Pacific) states to accept the proposed Cotonou Agreement between European Union and ACP states of June 2000. As provider of development, the European Union proposed to impose the principle of a readmission clause applying to their nationals and ACP countries, and envisaged extending it to migrants who would have passed through their countries. Under this arrangement, an ACP country would now have to prove that an expellable person is not its national; otherwise the expulsion would be lawful. In this way, readmission agreement could be avoided. As late as June 2010, Egypt pushed for the acceptance of this agreement, but fortunately it has been challenged successfully.

Before discussing the treatment of refugees in the North African states, it is important to state that one of the most traumatic experiences refugees face is that of crossing the Sahara. Hein de Haas wrote several articles on refugee experiences on the journeys across the Sahara Desert. He found that between 65,000 and 120,000 subs-Sahara Africans enter Egypt, Mauritania, Morocco, Tunisia, Algeria, and Libya each year. He said that between70 and 80 per cent entered through Libya and 20 to 30 per cent through Algeria and Morocco. He said they come mainly from Senegal, the Gambia, Sierra Leone.

Libya

Libya is a good example of a country that confused immigrants and refugees. Because of this confusion, we see that it often expected refugees to return to their home countries, and it is one of the countries that was used by Europe to be play the role of 'policeman' in the Sahara Desert and the Mediterranean Ocean. After the 1973 Oil Crisis, Libya became the destination of thousands of West African migrant workers. Between 1992 and 2000, Libya increased its relations with sub-Saharan countries because of the UN embargo. Libya invested a lot of the petrodollars in sub-Saharan Africa, and thousands of migrants came from Sudan, Chad, and Niger.

But the war in Sierra Leone (1991-2001); the civil war in Liberia (1989-1996) and (1999-2003); the fall of Mobutu in Zaire, now Democratic Republic of the Congo, in 1997; and the subsequent war in the whole Great Lakes region, the violence in Nigeria, wars in the Horn of Africa, and war in Côte d'Ivoire brought in refugees into Libya. Hein de Haas, who did research in the area, said that these new 'migrants' went there because of lack of choice: *Confronted with the lack of alternative destinations within the region, this prompted increasing numbers of West Africans to migrate outside the region to countries such as South Africa, Gabon, Botswana and Libya. (Irregular Migration from West Africa to the Maghreb and the European Union: An overview of recent trends. IOM Migration research Series 2008. P 16)* But Libya did not treat them as refugees and present them to the UNHCR. This was worsened by the year 2000 clashes between Libyan and sub-Saharan Africans which led to the death of dozens of sub-Saharan Africans. Libya's biggest problem with black people is xenophobia.

Xenophobia: Libya's xenophobia did not have a component of fear. It was only contempt, rooted on strong, popular resentment of sub-Saharan Africans. The xenophobia was expressed in blanket accusations of criminality, verbal and physical attacks, harassment, extortion, arbitrary detention, and possible torture. One Ethiopian man said that the older generation are better than the younger generation. Young men may just block your way and not allow you to pass when you go to the shops. Migrants have reported having stones thrown at them, being spit at, and being called abeed/'abd, Arabic for slave. Non Muslim women from sub-Saharan Africa are especially at risk in Libya, where they are often mistaken for sex workers. Marta T. An Eritrean woman said she had coca-cola poured on her head. 'I stayed in a private house with six other people in Tripoli. We couldn't outside because we were afraid. The one time when I went to buy something with my friend, they threw coca-cola on her head.' Yet migrants cannot take their cases to law enforcement.

According to de Haas, corrupt and abusive policemen, soldiers, and border officials take bribes and assets like mobile phones from migrants. This abuse is most evident in the detention and expulsion polices of a number of North African countries. Arrested migrants are often transported to detention camps in one of the three varieties of containers described by Fortress Europe as a pick-up car, another as equivalent to a minivan, and lastly as a 'real container, blue in colour, with three windows on each side, pulled by an articulated lorry.' Detainees face overcrowding in detention facilities, poor sanitation and food, not knowing the reasons for their detention and not having access to a lawyer or legal review.

Cruelty: Sub-Saharan Africans were forced to live in highly degrading circumstances, in overcrowded houses or sometimes in improvised camps. They were denied access to legal assistance, medical care and schooling. They were arbitrarily arrested, detained and deported. Some were taken thousands of miles into the desert and dumped there without basic needs for survival.

Non-refoulement: From 2003 to 2005 Libya deported 145,000 sub-Saharan Africans many of them from countries that were at war and where refugees were running away from. Libya made several agreements with countries of southern Europe to police the Sahara desert and the Mediterranean ocean for sub-Saharan refugees crossing into Europe. In August 2004 The Italian Prime minister and Libyan president agreed on the principle of 'reception centres' in Tripoli and Libya began to receive unprocessed returned refugees captured by the Italians in the sea or that had landed on Italian soil. In April 2005, European Parliament severely condemned Italy over its collective expulsions but Libya and Italy confirmed they would not discontinue the expulsion of unprocessed refugees. In December 2007 Italy and Libya signed an agreement which inter alia provided for joint marine patrols between Italy and Libya, coupled with provision of border control equipment and technical assistance by Italy to Libya. This saw the cracking down on smugglers' boats transporting migrants from Libyan shoes to Italy Italian. On 30 August 2008 Italian Prime Minister visited Libya again and they signed a Friendship Agreement in Benghazi. Italy officially apologised for thirty years of colonialism and agreed to pay damages. Italy committed itself to pay to Libya 5 billion dollars through investment over twenty-five years, that is, 250 million euros a year. Through this agreement the Italian company, ENI obtained an extension of its contract in Libya until 2021 for oil and until 2047 for gas. In return Libya agreed to a joint fight against refugees; setting up an electronic border surveillance system for Libya sea borders, 50 per cent of which Italy would finance, about $500 million and the European Union would be asked for the remaining 50 per cent. By June 2009 when Gadhafi gave the infamous speech in Rome when he declared that asylum claims were 'a widespread lie' only about 5 to 7 per cent of all immigrants reaching Italy arrived from Libya. In October 2009 an Italian firm won a tender worth 300 million euro to electrically secure Libya's immense southern border with Sudan, Chad and Niger. The funding was for three years and was to be paid by Italy and the European Union. Press reports quoted the Italian Interior Minister as saying, 'Until now, we had to get them, identify them, send them back to their countries of origin. For the first time in history, we were able to send illegal immigrants directly back to Libya' He called this a historic 'turning point' in the campaign against illegal immigration. The UN estimate that in the first tour months of the treaty alone, Italy sent back 1,000 Africans it had intercepted in international waters, without screening them for refugee status. Libya denied thousands of needy Africans the right to refugee status. Returned immigrants report adverse forms of treatment. 'I was arrested when I tried to leave Libya by boat', an asylum seeker who wanted to remain anonymous told Human Rights Watch. 'The steering wheel on out boat broke and the waves carried us back to land. Then the police caught us and beat me on the head and on the arms and then took us to prison.' Migrants consistently told Human Right Watch researchers of overcrowded dirty conditions, mistreatment by guards and indefinite lengths of detention in Libya migrant detention centres. (Refworld 7/5/2009).

As all this was happening to sub-Saharan refugees, there were no African politicians that said much to help their situation. The Association Malienne des expuls'es (AME, Association of Expelled Malians in Bamako reported the ill-treatment of their compatriots in Libyan prisons. Libya responded by expelling the Malian-153 immediately, 149 on 9 December 2009 and 150 on 3 May 2010. The Mali government did not respond. Libya has charted planes to deport large groups of migrants, and had been using cargo planes without seats to do so before other African governments complained. As in Novadhibou, Mauritania, Amnesty International representatives conducted interviews at a detention centre and found that most migrants detained had been robbed of some of their possessions and many said that they had been arbitrarily arrested in the street or at home when they were making preparations to get a boat to sail them across to Europe.

In fact Gadhafi went on to call a summit in Tripoli on 29 November 2010, attended by 80 representatives from Africa and Europe where he demanded a further 5 billion euros a year to stop him from opening the gates and flooding Europe with Africans. He said 'We do not know what will happen, what the reaction of white and Christian Europeans will be when faced by this influx of hungry and uneducated Africans'. African leaders did not take a united position to help the refugees in Libyan prisons

Refugees in Libya were to suffer their worst treatment when the Libyan 'revolution' started. Blacks were hunted; they were chased and persecuted by the 'rebels' as being mercenaries of the Gadhafi regime. The International Organisation of Migrants reported in August 2011, the forced departure of 670,000 foreigners from Libya, mostly to Africa-211,000 to Egypt; 286 000 to Tunisia; 127,000 to Niger, and a much smaller number to Europe across the Mediterranean Sea. Libya is one of the few countries of the world that has thus far not signed the Geneva Refugee Convention and the world has so far failed to persuade her to do so. Life is very difficult for all sub-Saharan Africans in Libya, especially those with no money to pay for transport across the Mediterranean, who then decide to look for work to raise the money. **Racism, xenophobia, discrimination, race-based violence are especially prominent.**

Morocco

For centuries, Senegalese had made pilgrimages made pilgrimages to the holy places in Fez honouring Ahmad al-Tijani, founder of a Sufi brotherhood that is mainstream Islam in West Africa. Their presence in Morocco was therefore tolerated, and migrants could count on networks of Senegalese pilgrims in major Moroccan cities. Even the arrival of Nigerians, Ghanaians, Malians and other sub-Saharan Africans was not a major problem in the early 1990s. Then in 1992 Morocco agreed receive immigrants returned from Spain. Although the agreement was to take back Moroccans, Spain began to send to Morocco sub-Saharan Africans from 2002. As Spain tightened entry routes more and more sub-Saharan Africans began to live destitute lives in Morocco. Secretly Morocco began to round them up and dump them in the desert, in Algeria. Algeria began to rescue scores of heavily de-hydrated people or find copses of people that died from hunger and thirst. Then on the 28 September tragic night when hundreds of refugees, tired of waiting for a chance to enter Ceuta stormed the fence, scaled it with ladders and in response both the Spanish and Moroccan security forces shot them down, killing five and wounding 100. Then on 6 October, refugees outside Melilla mounted their own assault at the fences, and again they were shot down. This time the figure of the dead was put at 10. Both countries were criticised by the international media. Spain then pressurised Morocco to act. Elie Goldsschmidt in *storming the desert* reported, *Infuriated by the heavy media coverage, Moroccan security forces hunted down undocumented Africans encamped in the mountains surrounding Ceuta and Melilla, arresting several hundred in just a few days. Initially, Morocco deported the detained to Algeria through an unofficial checkpoint at Qujda. Though the Algerian-Moroccan border has been closed since 1994, Qujda has become a main entry and expulsion point for clandestine immigrants to Morocco. Doctors Without*

Borders reported on 12 October that some migrants were also abandoned without food or water in a southern desert area. According to Interior Ministry official, Khalid Zerouali, an additional 3,600 Africans were subsequently placed on 22 direct flights back to their countries of origin. Daniel Pipes in *Europe under seige* reported that following this some 1,000 other Africans were in Moroccan southern desert. He said: *The removal was done with some brutality, dumping the Africans and leaving them to fend off the harsh elements almost without help.* Morocco then summoned the media and deported hundreds of sub-Saharan Africans into the desert. This was followed by several round-ups in the neighbourhoods and forests and repeated similar deportations. In 2003-2004, Morocco passed new immigration laws that institute severe punishment for irregular immigration and human smuggling . . . Although the new laws make reference to relevant international conventions, migrants rights ignored in practice.

In 2005 Amnesty International accused Morocco of entering desert parts of other countries and dumping over 500 people in uninhabited areas of the Sahara desert of various sub-Saharan countries. Amnesty International also discovered that a group of 35 homeless people that had been expelled from Morocco, who had then entered Libya and were being detained in a room 8 m by 5 m with only seventeen bunk beds for the thirty-five of them. A twenty-seven-year-old Malian detainee explained:—'You have to urinate in a bucket on the spot. For other personal needs, we are obliged to bang on the door and beg the guards to let you go to the lavatory. Sometimes they make us wait twenty to thirty minutes before opening the door for us.'

The scholar Hein de Haas in the article 'Irregular migration . . . European Union' cited above gives two conflicting disruptions of the 'irregular immigration' into North Africa. Initially he wrote that '*The trans-Sahara journey is generally made in several stages, and might take anywhere between one month and several years. On their way, migrants often settle temporarily in towns located on migration hubs to work and save money for their onward journey, usually in large trucks or pick-ups.*' (Haas.

p17). Later in the same article, he says, (Although migrants are commonly depicted as (passive) victims of 'unscrupulous traffickers' and 'merciless' criminal-run smuggling networks, the available empirical evidence based on research among the migrants concerned strongly suggest that trafficking is rare and that the vast majority migrate on their own initiative. Haas went on to write: 'In the process of crossing the Sahara to North Africa, migrants spend hundreds of dollars on bribes, smugglers, transportation, and daily necessities. In 2003, it was estimated that a boat crossing from Morocco to Spain cost US$200 for adults; to US$500 to US$800 for Moroccans, and up to US$800 to US$1,200 for Francophone and Anglophone sub-Saharan Africans, respectively (Lahlou 2003). Prices for the Libya-Italy crossing seem to be roughly similar (Haasp18)

It is unlikely that sub-Saharan Africans that have occupations that enable them to raise the money mentioned in the quotations would like to leave these occupations to migrate to Europe where there are daily announcements of depressed economies, unemployment and settlement problems. They would also be unlikely to want to travel across the ocean in the dangerous vehicles discussed elsewhere. Perhaps Dr Haas was talking about the migrants from China, India, Pakistan and Bangladesh which he said were beginning to use the Saharan Trail. However Dr Haas was talking of immigrants, mostly what he called irregular immigrants. As observed earlier many scholars have discussed the movement of immigrants, 'irregular immigrants', illegal immigrants, refugees and asylum seekers as if they are one and the same thing. Indeed some scholars have led politicians to believe refugees and asylum seekers are criminals and even terrorists. Many laws passed in Europe of late have treated immigration, crime, and terrorism as closely related issues and have often used the same laws to cover them. This book is about refugees who do get this status after they have applied for asylum. The book aims to persuade people to discuss the plight of people in refugee camps in Africa and Europe. These are the people who sometimes have to work for years to raise money to escape the trauma at home.

CHAPTER 5

Facing the Mighty Mediterranean Sea

We saw that majority of the people that escape persecution in sub-Saharan Arica do not leave their countries and regions. We saw that most people from the troubled Rwanda, DRC, Burundi, southern Sudan, and Sudan did not leave the region. They moved from one area to another. It is not a coincidence that the majority of asylum seekers that reach Europe and the United Kingdom are from these countries. It also makes nonsense of the argument by some scholars that the majority of these people are wealthy Africans looking for alternative and better-paying jobs. A research carried out by the United Nations shows that 58 per cent of the people that crossed to the Canary Islands between 2006 and 2007 had never been to school and only half were literate. They came from the West African fishermen or fishing communities. (The Role of Organised Crime in the Smuggling of Migrants from West Africa to the European Union: United Nations Office on Drugs and Crime, Vienna: New York, 2011).

A minority of the people that suffer persecution in sub-Saharan Africa take the very difficult journey across the desert. Armed gangs of bandits, criminals, and thieves often lie in wait for these people. We have seen how many have lost lives and property and how some women have been abducted. This partly explains why there is a large group of unaccompanied minors that reach Europe each year. Des Haas estimates that only between 65,000 and 120,000 people from sub-Saharan Africa reach the Maghreb states each year. Most of these people will be looking for protection from the many forms of persecution they will have experienced at home. With the levels of Internet communications there is today, most of those that venture to cross the Mediterranean will do so because they have no choice.

We have seen how sub-Saharan Africans are treated in the Maghreb states, and we have seen how some people prefer to live in mountains in Morocco while waiting for the chance to cross the Mediterranean. Sorious Samura, a journalist of the *Insight News TV*, decided to become an illegal immigrant in Morocco and said about the asylum seekers outside Ceuta (Spanish) fence, 'Huddled together in cold, flimsy tents and hounded by daily police raids, the immigrants struggle to survive with no food, money or peace of mind.' He was with three friends, and one of the three, Gus, was captured. Samura left the Moroccan forest and met with Theo in Ceuta. Samura soon found that life for those that had managed to take the dangerous swim under the fence was not better in Ceuta. His suffering there was just as he was in the forest. One day, Samura discovered a derelict factory known as Longhouse, where those on the run from authorities lived. The conditions were horrifying. Another journalist, Tordue Salem, wrote that a Committee of the House of Representatives in Nigeria is reported to have estimated as many as 10,000 Nigerian teenage girls could be held captive by sex-slave traders in Morocco and Libya, many of them from Edo State. (Reps move to repatriate 10,000 Nigerian girls from Libya and Morocco: Vanguard (Nigeria) 26 June 2009). Orji Ogbonnaya Orji about modern slavery in Libya: *When we visited the country in company with the President of Nigeria, Olusegen Obasanjo, in August 1999, we have come face to face with what could be regarded as modern day slavery. We saw hundreds of Nigerians, mainly young boys and girls who were lured with the promise of being taken to Europe but abandoned instead in Libya where they were subjected to a lot of horrifying experiences.*

In the following month, September 1999, the Government of
the Libyan Arab Jamahiriya announced at a summit meeting of
the Organisation of African Unity that it welcomed immigrants
of African origin. At about the same time, the Libyan Arab
Jamahiriya was estimated to be home to some 449,000 regular
migrants and no fewer than one million irregular ones, out of
the population of less than 6 million. A major outburst of popular
violence directed at immigrants in 2006 resulted in hundreds of
deaths and caused some sub-Saharan Africans living in Libya
to move elsewhere. Many of the Nigerians whom President
Obasanjo had met in 1999 were forcibly returned allegedly after
being stripped of all their belongings before being bundled into
aircrafts. (Inside Aso Rock; Ibadan, spectrum Books; 2003, p.
114)

Facing the Mighty Mediterranean Sea

So people chose to cross the Mediterranean as a last option.
Many knew that they would probably lose their lives in the
attempt. In the earlier years, many often managed to reach
Europe because 'at that time, many boat migrants made little
effort to avoid detection once they had reached European
territory, since they would normally be transferred when
apprehended to a major city for processing' (United Nations
Office on Drugs and Crime, Vienna: New York 2011). But since
the year 2000, the southern European states, Frontex, and
some Maghreb countries joined forces to arrest and deport
immigrants even before processing them and to force boats to
sail back to Africa without replenishing their food and water
supplies and replacing their makeshift boats. As a result, there
has been rising numbers of deaths of sub-Saharan Africans on
the sea each year, and not even the UNHCR is concerned enough
to do something about these deaths. The International Centre
for Migration Policy Development (ICMPD) reported that only 30
per cent of irregular migrants who are intercepted while trying
to cross the Mediterranean are from south of the Sahara. ICMPD
also reported that in 2005, it estimated that some 830,000
migrants travelled annually from the African continent to the

then-twenty-five countries of the European Union, of which only 100,000 to 120,000 crossed the Mediterranean. In the same report, Spain said that only 8 per cent of irregular arrivals were by sea. What has been happening is that in the last decade the poor sub-Saharan African boats had either broken down, sunk, or got damaged by sea storms and increasing numbers of sub-Saharan Africans had perished. Richer migrants from Asia, eastern Europe, and South America now fly into the Maghreb countries and hire speedboats to enter Europe illegally. But the numbers of sub-Saharan asylum seekers and refugees have perished in the mighty sea of North Africa. Several people and organisations have tried to make the world aware of this tragic loss of human life unsuccessfully. One organisation *united* for Intercultural Action, European network against nationalism, racism, fascism, and support of migrants and refugees and came up with the following figures for the years 1993 to June 2011:

Year	Total	Drowned	Suicide	Police Cruelty	No Medication	Froze to Death	Stepped on Mines
1993	62	20	14	18	3	1	0
1994	125	84	20	3	0	2	0
1995	156	93	33	20	4	0	4
1996	458	399	27	19	0	0	5
1997	384	341	9	12	0	0	0
1998	390	343	18	15	0	1	0
1999	519	436	14	41	6	0	6

From 1999 the deaths on the Mediterranean dramatically go up as victims of the Somali wars, Sierra Leone (1981-2001), Liberia (1999-2005), and DRC (1997-2005) found that they were not welcome in North Africa and decided to venture across the mighty ocean. Because they did not have money, they managed to hire only the small and unreliable makeshift boats. A small number decided to use the Turkish route. These are the asylum seekers that stepped on mines between Greece and Turkey.

Year	Total	Drowned	Suicide	Police Cruelty	No Medication	Froze to Death	Stepped on Mines	Starvation
2000	598	411	18	19	4		2	2
2001	474	419		11	3	4		
2002	795	708	16	17	6			1
2003	1301	1152	30	11	3	10	8	93
2004	993	844	16	22	8	23	4	
2005	912	829	12	27	4	1	5	
2006	2021	1975	21	6	5	4	3	130
2007	1839	1755	13	7	16	8		23
2008	1266	981		38	16	2		54
2009	1435	1318						
2010	273	185						
2011	1517	1507						
Total	15518	13799						

Although the document shows incidents when asylum seekers from sub-Saharan Africa were assaulted and killed by the police and security guards when they sought asylum in North Africa and the southern European states, most of them were individual cases. The document, however, cites five cases where large numbers of people were killed for claiming asylum, and most of the incidents were in Libya. On 9 August 2009, Libyan police massacred eighteen Somali prisoners detained in Benghazi. Twelve died instantly, but majority managed to escape. The police mounted a follow-up exercise in which they killed six on the same day and twenty the following day. On 30 May 2010, the Libyans, according to this document, executed twenty people from Chad, Egypt, and Nigeria for criminal offences. The Moroccans, on their part and as part of an arrangement with the Spanish government, shot dead several people that attempted to scale the razor wire fence protecting Ceuta and Melilla from the Africans. The most notable incidents were that of 28 September 2005 when they shot and killed five people and the well-documented incident in October 2005 when they were joined by the Spanish guards to kill eleven people at both Ceuta and Melilla. Turkey also shot asylum seekers, their largest being on 10 May when they shot dead nine people attempting to cross the border illegally.

While thousands of people died in the desert after their vehicles broke down, most of them lost lives in the earlier years. In later years, people often were better prepared and in most cases travelled in a convoy or behind army vehicles. So to have people dying in the Algerian Desert suggest that the people were forced out of the normal routes were victims of dumping. Most North African states signed repatriation agreements with southern European states, but because many of the people that were repatriated did not have proper documentation or could not be received by their home governments, some of the North African states adopted the habit of dumping these people in the desert. On 12 September 2008, some twenty-five bodies of decomposing sub-Saharan Africans were discovered by the Algerian police in the Sahara Desert, and on 15 August 2010, the police found fifty survivors out of a group of sixty that was stranded in the desert: three people from Cameroon, three from Mali, two from Senegal, one from Gambia, and one from Guinea who were part of the group of twelve from each country; they had died of thirst.

The document shows a surprising large number of persons that died from starvation and thirst on the Mediterranean Ocean. These were most probably people whose boats were not allowed to dock and forced back by guards on the southern European coast or people that got lost after taking a different course from the original and familiar one. The report has about a dozen of reports in which hundreds of sub-Saharan people lost their lives in the sea. On 19 October 2003, some sixty-three Somalis died of cold or hunger, hypothermia, and starvation on a boat from Libya to Lampedusa. Fifty of the bodies were thrown into the sea when found by the Italians. Most sub-Saharan Africans that died at sea were thrown into the sea. No country was prepared to be responsible for their burial. On 31 March 2005, some fourteen sub-Saharan Africans died of starvation on a boat drifting off the Egyptian coast, and on a boat that was destined for Spain, a child died of hypothermia in its mother's arms on the next day. On a boat drifting off Lampedusa, on 27 July 2006, out of the total of twenty-eight occupants, half died of starvation before the boat was allowed to dock. On 14

October 2006, twenty-eight people died of hunger between
the Senegal and the Canary Islands, and one person died of
starvation in the Mauritanian Hospital after the rescue operation
came too late to save him. On 12 August 2006, the Spanish
coastguard refused a boat to dock and forced it to return to
Africa. Twenty-eight sub-Saharan Africans died as a result of
this action. Some eighteen Senegalese had just died on a ship
off Dakar from gas explosions from bottles on the ship. The
report also gives the death of fifty Senegalese who started off
from an Egyptian port but died of starvation on the sea trying
to reach Europe. The last report of large numbers dying of
starvation in 2006 was one on 20 December when twenty-four
died off Mauritania on the way to the Canaries. There are three
reports of large groups dying of starvation in 2007: On 21 August
2007, six sub-Saharan men died on their way to Lampedusa;
on 7 November, some fifty sub-Saharan people, mainly from
Gambia, Mali, and Senegal, died of starvation and dehydration
on their way to the Canary Islands; and on 2 December, some
forty sub-Saharan asylum seekers died of starvation on a ship
from the Senegal to the Canary Islands. Three reports appear
for 2000: Fifteen sub-Saharans starved to death near Almeria
on 21 August 2008, and on 21 August 2008, in a ship of sixty
sub-Saharan people, thirty-five died of starvation and were
thrown into the sea before the boat which was probably forced
to return to Africa was rescued by the Moroccan coastguards.
In the boats that reached their destinations, there were cases
of fewer people that starved to death, for which we do not have
enough space to record.

But perhaps the largest numbers of sub-Saharans died on the
sea during the first six months of the Arab Awakening of 2011.
They were hated for being foreigners and accused of supporting
the status quo. Many of them, fearing a repeat of the suffering
they had experienced at home, took very dangerous risks to
cross the ocean. The document records the drowning of people
between March and April only, and they have the following
deaths: On 14 March, forty people drowned near Lampedusa;
on 37 March 308, 335 died near Italy; on 28 March 2011, a
boat from Sadi Bilal sank, and 241 people died; on 31 March,

seventy Somalis and Eritreans drowned near Lampedusa; on 2 June, some 270 drowned when their boat capsized towards Lampedusa; and on 6 June, a boat carrying 208 asylum seekers, mainly from Chad and Ivory Coast, drowned near Lampedusa.

The report is rich on the different forms of problems the asylum seekers experience trying to reach Europe by crossing the Mediterranean Sea face. Below is a description of what happens on the journeys across the ocean.

Crossing the Atlantic to the Spanish Canary Islands

One of the ways through which refugees have reached Europe and eventually the United Kingdom is through crossing from West Africa to the Spanish Canary Islands. Tens of thousands of men, women, and children attempt to make the perilous trip on one of the heavily crowded makeshift boats and make treacherous sea crossings to the Canary Islands. Many do not survive the journey. Despite the fact that several measures by European governments and EU organisations to stop the boats from reaching the Islands have been enacted, arrivals dropped only from 32,000 a year in 2006 to 13,424 in 2009.

When compared to the North African route and despite the fact that tens of thousands of West Africans have lost their lives in the Atlantic Ocean, this route can be regarded as safer and a lot easier than the northern alternative.

Crossing the Mediterranean Ocean: While sub-Saharan African have crossed the Atlantic to the Spanish Canary Islands or scaled the fences to reach the African Spanish towns of Ceuta and Melilla, the main route used and the route where the majority of those that have lost their lives is the route across the Mediterranean Ocean. Thousands of sub-Saharan Africans had started from the Libyan towns of Tripoli, Benghazi, and numerous other sea coasts and the Tunisian towns of Tunis and others in heavily overcrowded and dangerous makeshift boats owned by smugglers to try and reach the island of Malta or Italian islands of Lampedusa and others. Many Libyan fishermen have stopped fishing and now depend on smuggling people across the ocean. But because these boats are small, unsuitable for human transport, and often very much overcrowded, many of them break down in the middle of the ocean, get damaged by ocean currents, and sink. Malta, Spain, and Italy have found it expensive to monitor the ocean by air and patrol boats. This is complicated by the fact that the country that saves the sinking boat becomes responsible for the refugees, so often sinking boats are often not saved by anybody. Writing in a Roman newspaper Peter Popham described in these words the type of boats used by some of these adventurers: *In October 2003, they boarded a boat dilapidated wooden fishing boat—in mid ocean where the dead and the still-just-alive were all mixed up together, the survivors wailing for help. When the copses had been removed, one young woman, unconscious and barely breathing but still alive, was found trapped underneath them. Fifteen survived and thirteen died but survivors said about 70 had already been tossed overboard. Earlier that year, in June 2003 more than 200 died when their grossly overloaded vessel sunk.* A different reporter said, since they had started collecting such evidence in December 2002, the number of victims had risen to 3899. Out of these, 588 persons died in 2003; 296 in 2004; 343 in 2005; 653 in 2006; 732 in 2007; 628 in 2008, and 431 in 2009.

Malta

Malta, with a population of on 400,000 and many problems including shortage of water, is overwhelmed by the large numbers of illegal immigrants arriving on its coast every day. Its economy, which based mainly on fishing and tourism, has been badly affected. This, however, does not justify the manner in which they have treated the refugees. Maltese fishermen do not report sinking ships to the government. *According to representatives of the country's main fishermen association (Ghaqda Kooparative tas-said), Maltese fishermen, who often sail with a crew of only two or three, usually avoid coming too close to a boat carrying 20 or 30 migrants, as they fear being overpowered. Moreover if they alert authorities, it may take several hours to arrive on the spot, meaning that the fishermen's day of work is lost without compensation* (Centrum für Europäische Politik/www.EU-27 Watch). Maltese authorities put the number of deaths in the Mediterranean at 600 a year, but they also say the number could be much higher. They try as much as they can not to be responsible for any deaths that happen outside their waters. On 4 June 2007, *The Independent* reported that the Maltese government could not receive fifty-three corpses of Eritrean immigrants who had been identified to be in distress ten days earlier by their surveillance plane. The paper wrote: *When the boat crammed with fifty-three Eritreans was photographed by Maltese monitoring plane, it was only eighty miles south of the Island, perhaps three hours sailing time for the sort of vessel fast off shore patrol vessels Malta can deploy. When the patrol boat turned up, nearly nine hours later, there was no trace of the Eritreans. The Maltese refused to accept the 21 bodies later found in advanced decomposition. They were accepted for burial by the French maritime authority.* The paper goes on to report that two days later, the Maltese refused to accept twenty-seven Africans who spent three days and nights clinging to the walkway around a tuna pen at the sea. They were finally rescued by the Italians. All new arrivals are detained for twelve months if their asylum claim is still pending. Those who do not apply or whose applications are rejected can end up in custody for eighteen months under appalling conditions. In 2002 alone, some 12,000 immigrants were detained. UN Representative Ms Carmena Castrillo found an eight-year-boy in detention rather than in school and a Somali man, suffering from HIV and chicken pox, was found vegetating in a cell in complete isolation rather than in a hospital. There is a fast track procedure to release families with children, unaccompanied minors, pregnant women, breastfeeding mothers, and people with disabilities, but there are no more places to put them. *Euronews* reported on 4 July 2006 that over 700 illegal immigrants were being detained in an overcrowded former school that was never designed to accommodate so many people. University of Malta did a research on the rise of anti-immigrant, racist movements and activities. I found that the feelings were on the rise, but they had not yet become xenophobic. 'In 2006, for the first time, a number of violent acts were committed against the Jesuit Refugee Service (JRS) in Malta, and the houses of two journalists who had written articles condemning racism were also attacked. According to a survey done in 2005, 95 per cent of respondents had no objection to having European neighbours, while an equally high number were unwilling to live next to Arabs (93 per cent), Africans (90 per cent) or Jews (89 per cent). More than 75 per cent said they would not give shelter to refugees who had fled their countries because of political persecution, war, hunger or poverty.'

Italian Island of Lampedusa

Lampedusa is one of the small islands that are part of Italy. Most of the refugees there are rescued by the Italian Navy in the Mediterranean. Peter Popham said that the reception centre next to the airport was full to bursting. He said the centre is equipped to accommodate only 190 people and that there are only eight toilets which do not work well. He said there was no place for fresh arrivals to sleep. He said sometimes bodies of African migrants are washed out of the sea and pile up around sunbathers. His article says that the Italians wanted to see an end to the constant flow of arrival, and he quoted what a hard-hearted ally of Prime Minister Berlusconi said about the 200 Africans whose boat had sunk off the Island. *They died while travelling like many people on the roads . . . I want to hear the roar of cannon! The immigrants must be hunted down for better or for worse. Fire the cannon at them. Otherwise this will never stop.* These comments summarise the felling of many Europeans, although most did not think that shooting them down would stop them. There are three main ways asylum seekers can cross the oceans and enter Europe. Since this book is aimed at helping asylum seekers that want to reach the United Kingdom, the first two can be called the Anglophone routes. *Sail in*: Fewer asylum seekers from former UK colonies go to North Africa than to West African coast. Majority of the Anglophone Gambians, Ghanaians, Sierra Leoneans, and Liberians that sail across the Atlantic in makeshift boats go to the Canary Islands.

Fly in: Asylum seekers from South Africa usually have to fly into the United Kingdom. This is the most difficult way, not least, because the Home Office can easily control this form of immigration through regulating the airlines. It is also very expensive. Most asylum seekers that use it have relatives already in the United Kingdom. There are asylum seekers that have had to enter non-visa countries, change citizenship to that of the host country before flying to the United Kingdom to seek asylum. The United Kingdom has replied by withdrawing the non-visa conditions of all African countries. Most asylum seekers from South Africa have had to seek asylum in South Africa. South Africa has over three million Zimbabwean asylum seekers. It also has tens of thousands of Angolans, people from the DRC, Rwanda, Malawi, Somalia, and Nigeria. In fact, South Africa has a bigger immigration problem than the United Kingdom.

CHAPTER 6

Southern European Surprise
Reaction to New Arrivals

On the fiftieth anniversary of the founding of the UNHCR in 2001, the international body raised four issues affecting the host countries today essential to this study. The first was about the challenges facing the host countries. The UNHCR said:

The recurring cycles of violence and systematic human rights violation in many parts of the world are generating more and more intractable displacement situations. The changing nature of armed conflict and the patterns of displacement and serious apprehensions about 'uncontrolled' migration in the era of globalisation are increasingly part of the environment in which refugee protection has to be realised. Trafficking and smuggling of people, abuse of asylum procedures, and difficulties in dealing with unsuccessful asylum-seekers are additional compounding factors. Asylum countries in many parts of the world are concerned about the lack of resolution of certain long-standing problems: urban balance in burden-and responsibility-sharing, and increasing costs of hosting refugees and asylum-seekers. (Refugee protection: A guide to International Refugee Law: By Kate Jastram and Marilyn Achiron: UNHCR 2001, p. 3.)

The issue of violence and human rights violations will remain a third world problem for a long time. There are too many countries that were created in the Victorian times on foundations that failed to respect ethnic and cultural divisions that had survived for centuries. Many Third World countries created by the colonial system were based on availability of exploitable natural resources, and local communities were forced to accept them. The concept of democracy was new to these Third World communities, so since independence, traditional leaders have been fighting to repossess their power, hence wars such as those in the Great Lakes region and extreme violence such as that which resulted in the genocide in Rwanda. To most of the current African politicians, democracy is a very new concept, and democratic elections have generally led to the creation of autocratic regimes, military governments, or absolute chaos. In some sub-Saharan countries, governments are so weak that different parts of countries are controlled by different armed bandits, and some military officers serve the government during the day and bandit groups during the night.

The result has been uncontrolled migration. While sub-Saharan African countries that host refugees from other African countries seem not to have problems in defining refugees and countries of origin, European host countries have, however, failed to agree on which countries have violence that has led to the need to protect its people as refugees. European countries do not agree on which Third World countries are safe countries. Many European countries have problems of distinguishing between a refugee and a migrant. Scholars have confused the issue further by creating the name 'irregular immigrant'. So now we have immigrant, illegal immigrant, refugee, and asylum seeker. These words are being used to suit individual host country situations and legal systems. In some countries, they are closely related to the economic benefits the host country gets from the country of origin.

The second issue the report raised was the argument that Third World or developing countries do shoulder most of the refugee burden because a displaced person becomes a refugee only after he has left his home country. In countries like Sudan, DRC, and South Africa, which are themselves so big that each of them is bigger that western Europe, it is very difficult for displaced persons to be able to travel out of their countries to become refugees. So the UNHCR officially can't help them. The passage reads:

Developing countries argue that the burden of asylum are not shared equally: while they host thousands and sometimes millions, of refugees, wealthier countries are restricting access to their own territories and reducing support to the countries of first asylum. (UNHCR op cit p. 9) The rich world has failed to appreciate that all the sub-Saharan countries that have had all these wars since the 1990s have large populations of IDPs. The figures below show that as late as 2010 the situation had not improved.

Country	IDPs (End of 2010)
Burundi	157,200
C.A.R.	192,500
Chad	131,000
Ivory Coast	3,672,100
D.R.C.	1,721,400
Kenya	300,000
Somalia	1,463,800
Sudan	1,548,000
Uganda	125,600

(UNHCR: Annex 6: 2010: Refugees and people in a refugee-like situation, excluding asylum seekers 2010).

The world has also failed to notice that sub-Saharan countries have had to host refugees from the neighbouring countries even as their own citizens look for asylum elsewhere. There are too many bandit groups controlling sections of countries, making it difficult for the central government to be able to protect all their citizens. Let us look at the example of the DRC, which as we have seen before has not had stability since independence and had the whole eastern provinces occupied by Rwanda towards the end of the 1990s. This led to the regional war where DRC, Angola, and Zimbabwe fought on one side and

Rwanda, Uganda, Congo, and CAR fought on another. Peace was only agreed in 2003. As a result of this war, the DRC is going through a difficult time as they try to defeat the bandit groups that are using the DRC mineral wealth to persecute DRC citizens as they force them to be or remain mining slaves. At the beginning of 2010, the UNHCR showed the world that the DRC was far from stable. DRC citizens were not coming to Europe because they wanted European jobs and enjoy Western civilisation. They had nowhere else to go. The UNHCR was failing to assist the large numbers that had claimed asylum in sub-Saharan countries. They published the following figures of where DRC citizens were claiming asylum in Africa in 2010.

Countries DRC citizens claimed asylum (2010)	Total Numbers
Angola	13,364
Burundi	24,614
CAR	20,899
Congo	103,213
France	10,841
Germany	6,093
Rwanda	53,647
South Africa	11,708
Sudan	19,709
Uganda	73,175
Tanzania	63,275
Zambia	21,965

But as all these citizens claimed asylum in other countries the DRC was able to host asylum seekers from the following countries:

Countries whose citizens sought asylum in DRC	Total Numbers
Angola	84 374
Burundi	17 585
Rwanda	80 525

The third issue relevant to the issue of the plight of refugees is the 1969 OAU Convention. The report says:

Any person compelled to leave his/her country because of 'external aggression, occupation, foreign domination or events seriously disturbing public order in either part or the of his country of origin or nationality'—This means that people fleeing civil disturbances, widespread violence and war are entitled to claim the status of refugee in states that are parties to this Convention, regardless of whether they have a well founded fear of persecution or not. (UNHCR op cit; p. 13)

Most countries outside Africa did not sign the OAU Convention. They, therefore, do not necessarily give asylum to victims of civil wars from Africa even though the UNHCR recommends that they should.

Lastly, the UNHCR emphasises that refugees must be protected. There must be non-refoulement: It says:

The state may not return a refugee, in any manner whatsoever, to the frontiers of territories where his/her life or freedom would be threatened because of his/her race, religion, nationality, membership of a particular social group or political opinion (the principle of non-refoulement). This is true even if the refugee entered the host country illegally.

After signing the 1951 Convention and the 1967 Protocol, how did Europe, as a host continent, address the four issues raised by the UNHCR? To answer this, let us look at the main legal framework used by the European Union in their handling of the immigration issues on the continent.

Between 1951 and 1985, Europe did little to restrict refugees. As we shall see later, Europe, in fact, encouraged them to come because the European continent was experiencing an economic boom. Many immigrants from eastern Europe and Asia remained in Europe and worked with limited restrictions mainly because their labour was cheaper and easy to dispose of. So besides signing the 1951 Refugee Convention, Europe had the 1957 Rome Treaty. The treaty was signed by six nations, and it created the European Economic Community (EEC). Through this treaty, freedom of movement of citizens of the countries was agreed upon. Then they signed the 1967 Protocol which extended the right of asylum to all refugees and removed the geographical application of the convention. Finally, they signed the 1985 Schengen Agreement between five member states. It allowed free movement within internal (Schengen) area and removed internal border controls to these members. But here is what Deirdre Hogan said of the Schengen Agreement: *The agreement was said to be about the freedom of movement over the internal borders between Schengen countries however in order to compensate for increased freedom of movement within the Schengen area, much of the agreement was about increased control of travellers coming in. Common rules regarding visas, asylum rights and checks at external borders were adopted and coordination of the police, customs and judiciary was increased. In fact while just four articles in the convention are about open borders, 138 are about increased control. (Deirdre Hogan: Building Fortress Europe: Increased integration of EU asylum and immigration policy (Sept. 2002)*

The Soviet Union collapsed in 1980 and triggered off revolutions throughout eastern Europe. Two great surges of refugees and asylum seekers from eastern Europe in the 1990s were experienced during the wars in Croatia and Bosnia (1992-1993) and the upsurge of violence and ethnic cleansing in Kosovo (1998-1999). In Africa, we have already seen that war broke out in Sierra Leone (1989-2001), Liberia (1999-2003), DRC (1997-2005), and Nigeria and Ivory Coast and refugees began the long journeys that led to the loss of lives for the majority of them either in their countries, across African borders, across the Sahara, or across the Mediterranean. But more and more of them began to arrive in Europe as we got to the end of the century.

The initial reaction of the European Union was to welcome them. Up to the 1990s more than 90 per cent of all asylum seekers in Europe were not granted full convention status but allowed to stay in member states under ad hoc conditions. They were given this partial status because they were either displaced from the wars of the Yugoslav succession or considered endangered by Home Office or national courts if they were forcibly repatriated, even if they could not meet the stricter standards of proof demanded by the convention to secure full refugee status. The European Commission argued that migrants were needed for the European economy and for the future viability of the continent's pension system. These needs were recognised, and the recruitment of workers from the rest of the world was officially sanctioned for the first time since the official stop in the wake of the 1973 oil-shock. But towards the end of the century, there was increasing demands from sections of Europe to restrict the flow of refugees. From the 1980s onwards, anti-immigration discourse towards refugees as 'bogus asylum seekers', 'abusers of asylum system', or disguised 'economic migrants' became and remain part of the 'common sense' of political discussion in western Europe. (Carl Levy: The European Union after 9/11: The demise of a Liberal Democratic Asylum Regime? p.33)

As a result, Europe began to make it really difficult for refugees that had managed to escape the brutalities of Africa; travelled across jungles and crocodile infested rivers; managed to cross the mighty Sahara desert; escaped imprisonment and torture in North Africa; crossed the Mediterranean in a makeshift boat; and claim asylum at a European station. Individual countries began to put restrictions to entry before going to the European Union with restriction proposals. For example, in 1986, the Danish government introduced the 'safe third country' concept, the Danish Clause; Germany and Britain introduced the carriers' sanctions in 1987; and many countries introduced visa restrictions to foreign national. The 1986 Single European Act allowed free movement of European people, implicitly European citizens. For the first time, crime is associated to (illegal) immigration. It created legal ways for setting up a working group to prevent the opening of borders from affecting internal security. The 1990 Dublin Convention removed the possibility of 'asylum shopping' by asylum seekers; only a single European state became responsible for an asylum application. A sub-Saharan African, for example, who spoke English only as the second language to his mother tongue, would find it almost impossible to reach the United Kingdom to claim asylum if he entered Europe by sea through the Mediterranean. He would be denied the right to claim asylum in a country he felt safe. But a number of disagreements remained on the issue of new arrivals. At a London meeting of interior ministers in 1991, they discussed the issues of 'safe third country', whether a 'manifestly unfounded' asylum claim should be rejected without the right of appeal and the concept of 'safe country of origin', where there is a presumption of no risk of persecution and where an expedited procedure could be used. There were no agreements on these issues. They had to be decided along with readmission agreements. So for much of the decade the issues remained on the table while different countries handled the issues individually and differently. Much of the concern of the continent was how to handle the issue of the large pool of illegal immigrants from eastern Europe. But towards the end of the decade came two agreements that have affected the lives of thousands, if not millions, of sub-Saharan Africans that have attempted to enter Europe since then. These were the Amsterdam Treaty on 1997 and the Tampere Agreement of October 1999.

The 1997 Amsterdam Treaty introduced the beginning of a new era in asylum policy. Title IV, Article 63 of the Amsterdam Treaty refers to the adoption of minimum standards on procedures in member states for granting and withdrawing refugee status and establishing of EU-wide binding minimum rules on asylum and immigration. In the same year (1997), the Dublin Convention clarified that individuals claiming asylum must make their applications in the first EU country they enter. This applied to the then twelve member states. But it was the Tampere Agreement in Finland in 1999 set the terms for a new asylum policy over the European Union. Although the conditions were to be implemented over a period of five years, some countries moved faster than others. The first stage was to harmonise the asylum policies in respect to the following: Minimum standards for the reception of asylum seekers (Reception Directive); criteria and mechanism of determining the member state responsibilities for examining an asylum claim (Dublin II); minimum standards for the qualification of nationals of third countries as refugees (Qualification Directive); and minimum standard on the procedures for making decisions on asylum claims (Procedures Directive). All were to be to be adopted by 2004. Prior to the expiry of the deadline, EU Justice Ministers met in Brussels and agreed to adopt a draft Directive on Minimum Standards for Member States' procedures for granting and withdrawing refugee status (the Procedures Directive) and Directive on Minimum Standards for the Qualification and Status of Third Country Nationals and Stateless Persons or Persons who otherwise need international protection (the Qualification Directive).

Positives of the Directives System

Qualification Directive clarifies that in the determination of protection, status of the persecution is irrelevant and can include non-state actors such as militia; it also allows for the recognition as a refugee of those persons who have a well-founded fear of being persecuted on account of their sexual orientation or gender.

Procedures Directive applicants, including the right to remain in the EU country pending examination and decision making (including legal assistance and representation, personal interview, and stating of reasons for rejection.

Nevertheless, the Directive has failed to achieve its overall objective of establishing a Common European Asylum System based on the full and inclusive application of the Refugee Convention. This is arguably because of fundamental weaknesses in the draft Procedures Directive which potentially seriously undermines the ability of asylum seekers and refugees to access protection.

Directive's shortcomings

The wide scope of inadmissible applications listed in the draft Procedures Directive leaves EU states free to refuse access to asylum procedures. It is cause for concern that Article 27's definition for 'safe third country' concept is open to criticism due to the ambiguous stipulation of whether the third country concerned is in reality safe for the particular asylum applicant. The scope for the applicants to challenge the application of the 'third safe country' concept on the grounds that he is subjected to torture, cruel, inhuman, or degrading treatment or punishment in that country is not only minimalist but is also at variance with the general criteria for 'safe third country' in the same article. Scope for inadmissibility under the notion of so-called super safe third countries allows for refusal of substantive examination of asylum applications submitted by persons entering through certain European countries outside the European Union. The criteria for designating such 'super safe third countries' are formalistic. (Tim Morris: Chequered progress towards a Common EU asylum policy).

Algeria, Tunisia, and Libya's choice to work with Europe rather than Africa is one of the reasons why many sub-Saharan Africans lost their lives in these countries, in the desert, and at sea. One reason was the fact that the sub-Saharan wars lasted long times, and the political leaders there did not care much about refugees from their countries. They were also under pressure from the European countries to receive back refugees that had managed to reach Europe through these North African countries. Europe was saying they should have protected their borders properly, hence the financial and material support they offered and were accepted by these countries. The key point, however, is that they chose to work with Europe, and this resulted in a lot more suffering of the asylum-seeking Africans than was necessary. Europe used a number of strategies to limit and remove Africans from Europe, and three of them involved working with governments of North and West Africa. The strategies are part of the European migration policy which we can understand better if we follow it from the 1951 Geneva Convention.

In September 1999, the Red Cross approached the French government to get permission to house the thousands of destitute persons spending cold nights in the open, in the old warehouse of the Eurotunnel construction company. The French government agreed, and the Sangatte Camp housed between 63,000 and 80,000 people: Kosovans, Kurds, Iraqis, Afghans, and others. The camp was near the Calais terminal of the Eurotunnel. Most of the people intended to cross into the United Kingdom to apply for refugee status. They waited in the Red Cross camp for an opportunity to enter England illegally by train or in a lorry.

In June 2001, the European Union agreed on a directive aimed at carriers travelling by air, sea, and land. Heavy financial penalties were introduced against carriers that transport people whose documents were not in order towards the European Union.

Asylum Conditions After 9/11

Then on 11 September 2001 came the terrorist attack on the city of New York which impacted a lot on European opinion of immigration. Once again asylum issues became the major victim of decisions to be taken from then on. On 20 September, the Extraordinary Justice and Home Affairs met and asked the Commission to examine urgently the relationship between safeguarding internal security and complying with international protection obligations and instruments. On 5 December 2001, the European Commission issued a working paper, which encouraged member states to scrupulously and rigorously apply the exclusion clause contained in Article 1F of the Geneva Convention in order to prevent persons suspected of terrorist acts from asking asylum. The Commission suggested: *Pre-entry screening, including strict visa policy and the possible use of biometric data, as well as measures to enhance co-operation between border guards, intelligence services, immigration and asylum authorities of the state concerned, could offer real possibilities for identifying those suspected of terrorist* involvement at any stage. (com (2001) 743 final, 'The *relationship* Between Safeguarding Internal Security and Complying with Internal Protection Obligations and Instruments' Commission Working Document, Brussels, 5 December 2001, p. 6). On 27 December 2001, the common position adopted by the European Union required that member states investigate refugees and asylum seekers for the purpose of ensuring that the asylum seeker has not planned, facilitated, or participated in the commission of terrorist acts. Thus, the competing policy tradition of the securitisation of migration and refugee policy in Europe once again became the agenda setter after 9/11. (2001/931/CFSP Council Common Position of 27 December 2001 on Combating Terrorism, Article 16). Thus, in just three months of 9/11, the European Commission approved a working paper, which legally did not conflict with the conditions of the Refugee Convention. This is because the UNHCR's definition for terrorism is very wide, so it was used to bring changes that affected the conditions of refugees. Article 1F of the 1951 Convention excludes from international protection individuals who have committed a crime against peace or humanity, a war crime, a serious non-political crime, or an act contrary to the purposes and principles of the United Nations.

A number of hasty proposals were put forward in different meetings in different towns, and some of these were as follows:

The creation of Frontex in February 2002

The Interior Ministers decided to establish a European border guard force. It was tasked with surveillance of EU borders with cooperation with third countries.

June 2002: The Seville European Council meeting

The Seville meeting set out two main goals: (a) The fight against illegal immigration would be an absolute priority; (b) and that from then on, development aid would depend on the goodwill that countries of emigration would display in stopping departures towards Europe and in readmitting their nationals. Certain member states, including the United Kingdom and Spain, called for sanctions against countries that posed a migration threat. France and Germany opposed this. These decisions were not implemented directly as they would be against sections of the 1951 Convention and 1967 Protocol.

August 2002: French Minister Sarkozy announced the closure of the camp at Sangatte. The French and British negotiated and agreed on the fate of the camp's residents.

27 January 2003: The Council Directive laid down standards for the reception of asylum seekers.

February 18 2003: The Dublin II Regulation

Only the first country reached by an asylum seeker would be responsible for processing an application. This meant that most sub-Saharan Africans would have their asylum applications processed in the southern European states, mainly Spain, Italy, Greece, and Portugal. They would also be processed on the Spanish enclaves of Melilla and Ceuta and the Canary Islands. They would also be processed on the Island of Malta and Italian island of Lampedusa.

February 2003: The European Union agreed to start a neighbourhood policy for co-management of borders with neighbouring countries for surveillance, information exchange, and training. This became a very useful decision for the British and French who assisted each other, especially at the Eurotunnel. The European Union also agreed on 'Reception Directives', which set minimum standards for receiving asylum seekers. Countries were free to limit applicants' movement and access to employment.

March 2003: Tony Blair's 'Vision for Refugees' speech

In the wake of Tony Blair's speech on 'Vision for Refugees', European leaders endorsed at the Florence Summit in October 2004 the concept of building 'transit processing centres' for potential immigrants outside European frontiers. In practice, and spurning the Geneva Convention, people entering the European Union illegally would be collectively returned to the borderland states, without person-by-person checks of nationality, migration route, and reason for seeking shelter in the European Union, and after being confined in special detainment spaces. These spaces already exist in the European Union, in transit zones at airports, where the UNHCR and human rights organisations have little access, as well as at border camps in Ceuta, Canary Islands, on the Italian Island of Lampedusa, and on some Greek Islands. Before the idea was endorsed, the Germans and Italian Interior Ministers launched the proposal in August 2003 and invited the European Union to create 'emigration platforms' or 'processing centres' in order to screen migrants and asylum seekers outside the European Union.

September 2003: Family Reunion Directive

It had been discussed for three years, and it was agreed to restrict the rules of family reunion.

January 2004: Eurodac Regulations come into force

This was a unified database for the purpose of making Dublin II Regulation enforceable.

29 April 2004: Qualification Directive

Council Directive of 29 April on minimum standards for the qualification and status of third country nationals or stateless persons as refugees or as persons who otherwise need international protection and the content of the protection issued was published.

December 2005: Directive on 'Asylum Procedures'

Although EU states do not agree on the application of some of the principles agreed on this day, they all apply all of them, and this has had very negative effects on the application of asylum. The principles were criticised by European Parliament, the Council of Europe, UNHCR, and some NGOs, but criticism on its own has often not been enough to bring about change. The European Union agreed that States may detain applicants in special facilities. Asylum seekers had in the past been detained in special places, namely in prisons, detention centres, on board the ships they had arrived in, in windowless containers, and even on open land. Detention for asylum seekers was almost always accompanied with physical abuse: being beaten, raped, insulted, and even being killed. So authorising the habit was a very negative development in the asylum process. The second decision was that asylum requests would not necessarily result in the right to live in the country. This was to make detention at and deportations from the airports, seaports, and train stations acceptable. In essence, this decision was an indirect authorisation of refoulement, which was against the terms of the 1951 Convention. The next stated that exceptional procedures were to be envisaged, namely, rejection of manifestly unfounded applications and fast track and priority procedures. Among the criteria for rejection, notions of 'safe country of origin', 'first country of asylum', and 'safe third country' were placed on the spotlight. Then, of course, they stated that there would be the right of appeal but that the right would not suspend deportation.

Different European groupings continue to meet regularly and change aspect of the laws affecting the entry of refugees into Europe. Most of their decisions are on immigration and illegal immigration. The deaths *barely register on Europe's conscience. Instead, the problem of in criminological terms, focusing on the links with organised crime, rather than the rights of refugees. But policies of deterrence, which assume tougher penalties and tighter border controls can reduce movement of people, do not work. Instead such policies create a market for the services of trafficking and smuggling, which are now essential for refugees who want to enter the EU (Institute of Race Relations Release: 29 July 2003: The other asylum statistics: Governments count the numbers coming in, But who counts the numbers that do not make it?)* The European Union has not until now separated asylum from immigration, a deliberate act which want the world to believe there are no refugees coming from Africa. As a result, genuine asylum seekers are returned to countries where they suffer persecution. There is a current school of thought that the rich northern Europe is pushing the burden of asylum seekers to the poorer south who, in turn, are no longer processing them properly but signing repatriation agreements with North African countries to deport these people without going through the normal assessment of their refugee conditions. But even as we blame Europe and North Africa for failing to implement sections of the 1951 Convention and 1967 Protocol, we also must question UNHCR on what it has done to assist the tens of thousands of sub-Saharan Africans dying of hunger and thirst in the deserts, being ill-treated in North Africa and being captured like criminals, harassed, and deported into countries they have never been to. Where is the UNHCR? Yes, they have issued a few statements, but is that enough?

This book is following the journeys of asylum seekers from different parts of sub-Saharan Africa, the difficulties they meet as they travel through Africa and Europe on their journey to the United Kingdom and the difficulties they face as they apply for asylum there. The book will not dwell much on the European section of that journey because of the fact that travelling between EU countries has been made easier by the creation of the European Union. It is, however, necessary to look at how the southern European states are handling the sub-Saharan Africans that arrive there, not to claim asylum but to find a way to proceed to the north. We will, therefore, have a brief look at how Spain, Italy, Greece, and the island of Malta are handling asylum arrivals, most of who do not want to claim asylum in their countries but to move to other European states, and how they are handling those captured in the international waters.

Spain

For many years, the people of North Africa provided cheap seasonal labour to the farms and industries of southern Europe. They did not need visas. In the 1960s, thousands of such migrants crossed the Strait of Gibraltar from Morocco, through Spain to France. Spain did not ask them to obtain visas. They minimised the paperwork because they wanted to expedite the movement of the workers who were urgently needed in France.

Spain did not even take the issue of asylum seriously because it only ratified the 1951 Convention relating to the Status of Refugees and its 1967 Protocol in 1978. Spain ratified the 1950 Council of Europe Convention for the Protection of Human Rights and Fundamental Freedoms in 1979; it ratified the 1954 Convention Relating to the Status of Stateless persons in 1997, and it ratified the Council of Europe Convention on Action against Trafficking of Human Beings in 2009.

But as civil wars broke out in sub-Saharan Africa and refugees began to arrive, Spain introduced visas in 1991. By the end of the 1990s, nearly all the migrants trying to enter Spain became sub-Saharan Africans. One scholar said the number of sub-Saharan Africans intercepted along the coast of mainland Spain reached 17,000 in the year 2000.

Ceuta and Melilla

One area where refugees found easy to enter and find refuge were the two Spanish enclaves of Ceuta and Melilla. Spain had occupied these two Moroccan coasts for over 500 years, and they became the easiest points through which refugees could get protection. In 1993, Spain built high fences around both enclaves. *The fence is defined by two walls that have actually been raised to 6 metres in height from the original height of 3 metres, throughout their length (about 10 kilometres in Melilla and 8 kilometres in Ceuta). The 30 million euro razor wire round Ceuta was financed by the European Union. It consists of 8 kilometres of 3 metre fences topped with barbed wire, with regular watchtowers and a road running between them, to accommodate police patrols. Underground cables connect spotlights, noise, movement and infrared sensors and video cameras to a central control booth. The Melilla border fence cost Spain Euro 33 million and closely resembles the Ceuta fence. (Guido Cimadomo and Pilar Martinez Ponce: Ceuta and Melilla Fences: A Defensive System?)*

These are the fences that were scaled by the hundreds of hungry refugees that had travelled long distances across the desert and spent weeks, months, or even years in the mountains of Morocco waiting for a chance to claim refugee status. On the hundreds that scaled the Ceuta fence on 29 September 2005, very few managed to enter as they were fired at by security of both Morocco and Spain. Between 13 and 18 were shot dead, and fifty were injured. But the Melilla scaling was better planned. 700 entered Spanish territory, and six were shot dead. Unfortunately, all these people who scaled razor wire fence and were either killed or injured did not know that Morocco had Spain had reached an agreement in 1992 in which Morocco agreed to take back immigrants who had illegally entered Spain from its territory. And from the same year, Spanish guards at Ceuta and Melilla were returning sub-Saharan Africans to Morocco without even processing them. Returned sub-Saharan Africans were often imprisoned and assaulted and sometimes dumped in the desert. In fact, following the two fence-scaling incidents, Morocco invaded the mountains with heavily armed forces and arrested everyone they met walking about. The large-scale operations saw vehicle after vehicle loading arrested people into jails. *Spain may or may not have pressured Morocco to undertake the October 25 campaign of arrests and deportations. Human rights organisations are worried about a subtler and more systematic form of pressure: Europe has effectively conditioned the participation of southern and eastern Mediterranean states into the EU's Barcelona process of economic, strategic and cultural integration upon their cooperation in curbing immigration into Europe. (Spanish and Moroccan security forces were censured for having used live ammunition against people seeking refuge: September 12, 2005: By Eie Goldschmidt: Morocco and Europe's Anti-Migration Policy: Middle-East Research and Information Project)*

In fact, since the establishment of the Tampere Agreement of 1999 and The Hague programme in 2004, Spain started to work out agreements with the sub-Saharan African rulers. Spain took advantage of existing labour arrangements and then linked them with efforts to force the African states to agree to control emigrants from their countries. In July 2006, Spain introduced its 'Action Plan for Sub-Saharan Africans 2006-2008'. The aim was to bring Spain's diplomacy closer to sub-Saharan countries, mainly those on the African West Coast, and many of which had been established as the countries of origin and transit for migration flow into Spain. Fourteen countries, including Ghana, Guinea-Conakry, Mali, and Senegal, were prioritised.

Morocco Agreements: We saw earlier that Morocco and Spain had disagreements over the ownership on Ceuta and Melilla. But she decided to clear the mountains near Melilla and Ceuta of fugitive Africans following the attempt to scale the fences and the subsequent joint Moroccan-Spanish shooting down of the assailants, resulting in several deaths and injury of over 100 people. Morocco then dumped over a thousand of these people in several parts of the Sahara Desert without food and water. In May 2006, Spain agreed to provide new aid packages to Morocco in exchange for the latter applying more stringent border controls.

Mauritania Agreements: Under the code name 'Sea Horse' Spain established a project to control sub-Saharan Africans crossing from Mauritania to the Canary Islands. The 'Sea Horse' project included joint patrols of Spanish civil guard and Mauritanian police, as well as database Sea Horse Network, which aimed to track illegal immigration in real time. Spain aided Mauritania establish a detention centre in a former school in Nouadhibou that was used to confine migrants transiting Mauritania to take boats to the Canary Islands.

Gambia and Guinea Agreements: On 11 October 2006, Spain agreed to pay Guinea and Gambia £3.4 million each to prevent departures of their nationals and to support long-term development aimed at persuading young men to stay in their own nations. The two governments agreed to help identify their own nationals from among the hundreds who entered Spanish Canaries each week so they can be repatriated. Spain did not know that most of the migrants that reached Canary Islands did not come from the two countries. It emerged that only 156 sub-Saharan Africans that went to the Canary Islands in 2006 were from Guinea and only 500 or so were from the Gambia.

But the efforts to talk African politicians into making them arrest and detain their own people and refugees passing through their countries did not have expected results. The main reason is that Spain did not offer significant financial assistance, political, and other forms of advice to make these countries strong enough to control wars and human rights violations taking place in these countries and the subcontinent. In many cases, the very politicians Spain talked to were the main reason why the nations were at war. The task of addressing issues of corruption, ethnic violence, poverty, and civil wars in fourteen odd African countries would be too heavy for any one European country.

Spain, along with other southern European countries, monitored the seas to stop any boat they could find, arrest the occupants, and return them to Africa. Although against the 1951 Convention, refoulement was a primary method used to prevent the sub-Saharan Africans from reaching Spain. Different organisation have given figures of the numbers of sub-Saharan Africans captured and sent back to Africa, but the truth of the matter is no one knows the exact number. What we know, however, is that Spanish boats, helicopters, and other aircrafts were assisted by the EC either directly or through Frontex (after its formation in 2005), several UN organisations, and some North African states to capture and return to Africa as many of the refugee boats as possible. What we also know is that many of these acts of refoulement were never published because they were against the 1951 Convention. So tens of thousands of refugees were returned to Africa; many perished in the seas, and a few reached Spain.

Spain reacted by introducing a visa in 1991 for all African countries. It also developed the Integrated System of External Vigilance (SIVE). The southernmost tip of the Andalucia coastline is the Spanish side of the Straight of Gibraltar. This straight, which separates Europe from Africa by only 12 kilometres (8 miles), was the shortest point at which crossing would take place. Despite the rough sea at this point, refugee boats attempted and often perished crossing this short 8-mile journey.

Despite these deaths, many boats reached Spain through this point. In 1999, the Spanish government approved a plan for intensified surveillance at the Strait of Gibraltar, where the majority of unauthorised boats were arriving. The plan centred on the implementation of the Integrated System of External Vigilance (SIVE) and had a budget of about 150 million euro for the period of 1999-2004. Jordan Carling put this amount at about 1,800 euros for each migrant that was eventually intercepted during the five years in question. The key principles of the design of SIVE were early detection and central command. The system's functions can be summarised in the following steps:

1. A small boat with migrants on board approaches the coast.
2. A system of fixed and mobile sensors (radars, infrared cameras, and video cameras) detects the vessel 10 to 25 kilometres from the shore.
3. The control centre is alerted and can follow the vessel by remote control of the sensors. At a distance of approximately 5 kilometres from the coast, it is possible to estimate the number of people on board.
4. The vessel's course and time of arrival are estimated.
5. One or more interception units (boats, helicopters, and cars) are deployed in order to intercept the vessel close to the shore.

6. The passengers are apprehended and brought to the
   reception centre.

The Spanish government kept extending the area covered by
SIVE along the Strait of Gibraltar, both to the east and west.
By 2007, it covered the entire Andalucia coast. Spain installed
three fixed detection stations on Fuerteventura. Then the
system was extended to the islands of Lanzarote and Gran
Canaria.

But Spain was surprised by the changes that took place in
the boats' arrivals. First, there was a shift from the Andalucia
coast to the Canary Islands. In just two years following the
initiation of the SIVE on the mainland, the Canary Islands'
proportion of total interceptions rose from 12 per cent to 59
per cent, according to government statistics. Along the coast
of the Spanish mainland, a progressively smaller proportion
of migrant boats have crossed the narrow Strait of Gibraltar,
where SIVE was first installed and had had the greatest impact.
Instead, smugglers turned to crossing the westernmost part of
the Mediterranean Sea, known as the Sea of Alboran. Similarly,
on the Canary Islands, migrant boats' arrivals have avoided
areas with surveillance. The summers were usually marginally
affected, but the summer of 2001 received a third of all the
years' arrivals. On the Island of Fuerteventura itself, arrivals
shifted from the south, where the SIVE installations were
first located, towards the area around the capital, Puerto del
Rosario.

The overall result was that the problem of undetected
arrivals persisted. The migrants took longer to travel, but
they eventually arrived. Migrants arrived in areas without
established humanitarian infrastructure to receive them. Long
routes meant more difficulties on the sea. Engine failure,
changes in weather patterns, and other related problems meant
that more people drowned, died of hunger and thirst, and those
that became unwell did not receive urgent attention. But on the
other hand, smugglers adopted new routes and made technical
and organisational changes. They changed to larger and faster

boats. Wooden fishing boats were replaced by inflatable boats with outboard motors that travelled at a high speed and carried many more people. Smugglers also evaded the Guardia Civil by arriving in groups of several boats and fanning out when they reached the coast. Most importantly, the smugglers accepted the increasing likelihood of being detected and apprehended. They prepared for the possibility. Increasingly, the migrants being smuggled became mostly sub-Saharans, and it became more difficult for the Spanish government to return them to their countries of origin.

Detention: Much has been written about Spanish lenient policy towards asylum seekers, but records show that 90 per cent of sub-Saharan Africans that attempt to reach Europe through the Canary Islands and the Spanish mainland are captured, detained in very poor conditions, and deported.

Detention centres in Spain and on the Canary Islands.

The detention law, the Organic Law 4/2000, of Spain does not specify which particular agency can detain 'irregular migrants' for purposes of deportation, providing only that detention can be undertaken by a government authority or its agent for a maximum of seventy-two hours prior to referral to a judge to authorise the confinement or an irregular migrant at the officially designated detention centre. Migrants can only be detained under the following conditions: (1) For purposes of expulsion from the country because of all alleged violations listed under Article 53 and 54 of the Organ Law 4/2000, including being on Spanish territory without proper authorisation, pausing a threat to public order, and/or participating in clandestine migration. (2) When a judge issues a judicial order for detention in cases where authorities are unable to carry out a deportation order within seventy-two hours of its having been issued. (3) When a non-citizen fails to depart the country within the prescribed time limit after being issued with a deportation order.

A detained migrant cannot be held longer than is necessary for expulsion to take place, with a maximum detention period being forty days. Children may not be held in detention centres and are to be referred to Protection of Minor services, unless a judiciary authority, the Attorney General's office, and the parent(s) of the child (who must also be detained) in question request and agree to be accommodated together in a detention centre that contains appropriate facilities for family accommodation.

A network of migrant detention centres called Centros de internamiento de extranjeros was located in Andalusia, the Canary Islands, and major cities. There were nine (9) official detention centres located in Barcelona, Las Palmas (two centres), Tenerife, Malaga, Madrid, Valencia, Murcia, and Algeciras. In addition, the Lanzarote Airport Terminal has a transit zone detention centre, which has a capacity to accommodate an estimated 200 people.

Spain also makes use of several facilities it calls ad hoc because they are typically used only during the annual immigration surges in the Canary Islands and two North African exclaves. These facilities, which are otherwise not used as detention centres, include former military bases, retrofitted abandoned buildings, hospices, and tarps placed over parking lots.

Spain has been criticised for providing very poor conditions at these ad hoc centres, as well as for not adhering to its non-refoulement obligations and not ensuring the well-being and safety of detainees at these sites. Spain has also built and renovated old buildings and turned them into detention centres at the Port of Almeria and Las Canteras detention centre at La Laguna, Canary Islands. Spain has helped set up similar detention centres on the African coast such as a former school in Nouadhibou in Mauritania, which has been turned into a detention centre to receive refugees returned from the Canary Islands and captured from the African coast and waiting to be taken to African countries they came from or dumped in the desert where the homes could not be identified.

This report says that between 2004 and 2007, some 370,000 persons were deported, an increase of 43.4 per cent compared to the previous four-year period. In 2007 alone, some 55 938 persons were deported, and up to 4 per cent compared to a year earlier, despite the fact that the number of irregular migrants reached the Canary Islands fell by 61 per cent that year. Over the period 2004-2008, Spain increased the number of border police and frontier personnel by 25 per cent. (Most of the information on detention was got from Global Detention Project: Spanish Detention Profile; Last update May 2009).

Kjartan Dirdal confirmed reports, which indicated that up to the end of the 1990s, Moroccans were still crossing into Europe for seasonal labour. He said there were increasing numbers of sub-Saharan Africans escaping persecution in their countries that were beginning to use the Morocco route because it had become very dangerous to cross through Libya. He said that of the 56,400 foreigners apprehended in 2003 at the border, majority of them were Moroccans. However, there were 19,000 people of other nations intercepted at sea, 9,400 near the Canary Islands, and 9,800 in the straights between North Africa and southern Spain. Between 70 and 80 per cent of them were declared non-admissible. Below is what he wrote about the treatment of refugee in Spain. *We interviewed several residents in the centres. Their views on the conditions for asylum seekers in Spain were quite negative. Especially the first days in the centre, at the airport were a traumatic experience according to many of the interviewees. The period in hostels were also pointed out as a very difficult time. We were told stories about theft and fights inside the hostels without any attention paid by the police. One of the interviewee's experiences was that law and order did not exist inside the hostel. The residence also thought that the maximum stay in the centre of one month was not enough since the processing of asylum applications was not resolved within that period.* (Reception of Asylum Seekers in Spain: A report from the ENARO exchange programme in April 2005). Dirdal went on to say that the opinion of the UNHCR in Madrid was that worried about the treatment of sub-Saharan Africans at the detention centres of CETI in Ceuta and Barajas. *Only 10 per cent of the asylum seekers from sub-Saharan Africa in CETI are admitted to the asylum procedure. UNHCR also expressed their worry based on reports from asylum seekers that fundamental human rights are not maintained at the centres. The conditions are said to be poor and the legal rights also threatened because of lack of official translators in the asylum interview.*

In October 2009, a new asylum law was adopted in order to transpose the three most important European Directives: the Reception Conditions Directive of 27 January 2003; the Qualification Directive of 29 April 2004; and the Asylum Procedures Directive of 1 December 2005. In November 2009, the Department of International Protection Services of the UNHCR reviewed the asylum policy of Spain and produced a report. The report shows that by 2009, Spain had abandoned most of the basic conditions required in the 1951 Convention. Below is a catalogue of concerns raised by the UNHCR:

(1)   The new legislation limits the request and enjoys international protection to non-EU nationals and stateless persons. Such dispositions are contrary to the universal declaration of Human Rights, Article 14 on the right to seek asylum; the 1951 Convention, Article 14 on non-discrimination; and its 1967 Protocol, Article 1.3 on the lifting of the geographical limitations of the convention.

(2)   In the Aliens' Detention Centres, foreigners are kept under administrative detention for expulsion purposes. They can be kept there for a maximum of forty days after which they are released, if return cannot take place. To distinguish between detention centres used for this purpose and other regular detention centres, the above-mentioned Aliens' Detention Centres are often referred to as Aliens Interment Centres.

(3)   UNHCR was concerned with how Spain interpreted Article 1F (b) of the 1951 Convention to link asylum to all sorts of crime, not initially included in the scope of crimes for which countries would refuse to grant asylum status. UNHCR was also concerned about how the issue of terrorism was being used to deny

asylum to people. Secondly, the UNHCR was also concerned that Spain deporting people who had not been assessed for asylum. People were just rounded up and deported.

(4)　UNHCR was concerned that Spain was not taking seriously the 1951 Convention's Non-Refoulement Article 33(2).

(5)　Although leaflets on protection were being distributed in all detention centres on the conditions for protection, 'detainees often do not understand the protection leaflets due to their educational level and/or they may not be (sufficiently) literate in Spanish, French, Arab, and English; the only languages in which the leaflets are available. Moreover, detainees do not always have access to adequate legal counselling'.

(6)　UNHCR is also concerned about the difficulties that stowaways may be experiencing in getting access to asylum procedure. Although stowaways are entitled to pro bono legal aid if they indicate their wish to apply for asylum, the problem lies with the first contact between the authorities and the stowaways. In most instances, stowaways do not spell out clearly if they are in need of protection, and are not informed about their rights, thus being denied legal aid.

(7)　UNHCR is concerned about the prevalence of a crime-prevention approach to human trafficking issues, as reflected in the National Action Plan against Trafficking for Sexual Exploitation Purposes. The action plan approaches the issue of trafficking from a crime-prevention perspective. UNHCR recommends a more balanced strategy, including a focus on the protection, assistance, and compensation of the victims.

(8)　Two repatriation agreements relating to unaccompanied minors have been signed between the Spanish government and the Senegalese and the Moroccan authorities, respectively. UNHCR is concerned that the procedure for implementing these agreements lack safeguards that would ensure the identification of children (to whom these agreements apply) that may have international protection needs and the referral of these children to the asylum procedure. Age-assessment procedures are not uniform in the different autonomous regions, or even amongst the cities within Spain, and are generally inadequate. These examinations rarely incorporate cultural or ethnic considerations, individual maturity level of the children involved, or psychological issues, and they do not usually give children the benefit of the doubt. Spain does not have a procedure to determine the Best Interest of the Child, and a potential need for international protection is mostly analysed when dealing with unaccompanied and separated children. In relation to unaccompanied asylum-seeking children, there is lack of statistical information, and there is no segregation of data concerning sex, age, and other relevant information. The Asylum and Refugee Office has expressed its concerns about its inability to provide disaggregated data due to deficiencies of its computerised database.

(9)   In relation to the procedure in the cases of boats, 'pateras', and 'Cayucos' found in international waters, there is not much clarity about these operations and how eventual international protections concerns are assessed, before return to the last country of transit takes place.

(10)   Nationality determination procedures at the Aliens' Detention Centres also remain a concern, as there apparently do not exist any clear written standards or procedures governing nationality determinations (e.g., use of interpreters by the police, visits of delegations of consular officials).

(11)   As regards racism and xenophobia, authorities have singled out persons in street document checks with a view to initiate expulsion proceedings of irregular aliens. These practices have also affected persons in need of international protection. In some instances, persons with protection needs who feared that they

could become subject to such controls have avoided going out or refraining from carrying out certain activities, even if they were aware of their rights as asylum seekers. (Protection Policy and Legal Advice Section Department of International Protection Services: UNHCR November 2009)

Italy

The post-World War II reconstruction was heavily supported by migrant labour from eastern Europe and North Africa. There were very few sub-Saharan Africans involved until the 1990s. But from the end of the 1980s, large numbers of sub-Saharans began to arrive as they escaped from persecution in their countries. As happened in Spain, France, and Greece, these became a major source of cheap labour. Whether with or without proper work permits, most sub-Saharan Africans would not get employment in formal industry. They were taken by informal organisations. 'Italy's biggest Mafia clans with a global reach into fashion, real estate, waste disposal and drugs—hundreds of thousands of immigrants caught up in a brutal cheap—labour system of the Mafia runs for legitimate businesses from Milan to Naples.' (time world: African Immigrants in Italy: Slave labour for the Mafia by Nina Burleigh/Rome: January 15 2010). According to Saviano, an interviewee who had to be protected by the police after giving this interview, about 2,500 migrants live in the Rosarno valley in the southern Calabria region, moving with the seasonal agricultural jobs. Many have political asylum or are otherwise legally in Italy, but legal or not, the migrants are managed by a Mafia-run employment system, the *Caporalato*, which operates like a twenty-first-century chain gang. According to Saviano, those who object to low wages or poor working conditions are simply eliminated. 'It's a military system. The farm and factory owners employ the Mafia *Caporali* to bring the workers. The immigrants wait on the roads, the *Capolari* pick them and take them to work. If they complain, they get killed . . . find themselves trapped in a system in which they work ten to fourteen hours for about $3 an hour. They live in tents or shacks pitched inside abandoned buildings, without appliances, plumbing or health care' (ibid.).

But since the 1980s, sub-Saharan Africans started to reach Italy despite the problems they faced in North Africa. Italy responded initially by waiting for arrivals at Lampedusa and Sicily, processing them quickly and deporting them back to Africa. But they had problems because many of the refugees and asylum seekers had lost their documents in the struggle to leave their countries, avoid the bandit groups along the way, cross the desert, and survive in North Africa and then cross the sea. African governments refused to receive people without proper identification. But from 1990s, Italy began to make agreements with Libya, Egypt, and Morocco, promising economic development in exchange for receiving captured and deported sub-Saharan Africans. The number of 'irregular arrivals' dramatically decreased during the period 1998-2005 and as even as the immigration issue gained increasing public even as Italy introduced stricter immigration controls. In 1999, 49,999 undocumented individuals were registered as having arrived on Italian territory; by 2005, the number of arrivals had decreased some 50 per cent to 22939. Italy wanted to see a complete eradication of the irregular arrivals problem, so they put in place legislation to enable the enforcers of controls to do their job. From the 1980s, immigration laws saw changes, radical changes, come one after another.

1986: Italy passed the first of the series of restriction legislation. The Norms for the Placement and Treatment of Migrants, Migrant Workers and Against Illegal Immigration was passed in 1986 to restrict immigration.

1989: The country adopted the Legge Martelli (martial law), which established provisions for the recognition of asylum seekers, legal procedures for the expulsion of irregular immigrants, and time limits when the non-citizens must depart Italy after being issued a deportation order.

1998: Legge Turco-Napolitano (Turco-Napolitano Law): The government of Prime Minister Romano Prodi introduced mandatory detention for irregular immigrants in 1998. This change in immigration law led to the publication of a unified text on immigration, which contains provisions against illegal migration (Article 13). It also contained the grounds for issuing an administrative expulsion order, including for overstaying a visa by more than two months and entering Italy by evading border controls (Article 13). Article 14 of the Testo unico established that irregular migrants (as well as asylum seekers) can be detained at specified facilities for a period strictly limited to the time necessary to determine the identity and qualification for remaining in Italy and for determining whether or not they should be deported.

2002: The 2002 Legge Bossi-Fini (Bossi-Fini law) made further changes in detention policy. It established plans to expand and strengthen immigration detention (assistance and infrastructure) with the allocation of over 70 million euros between 2002 and 2004. Article 35 of the legislation provides that the Central Directorate of the Immigration and Frontiers Police be authorised to carry out all border control activities, including expulsions. In addition, this law set out maximum length of detention—which was modified in 2009—at thirty days, a period extendable by an additional thirty days when necessary to carry out deportations (Article 13).

2008: In May 2008, the then newly elected government of Berlusconi declared a 'state of emergency' in Italy, citing among other issues the 'present and extraordinary influx of non-EU citizens' and the presence of Roma and Sinti nomadic communities. The declaration had a significant impact on the country's immigration detention practices. Following the declaration, the government adopted a 'Security Package' aimed at facilitating expulsions, including a law criminalising unauthorised presence in the country. Among the penalties included were mandatory arrest and fast track trial for foreigners who remain in Italy notwithstanding an expulsion order and fines for illegal entry. The military was also commissioned to perform immigration—related police operations across the country; and the status of illegal migrants was added to the list of aggravating circumstances (Article 1F of the Italian penal code).

2009: In July 2009, the government adopted the (provisions relating to public safety), which amended the 1998 Unified Text on Immigration. Article 6 of the Unified Text was amended to introduce the crime of irregular stay in Italy, punishable with imprisonment of up to one year and a fine of up to 200 euros. Article 14 was amended to include provisions that allowed for imprisonment, for up to four years of non-citizens found to have remained in the country in violation of an expulsion order. Further, when a non-citizen's permit has expired by more than sixty days, and no request for renewal has been made, the non-citizen can be imprisoned for a period of between six months and one year. The new legislation also extended the maximum length of detention of irregular immigrants from sixty days to 180 days. This new maximum duration of detention is in line with the EU returns directive (Directive 2008/115/EC), to allow sufficient time for the identification of uncooperative migrants and to coordinate with their countries of origin for their return.

In March 2006, the Italian government finalised an agreement with UNHCR, IOM, and the Red Cross to put in place a pilot programme, requiring all the partners to maintain a constant presence at the detention facilities at Lampedusa (an island off the south coast of Sicily that serve as a key migrant interdiction spot in the Mediterranean). UNHCR helps identify asylum seekers and aid the processing of claims; IOM provides information to immigrants about Italian legislation on migration matters and assists immigrants who opt to voluntarily return to their countries of origin; the Red Cross takes charge of unaccompanied minors and provides general humanitarian assistance to detainees.

The Push-Back Policy

Since 6 May 2009, the Italian government, in cooperation with the government of Libya, initiated the so-called push-back policy by intercepting people, including those in need of international protection, on the high seas and returning them to Libya (not a signatory of the Refugee Convention). Italy also paid for chartered flights for Libya to send these people home. Some fifty chartered flights transported 5,668 people between August 2003 and December 2004. It is said that Italy had approximately thirty readmission agreements with some of the countries from where these people came, including Morocco and Tunisia. Italy signed many technical agreements with Libya to assist economic development and protection of the southern borders. The policy was a departure from the previous practice where Italian naval forces had regularly disembarked such persons in Lampedusa or Sicily. Observers have argued that this practice aggravated a growing humanitarian crisis of deaths at sea due to sinking migrant vessels. Below is a description by the UNHCR of how the push-back exercise started, who exactly was involved, and the numbers of asylum seekers, refugees, and irregular migrants were captured.

Most of the 'push back' operations appear to have commenced in the Strait of Sicily, within Malta's area of responsibility for search and rescue. The 'push back' operations were carried out by Italian forces belonging to the Guardia di Finanza (Tax and Customs Police), the Marina Militare (Navy) and the Guardia Costiera (Coast Guards). While such forces generally reported to different ministries for their main functions, for the purpose of these operations, they were coordinated by the Ministry of interior. Operational aspects were dealt with by the border unit within the Police Department, the Polizia di Frontier. Based on the information available to the UNHCR, it appears that the Tax and Customs Police played a major role in the operations of 6 May, 18-19 June, 4 July, 29 July, 12-13 August and 30 August. The Italian Navy carried out operations of 9-10 may (with the vessel Spica)and June 30—July 1, (with the vessel, Orione). Together with the Tax and Customs Police, the Italian

Coast Guard was involved in the first 'push back' operation of 6 May and 4 July. To the best of the UNHCR's knowledge a total of 834 were captured in the following ways: 6 May 2009 (231 persons); 8 May 2009(77persons); 9-10 May 2009 (163 persons); 18-19 June 2009 (72 persons); June 30—July 1, 2009 (82 persons); 4July 2009 (40 persons); 29 July 2009(14 persons);12-13 August 2009 (80 persons);and 30 August 2009 (75 persons). (UNHCR: Submission of the Office of the UNHCR in the Case of Hirsi and Others vs Italy (App No.27765/09). The UN Commission for refugees expressed 'deep concerns' regarding the fate of the interdicted migrants returned to Libya without proper assessment of their protection needs. 'Tomas', a twenty-four-year-old Eritrean man, interviewed in Rome on 20 May, gave Human Rights Watch an account of abuse, beating, a long journey in a packed airless truck, and ill-treatment in prison: *The (Libyan) navy force caught us and took us to . . . a place called Jawazat. It was an immigration prison. We were in the same room with 160 others-all in one room . . . We were only allowed to use the toilet once a day. Many people had skin problems. There was no soap. They gave us water in a jar to drink. Many of us had stomach problems. We had to beg the guard to take sick people to the toilet . . . After two months, they put us with another group of Eritreans-150 people in all. They put us in a big truck. It was packed with people. There wasn't room for anyone to sit down. We all remained standing . . . We started at 6 amand travelled all day and all the night . . . When they let us out of the truck, we were at Kufra prison. We spent on week there. They fed us food only once a day. Only rice. Ramadan was over. I had already experienced two months of hunger in prison. We were now 800 prisoners crowded in different rooms. We slept on pieces of cardboard . . . It was dirty . . .* Tomas said Kufra is Libya's deportation site and that the guards have an agreement with smugglers, who press the migrants to pay hundreds of dollars to return them to Tripoli. He said he failed two other attempts to flee Libya and suffered lasting damage from beatings: *I was beaten by wood and metal sticks by three guards. They beat me for more than ten minutes. They called me 'nigger' as they beat me. When I fell to the ground they kicked me. They beat me with a metal stick on my head. I have scars and pain inside my head. The metal sticks were thin but they did not bent.* **Tomas succeeded in fleeing to Italy on his fourth attempt, where he was granted humanitarian status. The full transcript of his account is available at http:// www.hrw.org/node/83699 (Human Rights Watch 9/6/2009). When Italians approach the crowded makeshift and/or small fishing boats, they give the impression they have come to rescue the sailors and make everyone believe they are going to be taken to Italy. But once the Italians have taken control of the vessel and transferred the people onto their boats, they begin to ill-treat the migrants. A number of witnesses told the UNHCR that they were placed in handcuffs prior to being handed to the Libyan authorities. The migrants reported they were assaulted with whips and rowing pads. According to these allegations, as a result of the June 30-1 July 2009 operation, six people from Eritrea reportedly required medical attention once handed over to the Libyan authorities. During the same (30 June-1 July) operation, witnesses further reported that their personal items (documents, money, and mobile phones) were seized. Eritrean and Somali witnesses reported to the UNHCR that they attempted to express and explain to the Italian authorities their fear of returning to Libya but were nevertheless handed over. There are reports of stressed people in boats who have chosen to die of hunger and thirst in the sea than be returned to Libya. Some have attempted to change directions once they realised they had been spotted. In many cases, several people jumped into the sea in order to escape the handover to the Libyan vessels, but most were eventually recovered by the Italian officials who forced them on board the Libyan ships. By 2010, the policy had become so successful that it had virtually stopped landings on Lampedusa, which has seen a 96-per cent drop in boat migration arrivals. In the first quarter of 2010, fifty-two irregular migrants were intercepted at sea compared to 4,450 in the first quarter of 2009. (Institute of Race Relations: Accelerated removals: a study of human cost of European Union deportation policy 2009-2010)**

Detention

Despite all these pushbacks and joint measures by Italy in collaboration with North African states, there were boats that managed to reaching Italy, but the numbers went down dramatically between 1998 and 2005. In 1999, the Italian government reported 49,999 undocumented arrivals. By 2005, the number had gone down 50 per cent to 22,939. Assistance on border controls, coastguarding, pushbacks, and deportations came from the European Union, mainly in the form of funding but also in the form of speedboats, ships, helicopters, vehicles, and aeroplanes. Frontex maintained a small team of workers who had their own guarding equipment. But Italy wanted to have a permanent solution. This is why they came up with new legislation, which empowered the state to imprison and detain foreigners. When Prime Minister Berlusconi came to power in 2008, he launched a crackdown on illegal immigration. He introduced new measures that made it an offence punishable by up to four years' jail to enter the country illegally. By the end of the year, there was an increase of 15 per cent prison inmates. Before the changes, some 20,000 out of the 55,000 prisoners were foreigners. Italy found it difficult to remove these Africans to their original countries. This is the reason why they had the oral agreement with Libya to deport all illegal immigrants of African origin to that country and then assist it to take them to their homes. But as we saw earlier, Libya sometimes just dumped them in the desert. (Italy illegal immigration 'soars' By David Willey: BBC News, Rome 15 August 2008)

Italy also increased the size and number of detention. By 2010, Italy had ten centres for identification and deportations: Bari, Bologna, Caltanissetta, Gorizia, Lamezia Terme, Milan, Modena, Rome, Turin, and Trapani. It created seven centres for asylum application: Bari, Caltanissetta, Crotone, Foggie, Gorizia, and Milano e Trapeni. There were four reception centres: Caltanissetta, Crotone, Cassibile, and Gorizia. In the first half of 2009, the Italian Parliament passed a law which extended the maximum period of detention within the Centres for Identification and Deportation from two to six months.

Doctors Without Borders reported in 2008, 'Serious state of overcrowding in the CARAs and CDAs (Reception Centres for Asylum Seekers and migrants). They reported that the situation had not improved since they reported it in 2003.' (On the Other Side of the Wall: A tour of Italy's Migration centres, January 2010: Doctors Without Borders Mission: January 2010)

Destitution in Italy: If a decision takes longer than six months, the individuals must leave CARA prior to receiving a decision on his or her claim. Regardless of whether their asylum claim is a positive or negative decision or whether it is still pending, the majority of those leaving CARAs became homeless. Unlike some European countries like Germany, Italy offers only a few publicly funded accommodation options for persons who have been dismissed from the first reception centres. The state-run 'Protection System for asylum Seekers and refugees' (SPRAR) (Siistem di Protezione per Richiedenti Asilo e Rifugiati) is supposed to work with the local partners across Italy to accommodate and intergrate persons with protection status and in part those seeking asylum. In reality, the system is totally overburdened. As set by decree, it only provides 3000 places despite the fact that the number of asylum seekers arriving in 2008 alone was around 31,000, and in 2009, around 17,000. The waiting list for SPRAR places in all areas, but particularly in the densely populated areas, it is so long that a significant number of persons with protection status have no realistic prospect of being housed in these areas.

Health care: Asylum seekers are entitled to health care under Article 35 of Legislative Decree No.286/1998. According to the JRS in Malta, in practice, however, they are treated as illegally staying third-country nationals and receive no special treatment to health care because they are still within the asylum procedure. Illegal migrants, asylum seekers, and unemployed foreign nationals are all regarded as third-country nationals who are in practice not allowed to benefit from health services. Even though the law allows illegally staying third-country nationals to get a STP code (temporary, present, foreigners), which can be obtained at the local health service to get medical care, some local health services do not issue STP codes with the consequence that most illegally staying third-country nationals do not get medical care after they have been given the initial compulsory preventive medical check-up and treatments. *One interviewee, who had lost all his front teeth after an accident, said he did not receive the necessary dental care because he was unable to pay (Jesuit Refugee Service: Report on Destitute Forced Migrants: Europe: May 2007)*

Not allowed to work: Asylum seekers are allowed to work six months after they have filed an asylum claim. In such situation, a work permit is issued at the discretion of the local Police Headquarters in accordance with Legislative Decree 140/2005. But many local police headquarters do not issue the work permits. The system has many inconsistencies. In fact many asylum seekers fear being arrested and sent for deportation because people are sometimes just rounded up and sent to the vessels ready to sail and pass the passengers to the Libyan vessels on the other side of the sea. Moreover asylum seekers who have lost their cases and are in appeal are treated as illegal immigrants. Appeals do not stop deportations. Many people therefore chose a life of destitution; working illegally under Mafia organisations; sleeping at the train stations; in abandoned homes or closed factories. Interior of the occupied office block, Anagnia. Hanging sheets and cloths between mattresses was the only way to get any privacy.

Somalis in Rome count themselves lucky because many of them sleep in the former Somali consulate.

Greece

Since the 1990s about 90 per cent of all undocumented immigrants that enter the European Union by crossing from Turkey into Greece. (Hans Lucht: Greece must not leave asylum seekers at the mercy of extremists: As Greece struggles to avoid economic meltdown, immigrants have become scapegoats in racially motivated attacks: The Guardian: 29 December

2011.) (Harriet Alexander Orestiada: Fortress Europe's busiest frontier is awash with illegal immigrants-despite mines, forest and razor wire: 4 December 2010). According to the Dublin II Convention, asylum claims must be processed in the country of entry to the Schengen area, placing a heavy burden on Greece's infrastructure. Between 1993 and 2008, the number of immigrants to Greece quadrupled. Greece replied with a number of measures: passing a very restrictive immigration law; hardening border controls; mounting an anti—immigration rhetoric; stepping up expulsion efforts and dramatically increasing apprehension and detention of both irregular migrants and asylum seekers. Greece also invited Frontex who sent in 175 border officers to work alongside their Greek compatriots and sharing the Greek shame. Greece also constructed a barbed wire wall on the Turkish border and increased the border police by an extra 1,800 men. In 2005, approximately 40,000 apprehensions were made. The number went up each year.

Law 3386 (2005): The law legalised imprisonment and/or expulsion of foreigners for a number of infractions related to their residence status. It legalised the administrative expulsion of a foreigner if he/she committed certain offences or served a prison sentence of at least one year. Anyone who illegally enters Greece is subject to a fine of 3,000 to 10,000 euros and a three months prison sentence. Under Article 83 of Law 3386, third-country nationals who attempt to enter or exit Greece without authorisation, are subject to a prison sentence of at least three months and a fine of at least 15,00 euros. Where immediate expulsion is not possible, the third-country national can be held in administrative detention under Article 76 and 83. The maximum period for such a detention was raised in June 2009 from three months to six months. Regarding detention facilities, Ministry of Interior has overall responsibility for immigration issues. Specialised centres for administrative detention ad hoc facilities and persons can be designated a number of additional ministries, including the Ministry of Public Administration and Decentralisation, the Ministry of Health and Social Solidarity, the Ministry of Public Order, and the Ministry of Economy and Finance. Police and border guards were authorised to apprehend non-citizens and carry out expulsion orders which could be issued by the public prosecutor or a relevant police director. Police were also made responsible for security arrangements in detention facilities. The European Committee on the Prevention of Torture noted during a 2008 visit to Greece that there was a lack of coordination between the various agencies involved in immigration detention.

Sub-Saharan asylum seekers and other refugees: Although Law 3386 provides that asylum seekers are exempt from expulsion (Article 79), Amnesty International observed that they were being detained for up to sixty days. In addition, observers noted that many asylum seekers were being prevented by the police from filing asylum claims (Brothers 2007). A particularly violent example of such a practice is provided in Amnesty International's 2009 report. 'On 26 October 2008, police officers outside the Aliens Directorate in Athens attacked a crowd of asylum seekers waiting to file applications, killing one man and injuring several others . . . The Directorate has reportedly been refusing to accept new applications for the past two months. (Amnesty International 2009 p.157) Violence against asylum seekers has always been a part of the Greek system of handling immigrants, especially against black sub-Saharan Africans. About 10 per cent per cent of all refugees that enter the European Union through the Greek or Turkish border are Africans. But this route is very dangerous for them not least because of the open racism practised in Turkey and Greece and because, like in the Maghreb of North Africa, Turkey also has problems of tribalism and religion. Sub-Saharan Africans, even if they are Muslim, find it very difficult to survive in Turkey. Human Rights Watch reported how Africans were dumped out of Turkey by state officials.

On 14 July 2001, approximately 25 African immigrants and refugees, detained at various points only on racial criteria in Istanbul were dumped into the border line between Turkey and Greece. Turkish gendarmerie have been forcing them into the Greek side, while the Greek border police have been forcing them back into the Turkish side. It is alleged that three of them died, two of them have been raped, and the others are starving. They may be facing death and other dangers to their safety.

The only criterion in this collective detention practice was the colour of the persons. They were not questioned under detention on the grounds of leaving their countries and staying in Turkey; neither were they questioned on their legal status in Turkey. There were no charges made to them, including the usual charge that they were illegal immigrants.

The detainees were forced to sign a statement in Turkish saying that they entered Turkey from Greece and that they wanted to go back on their own will. It is reported that 7 of these persons are still under detention as they did not sign those statements. It also reported that the police tore down the pages of passports which contained the Turkish visas.

They were forced to run into the Greek side and warned by the Turkish gendarmerie that they would be shot if they returned. The Greeks send them back and now some of them are living in the bush without food and water. (African migrants and refugees face imminent death in the border zone: Human Rights Server: Istanbul 21-23: July 2001)

Harriet Alexander Orestiada described this border in the following words: The border is marked by a fast flowing river, and was once peppered with 25,000 landmines from Greek-Turkish conflicts. At least 82 illegal immigrants have been killed by mines since 1994, and much of the frontier is lined by thick forests and razor wire.

Because the immigration issue had been so politicised, it is not surprising that *One morning of 25 May (2011), Kelly from Ghana was on the bus going to the pickup place at the outskirts of Athens, where African immigrants and asylum seekers go to look for work, when he was attacked by a mob. He saw them from afar, standing at the bus stop—a group of about 10 young men—but thought nothing of it. They were probably going to one of the demonstrations, he supposed. But as they entered the bus, they pulled out bats, iron rods and knives and attacked him. Kelly knew he had to avoid the guy with knife that came straight at him. He however managed to wrestle the knife from his hands—he is a big guy and a boxer in Ghana—while the others assaulted a black woman sitting behind him. The lady was beaten very badly, said Kelly. Blood was flowing down her face. She tried to call for help in their language. But no one came. They were all afraid. After the attack, the Africans went their separate ways, filing no report with the police. (Hans Lucht op cit)*

The word asylum is from the Greek word 'asylos', which has three main meanings. It may mean an institution for the maintenance and care for the mentally ill, orphans, and other persons requiring specialised assistance. It can also mean an inviolable refuge, as formerly for criminals and debtors. The third meaning is what cannot be seized or a place of refuge, a sanctuary. While we appreciate that the Greeks were the founders of modern democracy, we must also understand they were not the first to stop slavery. So it is quite possible that the majority of Greeks still look at asylum seekers as criminals running away from their debtors or similar concepts. This is clearly explainable from the manner they received irregular immigrants from especially after the year 2000.

Apprehensions: As soon as they enter Greece, new arrivals are arrested and detained in Border Police Stations, places totally inappropriate and unprepared to detain large numbers of people. These detention centres were and still are overcrowded, operating at two to three times their capacity. People have to sleep on the floor, with no space to move. The situation is further aggravated by the sub-zero temperatures, the more so as the heating in the cells does not always work and a number of migrants do not have blankets and warm clothes. The CPT noted during its 2008 visit that many persons, in particular irregular migrants would remain locked up under such conditions (in conditions intended for short-term detention) for months on end. The situation observed could in some cases, such as the

Xanthi Police and Border Guard Station, amount to inhuman or degrading treatment (CPT, 2009).

Detentions: There were nineteen detention centres listed in 2009: Amygdaleza Special Foreigners Holding Centre for minors in Attica. Its capacity was put at forty; Aspropyrgos Holding Facility for Irregular Migrants also in Attica and with a holding capacity of 140 adult males; Feres Border Guard Station in Alexandroupoli for both men and women without gender segregation. Its capacity was not disclosed, but when a one-day visit was made by EU inspectors, there were ninety-five men and women in detention; Fylakio Detention Centre in Fylakio, which has a capacity of 370 men, women, and children and gender segregation for the minors only; Lasmos Border Guard Station at Rhodopi with a capacity of twenty adult females and minors; Isaakio Border Guard Station at Orestiada; Kordello Border Guard Station at Thessaloniki; Mersinidi detention Centre at Chios (Hios) with a capacity of 200; Metaxades Border Guard Station with unknown capacity but holding ten minors; Neo Himoni Border Guard Station in Orestiada; the notorious Pagani Mytilini Special Facility for Irregular Migrants (Levtos reception centre) at Mytilini, Lesvos. In 2009, it had a capacity of 300, but when visited in on a day in August 2009, there were more than 900 detainees. The inspection team returned in November, and the number had gone up to 990. In 2008, the place had a capacity of 400. When visited in July of that year, there were 800 detainees, and by October, the number had gone up to 830. The detention centre was for males, females, and children. Although it was designed to have gender segregation for minors and family units, that was not possible because of the overcrowding. Another overcrowded centre was the Petrou Ralli Street or Kentrikou Holding Facility for Irregular Migrants, in Athens, Attica, which had a capacity of 358 and was for adult males and females; the Samos Detention Centre on the Island of Samos. It had a capacity of 400 in 2007 and was for both males and females; the Soufli Border Guard Station at Alexandroupoli. It capacity was not given, but it had thirty detainees and was for both men and women with no gender segregation; the Thermi Birder Guard Station in Thessaloniki, whose capacity was not given but was holding eight inmates, all women; the Thessaloniki Detention Centre in Thessaloniki, whose capacity was not given but had 108 adult males when visited in 2008 and 181 when visited the previous year; the Tichero Border Guard Station in Orestiada; the Vienna Detention Centre in Vienna with a capacity of 300 and the Xanthi Police and Border Station in Xanthi with a capacity of thirty but holding seventy when visited in September 2008. Additionally, there have been reports of foreign nationals being held at airport facilities and ad hoc sites located at the Academy of the Merchant Navy and at hotels (Special Rapporteur on the Human Rights of Migrants 2003; Amnesty International 2002). Prisons are used to confine irregular immigrants who have been prosecuted for criminal offences. The police and border guard stations are usually for short-term detention following apprehension, and the detention centres or special centres for hosting foreigners are for foreign nationals awaiting deportation. A large number of these detention facilities were and are still placed at the border with Turkey.

Detention facilities are prisons: Amnesty International reported in 2005 that detention centres in Greece bear a striking resemblance to prisons, arguing that there is little difference between incarcerations of criminals and administrative detention on non-criminal grounds (AI 2005 p25-26). Similarly during its 2008 visit to Greece, the CPT noted that detained irregular migrants continued to be provided with the same regime as criminal suspects; the drafting of minimum operating standards for special facilities for irregular migrants, as represented in Article 81 of the Law 3386, is still ongoing (CPT 2009). There is lack of transparency with regards to Greek detention practices. Detainees reportedly are often not provided information regarding the process of appealing detention, and it's difficult to track conditions at centres because civil society groups are prevented from accessing them (European Parliament, 2007, p. 93). Finally, the treatment of minors within the framework of immigration detention has been criticised by various international actors. UNHCR reports that refugee protection afforded to minors in Greece is arbitrary. Minors

may be detained for expulsion and unaccompanied minors are
held together with adults.

Inhuman facilities: Reports from human rights bodies have
noted that Greece's specialised detention facilities suffer
from overcrowding, poor hygiene, deficiencies in access to
health care, and lack of segregation of men, women, and
children (CPT2009; AI 2005; European Parliament 2007, p. 3;
Kehayiooylou 2009; MSF 2008 a and b; pro Asyl 2007, p. 23;
HRW 2008). Here are some reports from the different detention
centres across this country.

(1)   Athens: Currently there are seven reception facilities
      for unaccompanied minors and four for asylum seekers,
      respectively, offering 340 and 525 beds. The total of
      865 places for the housing of refugees is completely
      insufficient. In total, it is estimated that about 100,000
      to 150,000 undocumented refugees and migrants
      enter Greece each year, among them around 10,000
      unaccompanied minors.

(2)   Feres: The police station at Feres was visited by
      Bill Frelick of the European Voice on 22 September
      2011 who found that Feres, with a capacity of
      thirty, held ninety-seven detainees in squalid and
      dangerous conditions. As observed earlier, Feres has
      no gender-segregated facilities. Bill interviewed a
      fifty-year-old woman detainee, who said, 'You cannot
      imagine how dirty and difficult it is for me here. It is not
      appropriate to be with these men. I don't sleep. I just sit
      on the mattress' (Sharing Greek's asylum shame: The
      European Union's border agency should not be sending
      migrants to camps deemed abusive by Europe's top
      human rights courts. By Bill Frelick: European Voice:
      22 September 2011).

(3)   Fylakio: This is one of the first stops for many
      undocumented arrivals arrested as they cross the
      border into Greece. Designed to hold 300 at times up
      to 1,000 detainees have been crammed into Fyalakio.
      When Bill visited Fylakio unaccompanied children

were held with unrelated adults in overcrowded cells. Sewage was running on the floor, and the smell was hard to bear. Greek guards wore surgical masks when they entered the passageway between the large barred cells. And conditions have not improved. This month (September 2011) detainees in Fylakio put their own lives at risk by burning mattresses to protest against their treatment (Bill Frelick op cit).

(4) Pagani, Lesvos: We saw earlier that irregular migrants and asylum seekers that enter Europe through the Island of Lesvos face perhaps the most tragic experience in the story of asylum. The detention places are permanently overcrowded; facilities are never adequate, and people are openly assaulted. Bill Frelick reported that the capacity of the detention centre at Pagani which stood at 400 in 2008 was not increased but reduced to 300 in 2009. There was not a time it had less than 800 detainees in 2008, and when he visited the place in August 2009, there were more than 900 detainees.

More than 700 men, women, and children are packed into the Pagani centre, which lacks space and adequate hygiene and sanitation facilities to cope with such a large number of people, many of whom might be asylum seekers and the concern to the UN refugee agency. There are unacceptably poor conditions, which include 200 women and children living in one ward with just two toilets and one shower. They saw damp mattresses soiled with water leaking from the toilets. The UNHCR reported that some 5500 irregular migrants and asylum seekers were detained in Lesvos during the first eight months of 2011 after crossing from Turkey, compared to more than 13 000 in 2008 and 6 100 in 2007. These people were often abused in Lesvos. In October 2009, UNHCR demanded an inquiry into the alleged beating of several asylum seekers, including a seventeen-year-old boy, after they had protested against the cramped and insanitary conditions of detention at Pagani Centre in Lesvos. (Braband 2009). UNHCR has a history of investigating these acts of violence but we hardly hear of what action they took to correct the problems. The driving of Africans into mined border areas; the beating of Africans in the bus in Athens, the beating of people lined up to claim asylum and this beating up of detainees. As early as 25 June 2001, Joseph Emeka Okeke, a Nigerian, was beaten when he resisted expulsion at the Athens Airport. And there are many unreported such incidents because most people chose not to report their abuse.

Doctors Without Borders visited detention facilities in Greece and reported on the serious health situation in the detention centres. According to Doctors Without Borders (MSF) medical data, more than 60 per cent of the medical problems faced by detained migrants—who have attempted to cross the border between Turkey and Greece—are directly caused by or linked to degrading conditions in which they are being held.

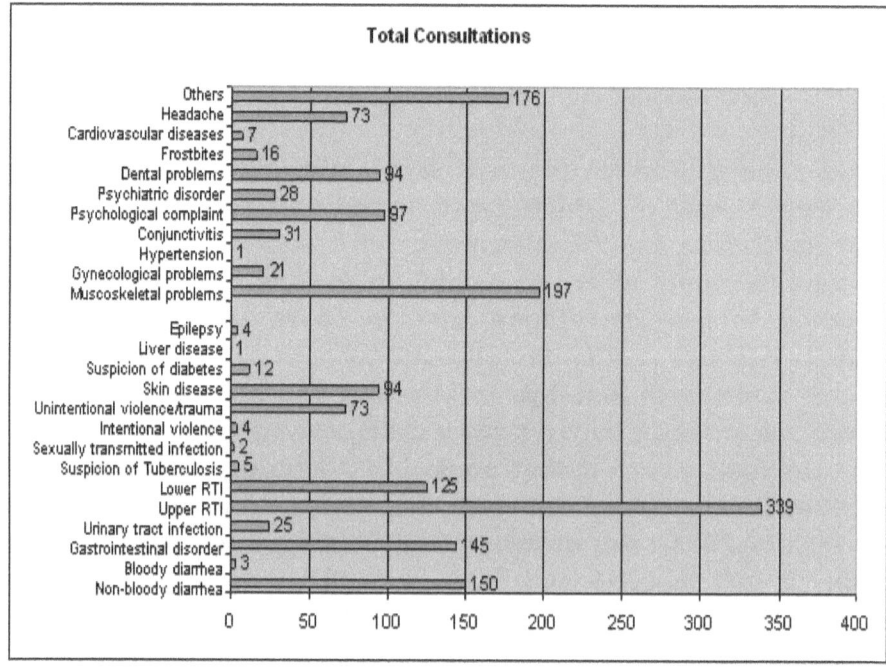

Out of the 1809 patients treated by MSF doctors between December 2010 and March 2011, 1147 were diagnosed with respiratory tract infections, body pain, diarrhoea, gastrointestinal disorders, psychological complaints, and skin diseases. 'Most of the migrants we treated were not ill when they first entered the detention facilities. They fell sick having being held in overcrowded cells lacking proper ventilation, with water and sanitation problems, no quality food and no possibility to spend time outside,' says Ianna Pertsinidou, coordinator of MSF's Project for Migrants in Greece. (Greece: Detention centres make migrants more ill. Doctors Without Borders: 16 June 2011) Doctors Without Borders were called to treat detainees on the Island of Lesvos. Reporting from there, the doctors said that sanitary conditions were very poor and health care inadequate. Psychosocial support was lacking. Vulnerable groups, including unaccompanied minors and pregnant women, were also detained in degrading conditions. Detention centres lack support staff and interpreters. Migrants and asylum seekers receive no or little information about their legal status or the detention system. (Medecin San Frontieres (MSF): Emergency Intervention in Migrations' Detention facilities in Evros: December 2010-April 2011).

Living in fear: Migrants, refugees, and asylum seekers that have managed to get permission to live in Greece or to wait for a decision on their application live in constant fear because they do not have the support of the state. They are living in extremely difficult circumstances, struggling to find food and shelter. Like living dead, they sleep all day to avoid hunger. Many survive on the discarded fruits and vegetables they collect in the marketplace and what they could find in the rubbish bins.

An African stares reluctantly while lying on his bed, in the main sleeping area of the refugee establishment of Patras, Greece.

Many sub-Saharan Africans sleep outside. Those that are lucky sleep on discarded mattresses as those in the picture above. Those lucky enough to find a room share with up to ten others. Those that are facing these problems communicate with relatives and friends and advise those still in detention. The sub-Saharan Africans live in constant fear. They know that they increase their chances of getting asylum if they are registered as coming from countries known to be at war. So they either refuse to disclose their identity after arrest or, say, they come from countries being offered asylum. *But if the immigrant refuses to speak, we have tricks like playing them a national anthem and asking them to sing to sing it. Or when they say they are Palestinian, we show them a bank note and say, 'How much is this?' Or if they say they are Somali, we say in French, 'Where is your money?' and when they go for their pockets, we know they are not Somali but from French Africa-probably the Congo or Côte d'Ivoire. (Fortress Europe's busiest frontier is awash with illegal 2010)*

Malta

Malta is a group of small islands in the Mediterranean. It has a population of only 400,000 people. Before the independence of African states and subsequent wars and before the collapse of the Soviet Union, Malta was hardly known to the world. But as African victims of war sought refuge in Europe, Malta increasingly found itself caught in between. The problems of immigration were probably one of the main reasons why Malta chose to join the European Union in 2004. But as early as 1970 when Malta passed the Immigration Act, Malta had a clear immigration policy, which has been through the years to suit the situation. The act stipulates a mandatory detention policy for prohibited immigrants. Part IV of the act describes a prohibited immigrant as "'inter alia'", any person who does not have the right to enter or reside in Malta, has been refused entry in the country; is unable to support himself or herself as well as dependents; suffers from a mental disorder; is convicted of a crime punishable for a minimum of one year; is a prostitute; or is a dependent of a prohibited immigrant'. Asylum seekers arriving without visas or other permits are therefore prohibited immigrants. The law says they must be immediately detained and so must apply for admission from detention. If there is no reply to their application after one and half years, then they should be released. If application is denied, there is room for appeal from detention. Failed applicants must leave Malta and return to home countries or be deported to these countries or countries that have signed readmission agreements with Malta. Article 10 of the act describes how people are detained in these words: 'Where leave to land is refused to any person arriving in Malta on an aircraft, such person may be placed temporarily on land and detained in some place approved by the Minister . . . until the departure of such aircraft is imminent. Where leave to land is refused to any person arriving in Malta by any other means, such person (may) be placed temporarily on shore and detained in some place approved by the Minister. Persons detained under this Act "shall be deemed to be in legal custody and not to have landed"' Air and sea carriers who transport passengers not in possession of appropriate entry documents can be fined and are required to convey undocumented migrants to another destination stipulated by law. Carriers must confine anyone refused entry to Malta on board their vessels. Anyone issued with a removal or deportation order may be required to pay any expenses incurred in connection with the maintenance, medical treatment, or expulsion of a prohibited immigrant or his dependents.

In a country with mandatory detention, one would expect the appeal procedure to be urgent—not in Malta. The Immigration Appeal Boart meets once a week for half a day. It discusses everything related to immigration, not detention only. It rules only on reasonableness, not legality. The Working Group on Arbitrary Detention (WGAD) reported in 2009 that the detention regime in Malta was 'not in line with international human rights law, as immigrants are subject to mandatory detention without genuine recourse to a court of law'.

Asylum seekers: Asylum applicants can be released only after eighteen months of continuous detention, for the rest time is not stipulated. Malta is a signatory of the 1951 Refugee Convention, and yet it keeps asylum applicants in detention for more than six months while waiting to be interviewed. A number of organisations have expressed concern about this. The International Commission of Jurists regretted that the administrative detention of asylum seekers and migrants was automatic, excessive, and disproportionate in length and duration (UN Press Release 2009). In the Jesuit Refuge Services, Malta published a research in which they raised the fact that automatic detention was very harsh. Detention 'follows a very long and difficult journey which in itself renders detainees in an even more vulnerable situation. For example, a detainee explained, "Seventy out of seventy-eight people on the boat died on the journey, and the newspaper said that the government said that the remaining eight should be released immediately, but six of us are still in detention. Why are we in detention? How long will I stay?"' (Becoming Vulnerable in Detention (The DEVAS Project) JRS, June 2010, p. 276) Asylum seekers who have been detained for more than twelve months together with undocumented non-citizens granted 'vulnerable people' (usually include the elderly, families with children, unaccompanied minors, pregnant and breast feeding women, and people suffering from disabilities and serious physical or mental illness) status or humanitarian protection are moved to non-secure reception centres that fall under the responsibility of the Ministry of Social Affairs and the Family. These centres which are run by private contractors have been described by a government minister as ghettos (The European Parliament Committee on Civil Liberties (LIBE) 2006).

Detention infrastructure: There are three detention centres, namely, the Lyster Barracks Closed Centre; the Safi Closed Centre, and the Ta'Kandja Closed Centre. When additional space is needed, migrants can also be detained in what are called correctional facilities and police headquarters. The approved places of detention for the purposes of the Immigration Act are as follows:

Quarters at the Special Assignment Group Complex

Approved place of police custody at the Victoria Police Station, Gozo

Lock-up in the building housing the courts of justice at Valletta

Lock-up at the police headquarters at Floriana

Approved place of police custody at the Malta International Airport

Approved place of the police complex at Fort Mosta, Mosta

The Hal-Far Immigration Reception Centre

Malta also operates a number of non-secure reception centres that provide accommodation for 'vulnerable' immigrants and those granted refugee or humanitarian protection. These centres act as transit for migrants who have come from official detention and who are free to move into society. These centres are reportedly run by either the Ministry for Family and Social Solidarity or society organisations. As of December 2007, there were 2,000 persons resident in them. These centres which are run by private contractors are the ones that were described by the government minister as ghettos.

Conditions of the detention centres: The WGAD, in 2009, found the Safi and Lyster Barracks detention centres' conditions to be 'appalling to the extent that the health, including the mental health, of the detainees is affected which affects their ability to properly understand their rights and follow the legal proceedings related them'. WGAD also expressed concern about the detention of families, including pregnant women and nursing mothers and unaccompanied minors (WGAD 2009 Annex.) In 2006, the LIBE Committee had recommended the closure of the facilities, stating that the situation 'is unacceptable for a civilised country and untenable in Europe, which claims to be the home of human rights'. (LIBE, 2006, p. 6). A 2009 MSF (Doctors Without Borders) report on detention conditions found that facilities were severely overcrowded, had poor hygiene, offered inappropriate shelter (particularly the Lyster Barracks, where some detainees slept in tents and containers), provided limited outdoor access, had no heating in winter and poor ventilation in summer, and provided lack of access to basic health care. Conditions fall 'far below the EC Directive laying down minimum standards for the reception of asylum seekers' (MSF, 2009, p. 8) and that 'without structural changes, and given the increasing number of new arrivals in 2009, the situation is likely to deteriorate further' (MSF, 2009, p. 3). The Council of Europe's Committee for the Prevention of Torture and Inhuman or Degrading Treatment (CPT) in 2010 described Malta's detention centres as amounting to 'inhuman and degrading treatment'. In the Hemes Block, a part of Lyster Barracks Detention Centre, the committee found conditions to be in a dilapidated state, describing it as being 'dirty and infested with rats'. 'Toilets and showers are in such a poor state of repair that it is practically impossible to ensure basic standards of hygiene,' says the committee. The CPT asked the Maltese government to shut down Helmes Block 'as a matter of urgency' until it is refurbished. In the New C Block, the committee found conditions to be particularly poor, with little or no access to running water. Moreover, the doors of B and C blocks are closed every day at 5 p.m., prohibiting detainees from accessing the outdoor exercise space. The CPT found the Ta'Kandja Police Complex detention centre to be 'a cage-like, oppressive and grim' place. At the end of their visit to Ta'Kandja, the CPT wrote, "Day-rot and mould could be observed on the interior walls of the two dormitories and the toilets and showers were in a dilapidated state. Immigration detainees were spending twenty-two hours a day confined to these two dormitories."' (CPT Brussels, 22 February 2010).

Members of the JRS talked to some of the detainee. Detainees at Safi Detention Centre complained about the dirty and broken-down facilities. In addition, '83 per cent highlighted the lack of privacy, stating that there is no space to even be alone in detention. A number of detainees feel that there is a direct link between living conditions and ill-health. "At times, we were 370 in a single warehouse. People are sick and they infect others. You are afraid that you get sick."'

Assaulted: 28 per cent reported as being physically assaulted while in detention, of which 68 per cent was by other detainees and 32 per cent by the staff. 18 per cent of these reported that they filed a complaint in case of physical assault, but none reported to have resulted in any charge. 40 per cent reported that they had been mocked, of which 58 per cent claimed to have been mocked by the staff. 'Whenever I try to speak to them, they tell me that I am a black animal and to go away from them. They keep telling me that we are illegal immigrants and Malta is to deport us back to our countries of origin.'

People: According to MSF, almost 50 per cent of the migrants and asylum seekers originate from Somalia. Others come from Sudan, Eritrea, Nigeria, and other sub-Saharan countries. Most of them will have been detained for long periods in Libya, yet only a very small portion of them (less than one per cent) are granted refugee status. The majority of them, 53 per cent, are granted humanitarian protection. The remaining 46 per cent are immediately deported, while those granted humanitarian protection stay a little longer.

Regarding arrivals, the records are not very accurate since some boats were forced to continue to the Island of Lampedusa when they found it difficult to dock without being arrested and charged for bringing in irregular migrants. Many migrants lost their lives at sea while waiting for the correct opportunity to land. However, the JRS in Malta collected records of the numbers of boats and passengers between 2001 and 2009, and they are as follows:

Year	Number of Boats	Immigrants
2001	1	57
2002	21	1,686
2003	12	2,003
2004	53	1,388
2005	46	1,822
2006	57	1,780
2007		1,475
2008		2,775
2009		1,475 (Up to Sep)
	Total	Total
		1,44,461

They analysed 2,704 arrivals as 2,298 males, 365 females, 32 children, and 9 infants. They also said that in the summer of 2005, at least 400 and probably between 600 and 700 migrants perished at sea trying to reach Malta.

CHAPTER 7

Northern Europe and the Birth of EU Asylum Law

We have seen that most of the sub-Saharan Africans that reached Spanish territories, Italy, Greece and Malta were arrested and detained in very unhealthy places and deported the Maghreb countries of North Africa that had readmission agreements with these southern European states. When one reads these tragic reports; stories such as 'The truth may be bitter but must be told' cited in Appendix 1, one is left with many questions. Why are sub-Saharan asylum seekers or any asylum seeker for that matter treated in such ways in countries that claim to be models of democracy? Why do the world and especially the UNHCR stand and watch as asylum seekers are openly persecuted and refouled in direct contravention of the 1951 Refugee Convention and the 1967 Protocol? Why does the world watch as people are loaded into windowless containers and taken and dumped at unknown desert places to die of hunger and thirst? There are scholars that would rush to put a racist label to it. But I think it is more than racism. Sub-Saharan politicians have not matured enough to protect their citizens against abuse both at home and away from home. Their state securities are so weak they cannot protect their borders. So North African vehicles can drive into their countries unnoticed and dump people in places they die of hunger and thirst unnoticed. Secondly when European economies are booming, southern European nations negotiate with sub-Saharan politicians for African labour which they treat differently. Until African leaders stand up for the human rights of their people, the journey to their human rights elsewhere will be long. This is in no way to condone the inhuman treatment sub-Saharan Africans are subjected to by the southern European nations.

Despite the arrests, detentions and deportations, there are some refugees that managed to reach the richer northern European states. There are many that choose not to apply for asylum in the southern European states. Some acquire false travel papers and travel to their chosen destination. There are a few with relatives already in Europe that are assisted to go and join them. Then there those that successfully get protection in the southern European nations but because these were not the countries they planned to apply for asylum, they leave these countries and move north. Black people began to settle in Europe before the great slave trade, but their numbers have never been significant. When their numbers are measured against the total populations of these countries, they remain a tiny minority. The latest figures collected from Wikipedia Free Encyclopaedia on the numbers of people of African descent in seventeen of the largest European countries show that except for 3 of them there is no country with a black population above 2 per cent as the figure below show.

Country	Country Population	Black and Mixed black	Percentage
Europe	738,856,462	>7,034,100	0.95%
France	62,752,136	3,000,000	5% (including overseas
Italy	60,020,805	>264,500	0.44%
United Kingdom	60,609,153	2,015,400	3.3%
Netherlands	14,491,461	507,000	3.1%
Spain	40,397,842	>200,000	0.5%
Germany	82,000,000	500,000	0.6%
Russia	141,594,000	40,000	0.03%
Portugal	10,605,870	201,200	2.0%
Norway	4,858,199	67,000	1.4%
Sweden	9,263,872	770,000	0.4%
Belgium	10,666,860	45,000	0.4%
Republic of Ireland	4,339,000	45,000	1.1%
Switzerland	7,790,000	740,000	0.5%
Austria	8,356,707	14,223	0.2%
Finland	8,340,783	20,000	0.37%
Poland	38,082,000	4,500	0.01%
Hungary	10,198,325	321	0.0%

Source: Wikipedia Free Encyclopaedia, 2012

The first conclusion one would derive from looking at these 2010 figures would be that sub-Saharan Africans are not the cause of the anxiety that Europe has shown in recent years over the issue of refugees and asylum seekers. Black people make less than 1 per cent of the European population, and only France, United Kingdom, Netherlands, Portugal, Norway, and Republic of Ireland do have black people that make more than 1 per cent of their populations. The majority of people claiming asylum in the European Union come from eastern Europe and Asia. Below are statistics of the figures for 2009 and 2010. Countries of origin of (non-EU-27) asylum seekers in the EU-27 Member States, 2009 and 2010

	2010	2009	Change 2009 to 2010		Ranking		
			Absolute (number)	Relative (%)	2010	2009	Change
Non-EU-27 total	258 945	263 990	-5 045	-1.9	-	-	-
Afghanistan	20 590	20 455	135	0.7	1	1	0
Russia	18 590	20 110	-1 520	-7.6	2	2	0
Serbia	17 745	5 460	12 285	225.0	3	16	+13
Iraq	15 800	18 845	-3 045	-16.2	4	4	0
Somalia	14 355	19 000	-4 645	-24.4	5	3	-2
Kosovo (UNSCR 1244/99)	14 310	14 275	35	0.2	6	5	-1
Iran	10 315	8 565	1 750	20.4	7	9	+2
Pakistan	9 180	9 925	-745	-7.5	8	8	0
FYR of Macedonia	7 550	930	6 620	711.8	9	47	+38
Georgia	6 860	10 500	-3 640	-34.7	10	6	-4
Nigeria	6 750	10 270	-3 520	-34.3	11	7	-4
Sri Lanka	6 470	7 380	-910	-12.3	12	11	-1
Turkey	6 350	7 030	-680	-9.7	13	12	-1
Bangladesh	6 190	5 970	220	3.7	14	14	0
China	5 655	5 800	-145	-2.5	15	15	0
Armenia	5 525	6 855	-1 330	-19.4	16	13	-3
Dem. Rep. of Congo	5 515	4 950	565	11.4	17	18	+1
Syria	5 010	4 750	260	5.5	18	19	+1
Guinea	4 895	4 485	410	9.1	19	20	+1
Eritrea	4 525	5 230	-705	-13.5	20	17	-3
Algeria	3 575	3 405	170	5.0	21	21	0
India	3 175	3 030	145	4.8	22	22	0
Zimbabwe	2 615	8 050	-5 435	-67.5	23	10	-13
Haiti	2 345	1 840	505	27.4	24	30	+6
Vietnam	2 320	2 460	-140	-5.7	25	24	-1
Sudan	2 295	1 955	340	17.4	26	27	+1
Bosnia and Herzegovina	2 105	1 330	775	58.3	27	34	+7
Azerbaijan	2 060	2 585	-525	-20.3	28	23	-5
Albania	1 905	2 065	-160	-7.7	29	25	-4
Mongolia	1 680	2 030	-350	-17.2	30	26	-4
Other non-EU-27	42 690	44 455	-	-	-	-	-

(1) Cyprus, data relates to applications instead of applicants.
Source: Eurostat (online data code: migr_asyappctza)

Secondly, Africans had migrated to Europe as slaves, workers, or traders from very early historic times, but they did not have a history of claiming asylum in Europe. It was only from the wars and the persecution of the post independence era that we see sub-Saharan Africans taking the painful and dangerous journeys to Europe. One would ask, 'Why Europe?' The answer lies in the pattern of countries chosen for the asylum. Africans went to countries of their former colonisers, because their representatives-preachers, politicians, and even businessmen talked of Europe as a land of democracy, justice, and peace. Secondly, the weapons now used by their new masters were not bows and arrows but guns, which came from Europe. So if there was any chance of protecting their families and of getting arms, they would be wise to go to Europe. When we count the numbers

of nationalities which went to Europe between 1996 and 2005 shown in the table above, we see that people of ten nationalities (Angola, Cameroon, Eritrea, Ghana, Guinea, Kenya, Nigeria, Senegal, Uganda, and Togo) went to Germany. France received Africans from thirteen nations (Angola, Cameroon, Congo, Côte d'Ivoire, DRC, Ghana, Sudan, Guinea, Nigeria, Rwanda, Senegal, Sierra Leone, and Togo). Five nationalities chose Belgium, and these were Angola, Cameroon, Guinea, Rwanda, and Togo. Only three nationalities went to Netherlands, and these were Angola, Congo, and Somalia. Sub-Saharan Africans from thirteen nationalities (Angola, Cameroon, Côte d'Ivoire, DRC, Eritrea, Ghana, Somalia, Kenya, Nigeria, Sierra Leone, Sudan, Uganda, and Zimbabwe) chose the United Kingdom. Italy was chosen by only five nationalities, despite the fact that a large percentage of the asylum seekers that went north or were returned under Dublin II passed through Italy. These nationalities were Côte d'Ivoire, Eritrea, Ghana, Sudan, and Togo. Eritreans were the only nationality that chose Sweden. Ireland was chosen by Nigerians and Zimbabweans only. Only Nigerian nationals went to Austria, and only Somalis went to Norway. Three nationalities—Guinea, Senegal, and Sierra Leone—went to Switzerland. Sub-Saharan Africans did not seek asylum in the rest of Europe. The figures show that if we compare with the numbers that sought asylum in Africa or chose to be IDPs, very few Africans went to Europe and that they went to very few European countries. Sub-Saharan Africans either claimed asylum in neighbouring African countries or moved from one area in their countries to another as IDPs. Except for Somalis, who sometimes had to be airlifted to certain European countries that were touched by their plight, very few sub-Saharan Africans set out for Europe from various parts of Africa reached Europe because of the traumatic experiences they faced on the journey, which often took years and where close to half of the people that started the journey died before their destination. The figures below were collected by the UNHCR. They counted the refugees in the popular countries shown below at the end of each year. As can be seen, not many people were added to the refugee population each year. According to the statistics below, Germany accepted a significant number of refugees from a few sub-Saharan African countries only in the year 2001. Thereafter, the admissions remained small. Records below also show the asylum applications that were made to the seven European countries between 1996 and 2005. When you consider that most of these European countries did not give asylum to more than 20 per cent of applicants, you can see why there was a problem of destitute people and why many of them had to go to the Dublin II Resolutions to try and solve problems of irregular migrants.

Based on UNHCR Statistics: Sub-Saharan Africans' European Countries of Refugee/Asylum Preference: 1996-2005

Country of Origin	Refuge/ Asylum	Country	1996	1997	1998	1999	2000	2001	2002	2003	2004	2005
Angola	Refuge	*Germany	-	-	-	-	-	-	3,334	3,288	3,272	3,753
	Asylum	France	232	269	263	538	611	993	1,590	1,409	996	851
	Asylum	Belgium	111	93	224	240	198	303	406	355	286	230
	Asylum	Netherlands	422	373	608	1,585	2,193	4,111	1,880	370	177	222
	Asylum	UK	365	195	150	545	800	1,025	1,420	1,155	550	190
	Asylum	Germany	764	653	288	434	346	471	585	353	183	147
Cameroon	Refuge	*UK	-	5	25	25	25	25	175	241	511	656
	Refuge	*Germany	-	-	-	-	-	-	1,223	1,742	2,138	1,841
	Refuge	*France	80	83	88	97	94	116	164	226	295	415
	Asylum	Belgium	60	99	166	267	417	324	435	626	506	530
	Asylum	France	47	58	81	161	404	416	639	806	611	383
	Asylum	Germany	450	494	544	597	739	923	1,205	910	618	327
	Asylum	UK	95	175	95	245	-	-	615	530	385	305
Congo	Refuge	*France	149	146	175	267	346	737	1,131	1,572	1,979	2,454
	Asylum	France	153	304	387	1,158	1,592	1,943	2,266	1,952	1,489	1,172
	Asylum	Netherlands	1	84	382	650	575	492	339	198	130	154
Côte d'Ivoire	Refuge	*France	17	-	14	-	-	42	111	317	647	1,075
	Refuge	*UK	15	60	120	120	375	410	500	678	754	831
	Asylum	France	25	13	44	101	350	727	600	1,420	1,106	1,147
	Asylum	Italy	-	-	-	-	6	14	93	348	183	586
DRC	Asylum	France	1064	1,348	1,778	2,272	2,950	3,781	5,260	2,093	3,848	3,022
	Asylum	UK	650	690	660	1,240	1,030	1,393	2,215	1,920	1,825	1,390

Country	Status	Destination										
Eritrea	Refuge	*UK	-	-	-	-	-	-	975	1,748	2,404	3,617
	Refuge	*Germany	-	-	-	-	-	-	2,553	2,754	2,974	2,746
	Refuge	*Italy	-	1	1	3	16	40	94	177	785	2,705
	Asylum	UK	-	-	-	-	-	620	1,180	1,070	1,265	1,900
	Asylum	Italy	-	-	-	13	33	276	927	1,230	830	1,313
	Asylum	Sweden	33	21	27	73	127	151	266	641	395	425
Ghana	Refuge	*Germany	-	-	—	-	-	-	1,308	1,435	1,491	7,136
	Refuge	*UK	471	422	380	240	1,785	1,845	1,855	1,897	1,873	1,877
	Refuge	*France	863	863	840	842	818	802	760	684	677	635
	Asylum	Germany	676	698	308	277	268	284	297	375	394	459
	Asylum	Italy	-	2	2	-	8	15	33	505	62	407
	Asylum	UK	675	350	225	195	285	200	275	360	375	250
Guinea	Refuge	*France	258	253	251	251	248	274	330	408	575	878
	Refuge	*Germany	-	-	-	-	-	-	703	841	891	723
	Asylum	France	150	139	205	313	544	745	753	808	1,020	1147
	Asylum	Belgium	250	165	336	342	488	494	517	354	565	643
	Asylum	Switzerland	148	193	335	388	455	679	751	652	412	211
	Asylum	Germany	373	444	419	128	232	478	360	413	349	210
Kenya	Refuge	*UK	55	80	90	110	1,085	1170	1,305	1,486	1,543	1,563
	Refuge	*Germany	-	-	-	-	-	-	179	227	217	290
	Asylum	UK	1,170	605	885	485	455	310	350	265	175	120
	Asylum	Germany	212	204	212	95	16	42	69	42	45	56
Nigeria	Refuge	*Germany	-	-	-	-	-	-	1,306	1509	1,607	5,984
	Refuge	*UK	54	145	305	310	1,475	1,620	1,785	1,932	2,012	2,111

Country	Type	Destination										
	Asylum	Ireland	9	665	1,729	1,895	3,405	3,461	4,050	3,110	1,776	1,278
	Asylum	UK	2,540	1,480	1,380	945	835	870	1,125	1,252	1,572	1,230
	Asylum	France	131	138	259	274	463	571	884	1,252	1,572	976
	Asylum	Austria	157	202	189	270	390	1,047	1,432	1,849	1,829	880
Rwanda	Asylum	Belgium	405	565	1,049	1,007	866	617	487	450	427	565
	Asylum	France	139	216	272	262	276	282	303	462	417	400
Senegal	Refuge	*Germany	-	-	-	-	-	-	140	148	61	311
	Refuge	*France	35	32	39	41	45	61	81	101	120	132
	Asylum	France	159	116	142	192	366	442	491	324	169	100
	Asylum	Switzerland	26	39	27	16	17	12	24	14	14	35
SierraLeone	Refuge	*UK	60	75	120	405	1,840	3,390	3,760	4,014	4,118	4,164
	Refuge	Netherlands	221	275	405	570	851	2,262	3,466	3,663	3,737	3,839
	Asylum	Netherlands	249	390	482	1,280	2,023	2,405	1,615	314	138	189
	Asylum	UK	335	815	565	1,125	1,330	1,930	1,155	410	255	165
	Asylum	France	12	58	117	276	512	823	545	386	198	160
Sudan	Asylum	UK	280	230	250	280	415	390	655	1,050	1,445	990
	Asylum	Italy	34	32	21	10	40	97	867	641	486	637
	Asylum	France	72	73	68	81	92	98	136	406	286	409
Uganda	Refuge	*UK	3,838	3,897	3,620	3,040	3,150	3,195	2,335	1,624	1,818	1,863
	Asylum	UK	190	220	210	420	740	475	715	775	445	230
	Asylum	Germany	58	72	53	49	41	72	99	115	89	49
Togo	Refuge	*Germany	-	-	-	-	-	-	5,743	5,778	5,579	5,988
	Refuge	*Italy	-	1	1	3	13	37	68	136	228	483
	Asylum	Italy	-	2	3	3	21	64	182	107	114	421

Zimbabwe

Asylum	Belgium	54	82	128	108	184	153	364	365	331	401
Asylum	France	29	30	47	57	83	136	327	408	255	344
Refuge	*UK	5	10	15	15	80	225	3,515	5,754	6,505	7,093
Refuge	*Ireland	-	-	-	-	-	1	175	271	312	342
Asylum	UK	115	60	80	230	1,010	2,115	7,655	4,020	2,520	1,390
Asylum	Ireland	-	1	-	4	25	102	357	88	69	51

Somalia

Year		1996	1997	1998	1999	2000
Refuge	*UK	14,768	16,706	19,156	18,266	26,891
Asylum	UK	1,780	2,730	4,685	7,495	5,020
Asylum	Netherlands	1,461	1,280	2,775	2,731	2,110
Asylum	Norway	180	552	938	1,340	910
Year		2,001	2,002	2,003	2,004	2,005
Refuge	*UK	31,366	34,131	36,106	36,700	36,319
Asylum	UK	6,465	6,540	7,195	3,295	2,105
Asylum	Netherlands	1,098	533	541	792	958
Asylum	Norway	1,080	1,534	1,623	1,315	667

Source: UNHCR Statistical Yearbook 2005.

Seeking asylum from countries that formerly colonised you is a grave mistake, not least because these people know your history. These people were forced out of their properties in your countries by the changes in political systems. In the case of countries like Zimbabwe, the ZANU-PF regime of Robert Mugabe was engaged in violent redistribution of land and other properties. Often they chose to kill rather than compensate previous property owners. So while the southern European states arrested, assaulted, detained, and deported asylum seekers that had managed to cross the Mediterranean, northern states combined the methods used by southern states with rigorous application of the numerous immigration laws they passed from the 1990s. While indeed there were many cases of abuse of asylum seekers as we will see later, northern states depended more on the application of negative asylum legislation implemented at both national and EU levels. One of the laws was the Dublin II Regulation, which we will shortly discuss in detail. What is important to observe is that 2005 was a turning point in the culture of providing sanctuary to sub-Saharan asylum seekers in Europe. The post 9/11 laws and changes brought between 2001 and 2005, namely, the creation of Frontex in 2002; the Seville recommendations of 2002; the Dublin II Resolutions of 2003; the Reception Directive of 2003; the Qualification Directive of 2004; and the Procedures Directive of 2005 brought such dramatic results that the numbers of asylum applications began to go down and have never again reversed the direction. If we analyse statistics collected from the UNHCR Yearbooks between 2006 and 2010, we see that almost all the main countries to which sub-Saharan Africans applied for asylum had decreasing numbers of people applying for asylum to them. The figures are shown below.

Country	2006	2007	2008	2009	2010
Belgium	16,820	17,575	17,026	15,545	17,892
Denmark	36,659	26,788	23,401	20,355	17,922
France	145,995	151,789	171,206	196,364	200,687
Germany	605,406	578,879	582,735	593,799	594,269
Greece	2,289	2,228	2,164	1,695	1,444
Ireland	7,917	9,333	9,730	9,571	9,107
Malta	2,404	3,000	4,332	5,955	6,136
Netherlands	100,514	86,587	76,600	76,008	74,961
Norway	43,336	34,522	36,101	37,826	40,260
Portugal	333	353	403	389	384
Spain	5,275	5,147	4,661	3,970	3,820
Switzerland	48,523	45,653	46,132	46,203	48,813
UK	301,556	299,718	292,097	269,363	238,150

By 2010 the UNHCR circulated a report, which in part read, *In Europe, the largest relative decrease in annual asylum levels was reported by the eight Southern European countries which received 33 600 asylum requests in 2010. This is a 33 per cent decrease compared to 2009. This decrease is mainly due to fewer individuals requesting international protection in Malta (-94 per cent), Italy (-53 per cent) and Greece (-36 per cent). (Asylum Levels and Trends in Industrialised countries 2010: Statistics overview of asylum applications lodged in Europe and selected non-European countries. 28 March 2011.)* But as you can see from the table above, there were countries which, in fact, increased the intake of asylum figures over the period 2006-2010 and beyond. There are reports which blame counting procedure saying that there were asylum seekers that were counted twice in some countries. But the UNHCR report above clarifies that. It states that while these countries arrested, imprisoned, detained, and deported asylum seekers coming from the south and fro Afghanistan, Iraq, Somalia, and Pakistan, they welcomed those coming from the eastern Europe. According to the report, France became the second only to the United States in the number of asylum seekers they accepted in 2010. France received 47,800 applicant, Germany, 41,300, and Sweden 31,800. The French increased their intake of asylum seekers from Georgia by 187 per cent, from Bangladesh by 118 per cent, and from Haiti by 37 per cent. Germany took many asylum seekers from Serbia and the former Yugoslavian Republic of Macedonia. They also took many Roma destitute persons. Swedish number of asylum seekers more than quadrupled from 1,800 claims in 2009 to 7,900 in 2010. One-fifth of all applications in Sweden came from Serbian citizens, mainly Kosovo.

Why did the numbers that claimed asylum go down from 2005? Was it because sub-Saharan Africans stopped entering Europe as asylum seekers? The numbers of Africans that chose to seek asylum in Europe did not go down as such. Interception in the Mediterranean Sea became better organised. The Italian or Libyan arrangement of stopping, inspecting, and forcing back to Africa any ship or boat carrying African migrants began to bear fruit. Frontex provided assistance to the southern states, where requested and those that managed to reach Europe were immediately detained and transferred to ships waiting to take them back to Africa. But as mentioned earlier, asylum seekers began to arrive in faster boats, began to land away from normal harbours, and did not ask for asylum in the southern European states. These are some of the reasons why asylum applications in these states dramatically went down.

Working illegally, assisted by humanitarian organisations and in some cases helped by relatives and friends already in Europe, many asylum seekers reached the northern European states. Some managed to reach countries they had wished to apply for asylum; others just asked for asylum in a northern European state in the hope to travel to a country of choice later. But most of the northern European states already had in place legislation, which made it illegal to enter their countries without a passport and/or a visa. While it is true that the 1951 Refugee Convention stated that asylum seekers did not need a passport or a visa, most northern European states argued that these sub-Saharan Africans were not asylum seekers but economic migrants. They needed to prove that they were asylum seekers. But many of the sub-Saharan Africans had destroyed their documents, lost them, or never had them in the first place. Some could not speak a European language. Some had never been to school. Some were unaccompanied minors. It was easy for European countries to deny them asylum for more than one reason. In fact, after 9/11, many were looked at as suspected terrorists. Europe had put in place enough legislation to detain them once they entered their countries. And so they were arrested and detained in detention places, at air ports, in prisons, in army barracks, or even at residential places. A quick survey of detention facilities in the popular destination shows that from 2005 onwards, detention facilities were always overcrowded.

Frontex in northern Europe

Frontex was mainly sponsored by northern European states, although initially its task was to assist southern states stop irregular migration ships and boats in the Mediterranean before asylum seekers in them had had even a chance to claim asylum. And as we have seen, by 2007, they had achieved that assignment. Although there were cases of people from other parts of the world going to Africa and using the Mediterranean routes to enter Europe, statistically, the Mediterranean routes were for sub-Saharan Africans and the Maghreb refugees. So the emphasis placed in assisting Malta, Cyprus, Italy, Greece, and Spain on removing people before they even arrived was primarily a scheme to stop sub-Saharan Africans from reaching Europe. I have already argued that sub-Saharan Africans were denied entry not because they were black but because they were poor. For centuries, in the history of northern Europe, Europeans did not discriminate Africans because of their colour but because of their economic status. The reasons why there are so many people of mixed blood in America and western Europe today is because many white men and women fell in love with black men and women, but they could not fall in love with their poverty. So when African asylum seekers arrived in northern Europe, few states wanted to accept them, educate them, and orientate them into Western systems. Poverty was misinterpreted as racism—religious racism, language racism, appearance racism, educational racism, and, on the whole, cultural racism. So it was African asylum seekers who were most likely to be subjected to group deportations (see Appendix 7 on the deportation of Nigerians). There is no other region in the politically unstable world where as many readmission agreements were 'forced' of home states than Africa. Using financial assistance to state and private institutions, military forms of support, and personal gifts and bribes, Italy sought and got readmission agreements with Tunisia, Ghana, Niger, Senegal, and Gambia, as well as its push-back agreement with Libya. Spain achieved readmission agreements with Cape Verde, Mali, Guinea Conakry, Guinea Bissau, and Nigeria. In some of these agreements, there are states that agreed to take sub-Saharan Africans that had passed through their countries on their way to Europe; in other words, southern European states had their own unwritten 'first third country' readmission agreements. But for the northern states, these were not as important as the new role Frontex, the Frontex chartered flights.

According to the European Council on Refugees and Exiles (ECRE), one of the most remarkable developments in 2009-2010 has been the transformation of the European Agency for the Management of Operational Cooperation at the External Borders, better known as Frontex. Although established only in 2005, as stated earlier, it has seen its annual budget and workforce increase yearly at alarming rate. In 2010, its annual budget had risen to 87 million euro and a staff of around 280. Irrespective of the economic climate, its steady amassing of finance and resources shows no sign of diminishing. In March 2010, the European Union published plans to enlarge Frontex's role so as to give it extra powers to charter aircraft for joint returns operations. Already in 2009, Frontex organised thirty-two joint charter flights for returns and doubled its operational days at air borders in comparison with 2008. By the end of 2009, twenty-seven flights deported 1,338 persons from the European Union coordinated and partly organised by Frontex. Nigeria topped the list in deportations, followed by Georgia, Kosovo, and Albania. Denmark, Sweden, Ireland,

France, and the United Kingdom all regularly expel by charter flights. Ireland has carried out at least sixteen expulsions by chartered flights to Nigeria and has been involved in joint charters with EU partners including the United Kingdom, Spain, Luxembourg, Slovakia, Italy, and Malta. Swedish Migration Board has speeded up group expulsions, with charter flights taking Iraqis to Baghdad and Mongolians to Ulan Baton.

Of the 5,866 million euro allocated by the European Union to what it calls 'solidarity and management of migration flows' for the period 2007-2013, nearly 300 million euro is allocated to external border controls and returns (with an additional 80 million euro annually going to Frontex from other funds amounting to a further 500 million euro over the seven years). Only 628 million euro is allocated to refugees, of which nearly 30 per cent is spent on voluntary returns, and another unknown proportion on removals among member states under Dublin II Regulation. (Institute of Race Relations, op. cit., p. 1). So when sub-Saharan Africans arrived in their different destinations, detention, 'voluntary' and involuntary repatriations, and deportations were waiting for them. Let us look at the country-to-country analyses of what went on.

Norway is a popular destination for only one sub-Saharan group—the Somalis. It had only one detention centre in 2010 with a capacity of 150 persons. They had a population of undocumented persons of between 10,500 and 32,000 in 2006. They saw claims for asylum double between 2007 and 2009. The country saw 24,400 claims in 2002, dropping down to 9,300 in 2005 and rising to over 17,000 in 2009. The number of removals sharply increased from 2008, rising from 2,300 in 2008 to 3,300 in 2009. But in 2010, the number of rejected asylum seekers forcibly removed in the first six months rose by a staggering 72 per cent. The country began to receive very few applications for asylum. In 2009, only 17,200 persons applied for asylum, and they granted asylum to only 4,500. (Institute of Race Relations, op. cit.)

Sweden is a popular destination for only one sub-Saharan African people—the people of Eritrea. Sweden had five dedicated immigration detention cites with a capacity of 185. But in 2008, they had 1,645 persons detained. This shows there was serious overcrowding at these sites. The country did not have a limit to the length of detention time. Asylum claims hit 33,000 in 2002, dropped to 17,500 in 2005, reached a peak of 36,200 (when half came from Iraq), and have since fallen, but a 42-per cent increase in orders to leave the territory took place from 2008 to 2009. Removals were down to 3,000 in 2007 from 12,500 in 2004 but rose to nearly 12,000 again in 2009. The country had between 30,000 and 50,000 undocumented persons in 2008. About 24,099 persons applied for asylum in 2008. In 2008, they deported 2,671 persons. Many of the flights were carried out by Frontex, which involved other EU members. The link between use of force and deportation flights for 2008-2009 were revealed by Swedish Migration Board statistics, which reported that the number of deportations had increased by 500 to 2,671—an increase of nearly a third.

Switzerland is a European destination for asylum seekers from three sub-Saharan African countries of Guinea, Senegal, and Sierra Leone. The country had five dedicated immigration detention facilities, two airport transit zones used for migration-related detention, three prisons used for migration related detention, and five semi-secure asylum reception centres. They also had a special space set apart for detained migrants awaiting deportation. In 2011, this special place could hold 476 persons. The population of undocumented persons was between 100,000 and 200 000. In 2010, they had some 12,916 asylum seekers. Swissinfo.ch reported that from January to March 2011, some 3,471 people applied for asylum in Switzerland—an 18-per cent increase on the same period in 2010. Most of the applicants were Eritreans (724 in all, up 35 per cent in 2010); Nigerians (428, down 32 per cent); and Tunisians (251, up 77 per cent). In March alone, there were 1,874 requests—a third more than March 2010. (Urs Geiser: Asylum in Figures: May 10, 2011). In reply, Switzerland has been involved in one of the most violent forms of removals in Europe. Between 2005 and 2010, Switzerland was involved in more than thirty flights organised by Frontex. Amnesty spokeswoman Denise Graf told Swiss Public Radio that Switzerland was not an example when it came to deportations, referring to an incident on 7 July 2011 when policemen clubbed and punched a Nigerian who resisted boarding an aircraft. (Swiss to assist EU border security agency. Swissinfo.ch. 20 July 2011). But this was not the only incident in which the Swiss had used violence against Nigerian asylum seekers. There had been three previous incidents. The most tragic was in March 2010 when twenty-nine-year-old Joseph Ndukaku Chiakwa, who had been on hunger strike, died shortly after he was forcibly restrained and placed in shackles at Zurich's Kloten Airport. Some insight into the police operation on the deportation flight that led to the death of Chiakwa was given to a Swiss newspaper by two other deportees, named only as Julius and Emmanuel. They said that a group of sixteen Nigerians were taken to Zurich airport at about 10 p.m. where they were met by sixty police officers. They said, 'They shackled our feet, knees, hands, hips, arms, and torso and made us wear helmets like those worn by boxers.' Julius said he was tied to the chair and carried into the plane by police, who then removed him from the chair and tied him to the airplane seat. Thomas Schnyder of the Association of Independent Doctors said, 'Forced immobilisation for more than ten hours, including having to wear a helmet, the inability to urinate or eat without assistance—these are not only inhumane and unworthy practices but also significant stress factors!' This was the third deportation death to have taken place in Switzerland during deportation flight from Switzerland to Nigeria. Six of the thirteen people who are known to have died in European deportation attempts since 1991 were Nigerians. Nigeria had bilateral agreement with Switzerland which it had to cancel because of the ill-treatment of its nationals. According to the Federal Migration Office, 1969 Nigerians applied for asylum in Switzerland in 2010. More than 700 of them were transferred to other European states under the Dublin II Regulation. Another 286 were rejected and returned to Nigeria, 165 voluntarily and 121 involuntarily.

Belgium is the main destination for asylum seekers from the DRC, and the numbers of those that sought asylum there between 1996 and 2005 are summarised above. It is also a popular destination for asylum seekers from Angola, Cameroon, Guinea, Rwanda, and Togo. Belgium's detention policy before 2006 is best summarised in the 'Tabitha Case' of 2006. In this case, the ECHR condemned Belgium for violations of Article 3 (prohibition of inhuman treatment), 5 (right of liberty and security), and 8 (right to respect for private and family life) of the European Convention of Human Rights. (Affaire Mubilanzila Mayeka et Kaniki Mitunga c. Belgique, 2006, para 58-9, 82, 87, 90-1, 103-5, 113-4). The case condemned the decision by Belgian authorities to detain a five-year-old Congolese girl who was trying to join her mother in Canada. The girl was confined to a closed centre for two months without an appointed guardian and then deported back to her country of origin. (Stateswatch, 2007). As a result, Belgium made extensive reforms to asylum, reception, and regularisation procedures which came into force in 2007. But even after the reforms, the detention conditions inside the closed centres remained severe and corresponded to a prison regime, with severe constraints. Living conditions are particularly bad in some centres. The transit centre 127 is dilapidated and insalubrious, and suffers from severe overcrowding with adults and children being forced to live together. The centres are equipped with isolation cells for detainees requiring a differentiated regime (isolation of people suffering from illness) or subject to a disciplinary regime (for those who cannot adapt to communal living). There is a risk that the differentiation between the differentiated regime and the disciplinary regime is unclear. Detainees' access to interpreters and information on their rights remains unsatisfactory. There are problems relating to the grouping together of people detained due to their administrative status and conditions and movements of people in and out of prisons. There are two types of closed centres managed by the Immigration Service. There are transit and repatriation centres (situated in international zones of the airport). These are closed INAD centres: centres 127 and 127b. Then there are three detention centres for illegal immigrants, namely, Bruges, Merksplas, and Votten. Belgium also operates open reception centres. These are hotel-like detention centres where asylum seekers are housed during the period over which their asylum applications are being considered. The provision of food, clothing, healthcare, education, social and legal guidance, daily welfare benefits, and community services is done by an agency, FEDASIL (Federal Agency for the reception of asylum seekers). The open accommodation centres for asylum seekers are directly managed by FEDASIL or by Belgian Red Cross. There are over forty centres with a total capacity of nearly 7,500 places. (Steps consulting study for European Parliament: The conditions in centres for third country national (detention camps, open centres as well as transit centres and transit zones) with a particular focus on provisions and facilities for persons with special needs in the twenty-five EU member states. December 2007). Belgium did not change its detention policy because of the 2006 Tabitha Case. It continued to detain both women and children in the same places and conditions as before. The JRS reported on 13 December 2011 that the ECHR once again found Belgium to be in violation of the European Convention of Human Rights by detaining a migrant mother and her three children; a violation of Article 3 (prohibition of torture and inhuman treatment) regarding the children; and a violation of Article 5.1 (rights to liberty and security) concerning the mother and the three children. In January 2009, a mother, Ms Kanagaratnam, and her three children—all Sri Lankan nationals—arrived at the Belgian border after travelling from Kinshasa, in the Congo. They applied for asylum and subsidiary protection at the border. Pursuant to Belgian law, the authorities refused them and decided to return them, on the grounds that the mother was in possession of a false passport. On the same day, the Aliens Officer placed the family in a detention centre, 127 bis, near the airport, pending processing of their asylum application. Appeals to the courts to be released were not successful. Ms Kanagaratnam told the Belgian asylum officer that she had been arrested in Sri Lanka three times for her alleged collaboration with the separatist movement. She fled with her children in fear of arbitrary arrest for her Tamil origins. The asylum officer refused her application on the grounds that her statements lacked credibility. After learning that she would be returned to the Congo, Ms Kanagaratnam applied for a temporary measure for fear that she would be subjected to inhuman treatment were she return to the Congo. In March 2009, the court issued a temporary suspension of the return. This was extended by a month after the family refused to board the airplane. In September 2009, the asylum officer granted her family refugee status. Belgium was found to be in violation of Article 3 for detaining children in a facility that was not age-appropriate. A similar ruling was made twice in prior cases. Belgium was also found to be at the centre of deportations both nationally and regionally. On 28 April 2010, Belgium organised a flight to deport sixty failed asylum seekers of the Congolese DRC origin, coming from different European countries. Deportation was arranged in a Frontex charter flight. In 2010, Frontex coordinated thirty-eight flights from Europe to Nigeria, Cameroon, Burundi and Georgia, Columbia, Kosovo, and Ukraine. From January to March 2011 alone, Frontex carried out seven flights to Congo, Nigeria, Georgia, and Iraq. Belgium is an active member of the European anti-migration policy movement. It organises something like twenty deportations a day and group flight for unwilling migrants. (Bristol No Borders: Belgium Activists block detention centres to stop a charter flight: 28 April 2011)

Netherlands is a European country destination for sub-Saharan Africans from Angola, Congo, and Somalia. The state adopted a very restrictive asylum policy which led to the numbers of asylum seekers dropping from 18,700 in 2002 to 4,550 in 2005. A new government in 2006 brought in the 'Law of Forgiveness' 28 which deported en masse 26,000 asylum seekers in 2006. In July 2007, they introduced new asylum measures, which are very harsh to the asylum seekers. The reception of asylum seekers was handed to the COA (Central Agency for the Reception of Asylum Seekers), an independent administration funded by the ministry of justice. They accommodate asylum seekers in the following reception places: three application centres in which newly arrivals must register before being sent to other centres. Asylum seekers are kept here between two days and one week; seven orientation and integration centres designed for asylum seekers waiting for an initial decision on their asylum application. They stay here between six months and one year. Each has a capacity of 400 places, except for the larger Dronten Centre; around forty return centres where asylum seekers who have received an initial application refusal from the Office of Immigration and Naturalisation and have begun appeal proceedings. The average duration of residence is two years; four centres for unaccompanied minors. The total number of people accommodated in these reception centres had gone down from 85,000 in the year 2000 to only 23,000 in 2010. Then there are seven detention centres under the direct authority of the ministry of justice. They are given the same supervision and security regimes and operation services as in prisons. One of these centres is for women. In 2008, the government completed the construction of two large penitentiary complexes for foreign nationals. Here they housed illegal immigrants, rejected asylum seekers awaiting expulsion and those refused entry onto Dutch soil. *The living conditions and conditions for those awaiting expulsion in the return centres are very harsh. The duration of residence may be up to several years, and there is a lack of privacy with residents forced to live together in small rooms and a lack of activities (training and cultural activities are no longer provided). This extended residence inevitably lead to tensions between residents, extended period of separation from the reception society and a risk of depression and a feeling of abandonment which affects children and adolescents most keenly.* (Steps Consulting Study for European Parliament: December 2007, p. 126). There is no legal limit to the duration of detention which depends on the decision of the tribunal, and has to be confirmed or quashed each month. Consequently, in 2006, the duration for detention on the prison ship in the port of Rotterdam exceeded three months for some detainees; one detainee broke the record of thirteen months detention. The internal detention conditions in some centres are extremely severe, identical to those found in prisons, with personnel made up of guards and police officers. The living conditions in some centres are particularly harsh, in a confined, overcrowded environment, where detainees' personal living space is reduced to a minimum. The pathogenic nature of detention: These conditions are considered to be a punishment which should not be the case, especially in cases where the wait can last for several months with absolutely no certainty concerning the outcome. Lack of contact with the outside world increases anxiety amongst detainees. (Steps Consulting Study for European Parliament: December 2007, p. 126). There were over 32,500 asylum claims in 2001 but only 7,100 first claims in 2007 rising to just fewer than 15,000 in 2009. But removal went up from 16,500 in 2001 to 23,200 in 2003 before dropping to just less than 9,000 in 2009. Orders to leave the territory rose from 31,700 in 2008 to over 43,300 in 2009. (The Institute of Race relations: European Race Audit: Briefing Paper No 4—October 2010: Accelerated removals: A study of the human cost of EU deportation policy 2009-2010)

Germany is a preferred destination for asylum seekers from Angola, Cameroon, Eritrea, Ghana, Guinea, Kenya, Nigeria, Senegal, Uganda, and Togo, and the figures above show the numbers that have sought asylum in Germany from 1196 to 2005. However, by 2010, Germany saw claims drop to a third of their 2001 level. First claims peaked at 88,200 in 2001, dropped to 19,000 in 2007, and then rose slightly to 29,000 in 2009. These asylum changes were due to the combined impact of the admission of new member states into the European Union, the implementation of the Dublin II Regulation, and the strengthening of external borders which accompanied the entry of new countries to the European Union. Asylum seekers were also frightened by the German policy of detention and removals. Removals also reached a peak of 44,200 in 2001 and started to go down until they reached only 12,000 in 2009. They were, however, replaced by indirect removals called orders to leave, which went up from 12,000 in 2008 to 14,500 in 2009. Germany has three closed detention centres located at airport transit zones; approximately thirty-two closed detention centres in other parts of the country; twenty reception centres for asylum seekers; around 900 community centres; and six open removal centres. Detention for readmission (Dublin II) has become widespread and allows for detention during the asylum application procedure, despite this being against the international measures in place. Furthermore, it is no longer possible to appeal against detention orders for asylum seekers, which deprives unaccompanied minors and separates family members and other vulnerable groups of their right to legal counsel. Although the detention pattern is generally similar, there are variations between the different regions of Germany. In Brandenburg, there were around 6,000 refugees housed mainly in thirty communal houses (Sammelunter Konfte) of the Federal State. The communal shelters are often located outside small towns and sometimes in areas as remote as in a middle of a wood, where accommodation is in buildings such as run-down former barracks. The living conditions are very poor. A camp called Waldsieversdorf in the district Märkisch-Oderland in Brandenburg is an example; the nearest bus stop is 4 km away, and the nearest shopping facility 23 km away. The inadequate conditions of the buildings contributes to health and hygiene difficulties, which are also produced by the fact that people who are not used to each other are forced to live close together and share kitchen and sanitary facilities. The potential conflict generated by such living conditions. (Aspects of contempt for Humanity in Europe: Berlin/Brandenburg, February 2007: deportation centre motard straße)

France is a favourite destination for asylum seekers from the sub-Saharan countries of Angola; Cameroon; Congo; Côte d'Ivoire; DRC; Ghana; Guinea; Nigeria; Rwanda; Senegal; Sierra Leone; Togo and Sudan. First asylum claims rose from 47,000 to 58,500 between 2001 and 2004, falling back to 29,400 in 2007. There were 38,400 asylum claims in 2009 and 25,200 in the first six months of 2010. In 2006, the French Interior Ministry instituted the controversial practice of establishing targets for deporting undocumented immigrants each year. Since then the government has increased police raids to arrest unauthorised immigrants and introduced legislation to make it harder for immigrants to bring their families (Lakoff, 2008). Accordingly in January 2009, the government announced that it had surpassed the 2008 target of 26,000 deportations by nearly 4,000 cases (Connexion, 2009). Additionally, asylum seekers who initially entered the Schengen zone through another country constituted about 8 per cent of detainees in 2007. According to the Dublin II Convention regulating asylum in the Schengen area, asylum seekers may be deported to the country through which they originally entered in the Schengen area or to the country in which they have already filed an asylum application. Nearly 200 children under ten years of age were placed in detention in 2007, including one three-week-old infant. It emerged in 2010 that over the previous three years, French Ministry of Interior, in conditions of secrecy, was using small rented planes for deportations, particularly of children. In an interview with France info, a police officer revealed that small rented planes, with a maximum capacity of fifteen, were being used for deportations involving children who were supported by activists. (<http: www.france-info.com/france-justice-police-2010-08-06-sans-papiers-des-petits-avions-pour-des-expulsions-plus-discretes-473175-9-11.html). The Global Detention Project has gathered data on some thirty-six detention sites in France (not including short-term holding facilities and other ports of entry). The number of persons detained per annum rose from 28,228 in 2003 to 35,008 in 2007. Removals increased from 8,600 to 29,300 between 2001 and 2009. (Global Detention Project 2007-2009: France Detention Profile: Last updated April 2009); (Institute of Race relations: European Race Audit: Briefing Paper No. 4—October 2010: Accelerated removals: a study of the human cost of EU deportation policies, 2009-2010.) Like in most northern European countries, asylum seekers were not received, given proper accommodation, and had their cases properly assessed. Minors are detained in same facilities with adults, of both sexes, and there is no provision for educating these young people. Asylum seekers are sent back to countries from which they ran away from persecution. Europe generally failed to respect the terms of the 1951 Refugee Convention and 1967 Protocol. Many of these abuses go unnoticed because they are carried out in secret. We only get to know some of these abuses when an asylum seeker gets someone to sponsor him to take the state in which he has been abused to court. Most asylum seekers do not have the means and the knowledge to do so, but the few cases we get reveal a lot of surprising decisions made by European states. One such

case was that of IMv France (Application no 9152/09). In this case, the European Court of Human Rights held a unanimous decision that there had been a violation of Article 13 (rights to an effective remedy), taken together with Article 3 (prohibition of inhuman or degrading treatment) of the European Convention of Human Rights. The case concerned the risks the applicant would face in the event of his deportation to Sudan and the effectiveness of the remedies available to him in France in view of the fact that his asylum application was dealt with under the fast track procedure. IM is a Sudanese national-born in 1976 and lives in Perpignan (France). In December 2008, he travelled to Spain with a view to crossing the border into France carrying a forged French visa. In Sudan, he had been arrested by the police on account of his activities within the student movement and his alleged link with rebel groups in Darfur. He had spent eight days in detention in May 2008 and a further two months under surveillance by the Sudanese authorities, who interrogated him on a weekly basis using violence. On his arrival at the French border, the applicant was arrested for illegally entering or staying in France and for forgery and use of forged documents. According to his submissions, he immediately said that he wished to apply for asylum but received no response. He was remanded in custody and appeared before the Perpignan Tribunal de Grande Instance, which sentenced him to one month's imprisonment for an offence under the alien's legislation. According to the applicant, he restated before the court his intention to claim asylum, but to no avail. While in detention, he challenged removal by prefecture on 7 January 2009. He wrote in Arabic, but the application was rejected on the grounds that no conclusive evidence had been provided to substantiate his claim that he faced a risk of ill-treatment in Sudan. The court also observed that he had not lodged an asylum application. On 16 January 2009, IM was placed in administrative detention with the view to his deportation. He was informed the same day of the possibility of applying for asylum. He lodged an application on 19 January 2009 with the assistance of CIMADE, an association which assists foreign nationals, particularly those in administrative detention. On 31 January 2009, he was notified of the refusal of his application.

He appealed against the decision to the National Asylum Tribunal (Cour nationale du droit d'asile). France began steps to deport him. On 16 February 2009, the applicant applied to the European Court of Human Rights under rule 39 of the rules of court (interim measure) seeking to have the order for his deportation suspended. On 19 February 2011, the National Asylum Tribunal granted the applicant refugee status.

Conclusion

The *Eurodac* fingerprint marching system has become one of the most useful tools of the Dublin II Regulation. The northern European states now have several options: The asylum seeker can now be detained for lengthy periods while awaiting deportation and can be deported using national airlines, locally chartered airplanes, or combined chartered Frontex airplanes. Dublin II opened an extra door. As soon as Council Regulation (EC) No 343/2003of February 18 2003 establishing the criteria and mechanism for determining the member state responsible for examining asylum applications lodged in the member state by a third country national was passed there followed applications by all Europeans to deport asylum seekers to countries where they made their first asylum claim.

Dublin II Regulation Statistics: Incoming Requests for January 2004 to June 2005

	January to December 2004				January to June 2005			
	Request	Accepted	Rejected	Effected	Request	Accepted	Rejected	Effected
Belgium					1,353	1,059	324	180
Germany	7,436	6,009	1,517	2,681	3,091	2,292	808	1,453
Greece	1,351	1,112	127	404	565	526	49	176
Ireland	133	87	32	59	56	32	9	15
Italy	2,701			6	1,238	96	7	248
Malta					117	Est66	Est15	35
Netherlands	3,385				1,225	759	324	550
Norway	2,180				3,989	3,478	500	N/A
Portugal	60	43	27	17	44	26	10	7
Spain	68			111	329	317	52	156
Sweden	3,596	2,642			1,523	1,111	391	N/A
U.K.					342	222	89	118

Dublin II Regulation Statistics: Outgoing Requests for January 2004 to June 2005

	January to December 2004				January to June 2005			
	Request	Accepted	Rejected	Effected	Request	Accepted	Rejected	Effected
Belgium					2,210	1,664	546	N/A
Germany	6,536	5,110	1,068	2,765	2,608	1,824	661	1,108
Greece	18	10	5	5	16	11	4	3
Ireland	292	261	27	74	261	193	28	78
Italy	616				354	66	4	11
Malta					N/A	N/A	N/A	N/A
Netherlands	1,862				932	636	145	503
Norway	3,175			2,099	5,925	5,749	646	503
Portugal	15	15	1	2	19	17	3	4
Spain	238			10	142	50	18	14
Sweden	6,188	5,242		4,225	1,999	1,646	317	N/A
U.K.					1,059	974	77	1,155

Source: ECRE: European Council on Refugees and Exiles: Summary Reports on the Application of the Dublin II Regulation in Europe: March 2006.

The asylum seekers we have been following from the sub-Saharan states who thought they had finally reached the countries they wanted to claim asylum found that there was a law which said they claim asylum in the first safe country. The asylum seeker

is confused about the word *safety* if he thinks of the way he was treated in Greece, Italy, and some of the countries of southern Europe. What is safety if you are forced to sleep in the open without food and denied permission to work? What is safety is your future is undecided and you face the possibility of abuse in the open or even in the places of detention? But the asylum seeker did not know that when he was fingerprinted; the fingerprints were sent all over Europe to stop him from what Europe called asylum shopping. So when he arrived at the border of the preferred country, he is captured and detained again. Unfortunately, one of the biggest weaknesses of the 1951 Refugee Convention is failure to legislate on detention. So people are placed in all sorts of unsuitable places while the countries do 'readmission shopping'. Countries exchange documents, and time is no longer an issue because the asylum seeker is now detained in a 'safe country'. As you can see above, many of the applications are rejected. Mike Van den Broeck described the Dublin II Resolution in the following words: *The Dublin system pledged to 'guarantee 'asylum applicants 'that their applications will be examined by one of the member states'. In fact, far too often, a Dublin transfer guarantees that asylum applications will not be meaningfully examined. During responsibility determination, the process of deciding which member state should assess an application, asylum seekers are detained as long as six months before their claim can be heard . . . Reception conditions also vary widely. NGOs, governments and the European Parliament have raised serious concerns at inadequate or even inhuman treatment of asylum seekers in several member states. States increasingly detain asylum seekers to try and complete transfers, families are kept apart, and refugees with serious health problems receive insufficient care.* (Dublin II-Convention and principle of non-foulement, International protection of refugees in the EU fails. Mike Van den Broeck: Progress Lawyers Network Antwerp-Brussels-gent: 2009) The host countries then try to have them accepted back by the countries from which they came. If they fail, they then shop around the African continent for a nation willing to accept them, even for a bribe. When they offer to support a country solve pressing economic or military problems, they usually get a country willing to take the unfortunate asylum seeker. When an asylum seeker is told he will be deported to a country, he escaped persecution or to a country he has never been to in his life, he is bound to resist. Using passenger planes has been found to be problematic as asylum seekers often shout, cry, attempt to commit suicide, and so on. European countries have chosen to combine efforts, either through the use of Frontex or use of charter planes from one of the member states. Under such conditions all tactics used to force prisoners will be employed. The United Kingdom, Switzerland, Ireland, Austria, and a few other nations use joint charter planes and in some cases private companies to deport unwanted asylum seekers. The Institute of Race Relations describes how it is done in the United Kingdom: *In the UK, according to a major investigation by the Independent newspaper, private security escorts (who may be recruited despite criminal convictions, including assaults) are authorised to use a variety of techniques to restrain deportees including a 'Goose Neck' wrist lock, 'thumb and strait arms locks' as well as a procedure entitled 'Nose Control'—which presumably refers to pressure or a strike on the base of the nose, and 'Head control'. The private company, G4S instructs its escorts on the type of restraints they can use, including 'rigid bar', 'chain link' and double-lock handcuffs are used by some specially trained police officers to put pressure on an individual's wrist in order to force compliance.* (Institute of Race Relations European Race Audit: Accelerated removals: A study of the human cost of EU deportation policies 2009-2010)

CHAPTER 8

The United Kingdom and the Five Ds (Desperation, Deterrence, Destitution, Detention, and Deportation)

Introduction

The United Kingdom is one of the top five recipients of refugees in Europe. The size of the refugee population in the United Kingdom is not known. It is best measured by the number of people that claim asylum. ICAR reports that in 2008, the United Kingdom had the second largest number of asylum applications in Europe. 35,200 applications were received in France; the United Kingdom had 31,300; Italy 31,100; Sweden 24,400; Germany 22,100; Greece 19,900; Switzerland 16,600; and Netherlands 13,400. Spain had only 4,500 applications. These applications included dependents. (ICAR Statistics Paper 1, December 2009 update). But a large percentage of refugees do not claim asylum because they fear detention and deportation. So the actual number of refugees is never known. All that government works on are estimations. In fact, until the World War II, almost all the colonies and former colonies of the United Kingdom did not need visas to enter the United Kingdom. But following World War II when Europe could no longer hold on to the colonies largely because they had to put most of their resources into rebuilding war-damaged infrastructure, this policy significantly changed. First, the main colonial countries, Britain, France, Spain, and Portugal, virtually abandoned most of the African colonies between 1957 and 1975. So African countries, which had been created by the colonial system to suit colonial pursuits, found themselves having to create governments using a selection model, 'parliamentary democracy', which did not exist in their history and did not accommodate traditional forms of leadership selection. (Sub-Saharan Africa had tribal leaderships based on common cultures and languages. These societies had limited knowledge of minerals in their areas. So their systems were based mainly on animal and agricultural wealth. When Europeans arrived, they created new countries based on availability and distribution of mineral wealth. They forced different and rival traditional groups to become parts of European designed and created new countries. There was little effort to integrate these tribal groups because this was not one of the objectives of creating colonies. In fact, the colonial systems encouraged tribal divisions because that weakened African opposition to colonial rule). These post-colonial democracies, especially those from the French and British colonial system, did not last. They were quickly replaced by dictatorships and by the army. From the 1970s, Africa has seen some of the worst forms of violence ever seen in world history and the victimisation of innocent people, as new governments tried to reconcile the traditional system with the colonial one. Majority of the victims have been women and children. So from the 1970s, Africa, especially Africa south of the Sahara, has seen unprecedented human displacement. Majority of the displaced have sought refuge in neighbouring countries, but with instability almost everywhere, many have been forced to go the countries that had political stability, and most of these were their former colonisers. This is the reason why so many sub-Saharan Africans have in the past half century been making all these attempts to enter Europe. Although the actual numbers of Africans that have reached Europe are small by world standards of immigration, Europe is reluctant to help solve the African refugee emigration. Europe has not helped African governments create true democracies. In fact, Europe is desperate to remove Africans refugees already in their countries. It has not been possible to study in detail the condition of immigrants in the whole of Europe because for a long time Europe used to turn refugees into cheap labour. With the coming of UN regulations on refugees, it has become difficult to continue to do so. So European governments now want to classify refugees as labour migrants that take European jobs, as criminals that bring instability to Europe, and, after 9/11, as terrorists. However, companies have not changed policies. They want the cheapest labour, no matter where it comes from. They continued to prefer refugees because they are cheaper. Some companies can even underpay them because their rights are compromised by politicians. Some sub-Saharan African refugees are very highly qualified persons willing to do jobs Europeans rejected. This study is based only on refugee experiences in the United Kingdom. The study will be divided into five sub-topic area: (1) Desperation, (2) Deterrence, (3) Destitution, (4) Detention, and (5) Deportation

(1) Desperation

Sub-Saharan Commonwealth Africans

The majority of sub-Saharan Africans that escaped persecution from home governments and sought asylum in the United Kingdom came from Commonwealth countries. This scenario changed significantly in the last decade because of the wars in the Great Lakes region, West Africa, Sudan, and the horn of Africa. UK immigration restrictions have tended to react to some of these changes. One could say there has been panic reaction from the United Kingdom. Before 1948, anyone born in the United Kingdom or a colony was a British subject. But after the United Kingdom gave independence to its African colonies, British laws began to change as it reacted to the rise in numbers that preferred asylum in the kingdom. The first reaction was to redefine Britishness. The British people were classified into five categories—citizens by birth, adoption, descent, registration, and naturalisation. Most sub-Saharan

Commonwealth people lost British citizenship as a result of this categorisation. They, however, could still enter the United Kingdom simply by being members of the Commonwealth. The 1962 Commonwealth Immigration Act removed this privilege. With very few exceptions, Commonwealth citizens' position can no longer be distinguished from that of other foreign nationals. But with many East Europeans migrating west, the United Kingdom found itself with a lot of labour for a very slow growing economy. The United Kingdom had to find an answer. Traditionally, they looked to the law for control of migration. The law had to make the United Kingdom as unattractive to asylum seekers as possible; the law had to create legislation on how to control entry and settlement in the kingdom, and the law had to find a way to return some of the asylum seekers to their or other countries. These three divisions created the concepts of destitution through legal deprivation of basic needs of asylum seekers; detention of all those the state could manage to detain; and deportation of all those the state would manage to deport even to states the UNHCR felt were not safe for repatriation.

The second significant development in United Kingdom is that the number of asylum applicants has been dropping significantly and continue to drop each year, and the number of refusals continues to be very high. The graph below show how dramatic the fall is.

Year of entry to the UK of Black African-born people, 1960-2007

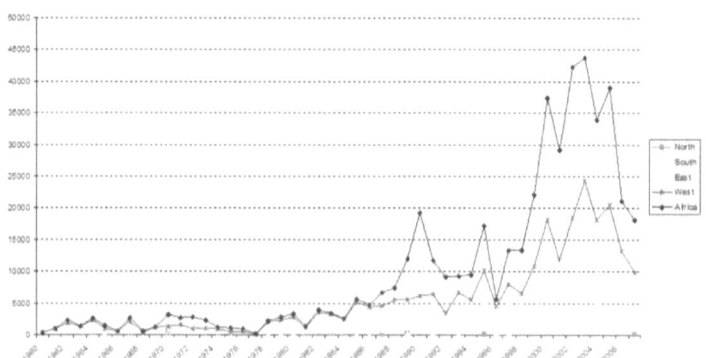

The graph on Africans reaching the United Kingdom for asylum begins in 1960 when the first African countries gained independence, and as you can see, up to the 1970s instability and the collapse of post-indepence democracies had not resulted in many refugees reaching the United Kingdom. By the end of the 1970s, African democracies were completely wipped out. The succeeding armies and dictators were nototious for their corruption and violence. People began to move out of Africa because there was hardly anywhere to look for refuge. We see the numbers of refugees reaching the United Kingdom rising until it reached its peak just after the year 2000. If we look at the graph above, we see a sharp drop from over 40,000 applications for asylum in the year 2000 to just over 15,000 eight years later. The trent is same for the South Africans who did not seek asylum in the United Kingdom before 1980 had to seek asylum after the Mugabe became the main force in the central African regional war involving Zimbabwe, Angola, and DRC on one side and Rwanda, Uganda, and rebel movements of northern DRC on the other. Tens of thousands of central Africans fled the region to seek asylum elsewhere, and many reached the United Kingdom. Mugabe followed the regional war with slaughter of his own people. After his election defeat in the year 2000, Mugabe created so much violence in the whole country so much that Zimbabweans became the main applicants for asylum in the United Kingdom in the year 2002. But as the graph below shows, the numbers of applicants dramatically dropped after that year in all the eight main asylum applying nations of sub-Saharan Africa. What did the United Kingdom do to enable this to happen? We know that it is not because there were political improvements in the systems of governance in sub-Saharan Africa. There is still much persecution of innocent people in the DRC, Zimbabwe, Uganda, Angola, Rwanda, Sudan, Eritrea, and Somalia. We also know that the United Kingdom has in its parliament passed numerous laws to control immigration. Many of these laws have, in fact, controlled refugees rather than immigrants. We will analyse the measures the United Kingdom implemented and see how they affected asylum seekers and refugees and find out if this increased their traumatic experiences in their struggle to receive protection from persecution. Because if you look at the asylum application for the eight countries that have suffered the worst political persecution in Africa between 1998 and the year 2008, there is no way this sudden drop in asylum application in the United Kingdom would reflect the truth about these eight African countries attempts to seek protection in the United Kingdom.

Trends in asylum migration from Africa,1998-2008

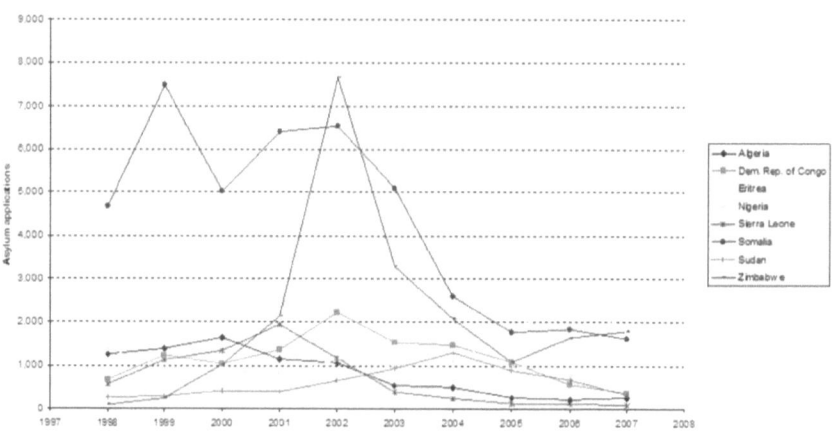

Secondly, it appears that when the refugees manage to reach the United Kingdom and apply for asylum, the United Kingdom seems to be turning down their applications using the argument that they are immigrants and not refugees. The figures below support the argument that despite the obvious drop in the numbers that claimed asylum from the world and from Africa, the United Kingdom has consistently denied the majority of the asylum. There is not a single year when less than 69 per cent of them were denied asylum. In 2004, the United Kingdom denied 88 per cent of all asylum applicants' asylum! Many of the people refused asylum have also been refused permission to work, turning them into destitute. We will see later the desperate lives some of these people now live in the United Kingdom.

Applications and Home Office Decisions (2000-2008)

Year	2000	2001	2002	2003	2004	2005	2006	2007	2008
No. of asylum applicants	80,315	71,025	84,130	49,405	33,960	25,710	23,610	23,430	25,930
No. of initial decisions	1,09,205	1,20,950	83,540	64,940	46,020	27,395	20,930	21,775	19,400
No. of total decisions	96,400	1,24,205	85,575	67,740	50,360	29,885	21,745	22,890	19,855
No. and percentage refused asylum	62,720 (74%)	89,115 (72%)	54,305 (63%)	55,890 (83%)	44,070 (88%)	24,730 (83%)	17,050 (78%)	16,755 (73%)	13,700 (69%)

(Source: ICAR Statistics, Paper I, p. 10)

Top Ten Nationalities of Asylum Applicants (2004-2008)

2004	2005	2006	2007	2008
Iran 3455	Iran 3150	Eritrea 2585	Afghanistan 2500	Afghanistan 3505
Somalia 2585	Somalia 1760	Afghanistan 2400	Iran 2210	Zimbabwe 3165
China 2365	Eritrea 1760	Iran 2375	China 2100	Iran 2270
Zimbabwe 2065	China 1730	China 1945	Iraq 1825	Eritrea 2255
Iraq 1725	Afghanistan 1580	Somalia 1845	Eritrea 1810	Iraq 1850
Pakistan 1710	Iraq 1415	Zimbabwe 1650	Zimbabwe 1800	Sri Lanka 1475
DRC 1475	Pakistan 1145	Pakistan 965	Somalia 1615	China 1400
India 1405	DRC 1080	Iraq 945	Pakistan 1030	Somalia 1345
Afghanistan 1395	Zimbabwe 1075	Nigeria 790	Sri Lanka 990	Pakistan 1230
Sudan 1305	Nigeria 1025	India 680	Middle East 825	Nigeria 820
Total 19,475	Total 15,720	Total 16,180	Total 16,705	Total 19,315

(Source: ICAR Statistics, Paper I, December 2009 update, p. 18)

Nationality of UK Asylum Seekers, United Kingdom (2008)

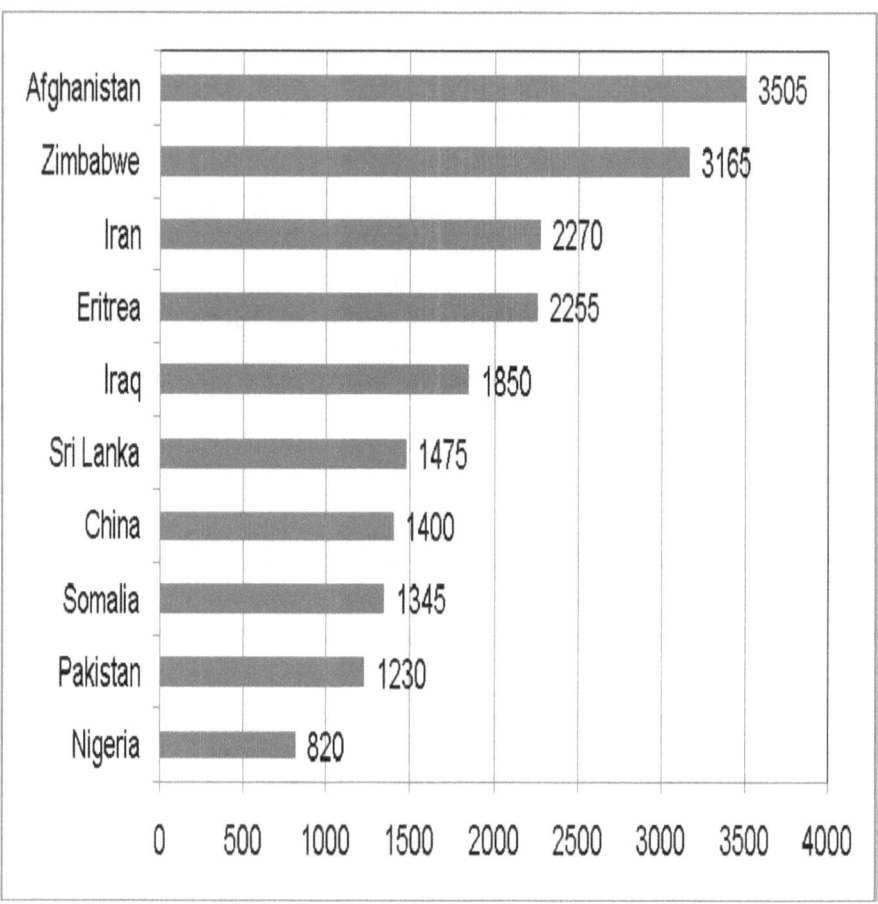

Source: Home Office (2009)

According to the ICAR, in 2008, the percentages of applications of the top ten countries were Afghanistan (14 per cent), Zimbabwe (12 per cent), Iran (9 per cent), Eritrea (9 per cent), Sri Lanka (6 per cent), China (6 per cent), Somalia (5 per cent), Pakistan (5 per cent), and Nigeria (3 per cent). In that year, over two-thirds (74 per cent) of all applications for asylum in the United Kingdom were from nationals of these countries. Many of these nationalities have featured consistently in the top ten for the last five years, suggesting that a significant number of asylum applicants in the United Kingdom originate from protracted refugee situations. David Owen in *African*

migration to the UK shows graphically that African migration to the United Kingdom went up significantly from the end of the last century but slightly differs with the ICAR on the nationalities and numbers. The difference may arise because Owen's study was of immigration and not asylum. The pattern, however, is similar. He said in 2008, there were six countries from which there were 20,000 or more black African migrants in the United Kingdom—Nigeria, Ghana, Somalia, Zimbabwe, Uganda, and Kenya. The largest was Nigeria with 125,000 migrants to the United Kingdom. Owen shows in the graph above that the majority of the people that entered the United Kingdom between 1998 and 2007 were from politically troubled nations. Somalia had a civil war which forced all the political leaders of the country to escape to neighbouring countries. Although the numbers of Somalis entering the United Kingdom has dramatically dropped, it is so because the United Kingdom has made it very difficult for Somalis to claim asylum in the United Kingdom as we shall see later. Similarly, Zimbabwe faced unprecedented violence when the MDC was formed and both parliamentary and presidential elections in the years 2000 and 2002. The incumbent leader refused to accept defeat and violence led to much loss of life and the mass exodus of refugees mainly into South Africa. The sharp rise in the graph above is of the numbers that managed to reach the United Kingdom to claim asylum. The DRC, Eritrea, Nigeria, Sierra Leone, Sudan, and Algeria all had civil wars that forced their citizens to look for asylum in other countries, including the United Kingdom.

If we look at the total migrant figures as shown in the bar graph below, we see that the number of women is often equal to or more than that of men. This is inconsistent with commercial migration from Africa or indeed from third world countries. In Africa, far less numbers of women have been given good enough education to compete on the international market. So if these movement were commercial, there should have been far more men than women. But the figures are consistent with immigration because women will not allow their children to die if they can manage to take them elsewhere. We will see later on that some of the women rescued from sinking makeshift boats are pregnant or travelling with little children, but hardly any man has been rescued with a child. In fact, many children have been rescued on their own in the company of many men who do not want to have anything to do with them.

Countries of origin of African migrants

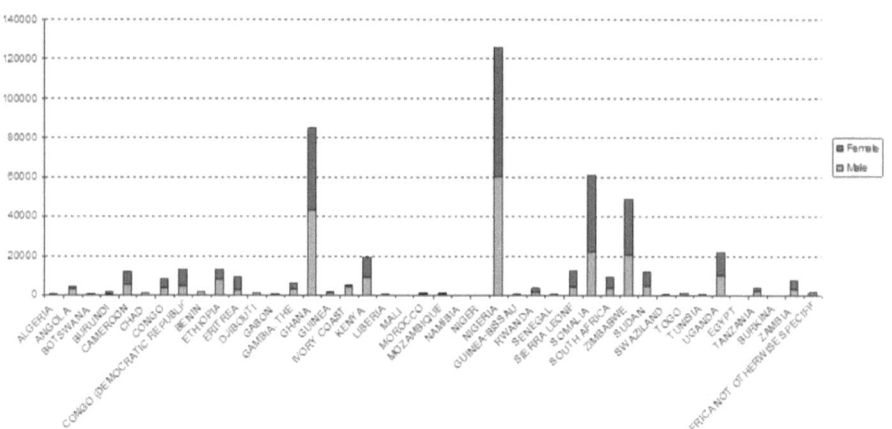

(2) Deterrence

United Kingdom's External Control Policy

Despite the fact that the United Kingdom is a signatory of the UN Universal Human Rights Convention (RC51) cited before and despite the fact that Article 14 of the Convention says, 'Everyone has the right to seek and enjoy in other countries asylum from persecution', the United Kingdom has in recent years created and enforced legislation to significantly reduce the flow of immigrants and virtually deny asylum seekers entry into the United Kingdom. The set of laws against immigration and asylum seekers passed, especially in the last twenty years, have been the main reason why there has been a dramatic drop in the number of asylum seekers reaching the United Kingdom. These regulations are helping to endanger the lives of refugees forced to remain or returned to the countries they face persecution. Below is a summary of how these restrictions have created outside the United Kingdom to make it impossible for asylum seekers to enter the United Kingdom formally.

Passports: The UK government expect every immigrant to have a passport. It is an offence punishable by a fine and up to two years imprisonment or both to fail to produce a passport on entry into the United Kingdom. Passports are also required of dependents of the principal applicants. But passports are issued by the home governments run by people from which refugees are fleeing. If these governments are the reason why the refugee is running away, it does not make sense for him to go to them for a passport. Many of the countries from which Africans run are governed by brutal armies or dictatorial regimes or are heavily involved in civil wars or cross-border wars. They often have no money for passport materials, and many of them cannot even make passports locally. Some passports take several months to produce. Refugees have often found themselves stranded. So in order to flee quickly or easily, refugees have increasingly turned to members of the community that claim to know how to assist victims of persecution—these are often experts in acquiring false documents, crossing borders clandestinely, or bribing immigration officials. They claim to be able to assist them in finding a safe passage to a country they can apply for asylum; in this case, the United Kingdom. Refugees have been forced to surrender their lives into the hands of traffickers that have stolen their money, abandoned them in forests or deserts, and even dumped them in the ocean. Yet the United Kingdom is a signatory of the 1951 Refugee Convention. Under the terms of the convention refugees do not necessarily require passports to claim asylum.

Visas: Most countries of sub-Saharan Africa are what are called visa nationals by the UK government. This means that their people will not be able to enter the United Kingdom without a visa. There are two initial problems with that. Firstly, visas are not transferable and/or interchangeable. If you enter the United Kingdom as a student, you cannot at a later date change your condition to wife or partner. If you enter as a visitor, you cannot change into a student. You have to go back to your country of origin and apply for a new visa. Secondly, there is no visa status called refugee visa. So refugees cannot enter the United Kingdom legally. In other words, refugees can only enter the United Kingdom as criminals first and then prove that they are not. The UNHCR said this to countries like the United Kingdom: *By requiring a refugee to obtain proper travel documentation before fleeing his or her country to seek asylum in another country, States in fact ignore the very problem which give rise to the need for refugee protection and in effect, deny the possibility of asylum to some refugees.* (UNHCR 2000a:10) Children, wives, partners, and certain members of the family visas are mandatory for all non-nationals. But even those that have got the visas will not be sure they reach the United Kingdom, because government representatives conduct checks while the traveller is still in his country of departure. At different points, during the journey through a combination of control measures, including airline liaison officers (ALOs), carrier sanctions, and port police, this traveller can be checked by a variety of actors positioned at key points, to decide if he or she is admissible to the United Kingdom and to prevent entry if necessary. In this way, visa restrictions form the frontline of immigration control and allow migration management to become detached from the physical border and to function efficiently at every stage along an individual's journey to the United Kingdom. A look at the visa restrictions imposed over the past twenty years suggests that they have been used to stop potential asylum seekers reaching UK territory.

1. In 1987, the government imposed visa restrictions on Sri Lankan nationals, following an increase in the arrival of Tamil asylum seekers.
2. In 1989, the government imposed visa restrictions on Turkish nationals in response to a rapid increase in the arrival of Kurds.
3. In 1992, nationals of the former Yugoslavia and, in 1994, nationals of Sierra Leone and Ivory Coast were required to obtain visas to travel to the United Kingdom.

4. In 2003, a visa requirement for the citizens of Zimbabwe was a direct response to the large numbers of asylum seekers from that country. The measure was effected even as the number of asylum seekers fell from 7,655 in 2002 to 3,295 in 2003 (Home Office, 2004:3)

The UK government does not hesitate to link the imposition of Airport Transit Visas with reduction in asylum numbers. In 2005, it claimed, *We have substantially increased the nationalities that require visas just to pass through the UK. This has had a significant impact on unfounded asylum applications.* (Home Office, 2005:25)

But as visa restrictions block the legal routes to the United Kingdom, many asylum seekers have fled to neighbouring countries where they do not need visas. Millions of Africans from different countries have flooded South Africa. Many are in Kenya, Ethiopia, and Zambia. Some have moved from one country to another; many have lost loved ones in the process, and many have lost their lives. But there are others that have been forced to use the more difficult routes and still reached the United Kingdom. The United Kingdom need to appreciate that there are countries like Somalia where there are no governments, so no one can give passports. There are countries like Eritrea where military service is compulsory. One can only get a passport after fighting in local or regional conflicts. There are many countries in Africa where women cannot get travel documents without the permission of the husband, so some women are forced to use forged documents to leave their countries of origin. There are countries where asylum seekers travel without documents for fear of being identified; do not get the documents because they do not have the time; where the documents were stolen; and where they have to use false documents and false names. The decision to classify most sub-Saharan countries as visa nationals have denied many Africans the asylum they are entitled to and has led to much suffering as some of them tried alternative routes. Some have lost their lives in the attempt to reach the United Kingdom through the alternative routes.

Out-posted Immigration Officials: The United Kingdom has placed several control officers in different countries to carry out several tasks that have resulted in the dramatic drop in the number of immigrants reaching the United Kingdom. These representatives take the form of Immigration Liaison Officers (ILOs), ALOs, Juxtaposed Controls, and, more recently, Migration Delivery Officers (MDOs).

ILOs: The United Kingdom began posting ILOs abroad in 1980s, and by 2006, the United Kingdom had ILOs in fourteen locations, covering twenty-six countries. In 2005, the United Kingdom announced that it was to invest £4 million to extend the ILO network to a total of forty-two officers supported by a 'fast response' team of thirty immigration officers, and to extend the IT system and technology. The locations of the ILOs are selected primarily on the basis of the numbers of inadequate documented passengers who arrive in the United Kingdom. Countries of origin or transit include Kenya, South Africa, Pakistan, Libya, Malaysia, and Egypt. Their roles and responsibilities of liaison officers are to reduce the number of improperly documented passengers travelling from or through the country in which they are posted; verifying documents on behalf on national authorities; providing advice on relevant legislation; and delivering training on identifying false documents. The ILOs are also charged with gathering information on irregular immigration and routes, including smuggling and trafficking, facilitating the exchange of investigative information between national authorities and enabling returns.

The ILOs keep no formal records of the numbers of intercepted persons—the reason why they wanted to leave their homes and why they chose the United Kingdom as their destination. In more cases than not, the ILOs are intercepting asylum seeker, and the UK government is aware of it. The United Nations has made the following comment about ILOs: *In some countries, efforts to control illegal migration are failing to make proper distinction between those who chose to move and those who are forced to flee because of persecution and violence. All too often we see refugees turned away at the borders of countries where they had hoped to find safety and asylum* (Antonio Guterres, World Refugee Day. June 2008). Between 2001 and 2007, the UK ALO network prevented 180,000 people with inadequate documentation from boarding aircraft to the United Kingdom (Cabinet Office, 2007). But the UNHCR Experts Roundtable said that it was impossible to be precise about the number of refugees who are denied escape due to the stringent checks by transport companies. In other words, many more people are turned away by airlines before the inspection of documents by the ILOs.

Similarly, refugees are being turned away by road transport companies, railway transport companies, and sea transport companies before the government immigration officers stationed at entry points look at their documents. The UNHCR Experts Roundtable said it was impossible to be precise about the number of refugees who are denied escape due to stringent checks by transport companies. The number is considered to be on the rise, however, not least, since transport companies have been assisted by Government Liaison Officers in verifying travel documents. The Refugee Council added, *Our research suggests that UK immigration liaison officers are indeed involved in the interception of refugees, and that they may be contributing to the refoulement of people of people in need of protection. For example one of our Zimbabwean respondents described the experience of a friend who tried to flee through South Africa at the same time as him but was intercepted by UK immigration officers based at the airport. They took him to the British Embassy in Pretoria and when he was there, there were South Africans that were called in and only to find out that . . . he is Zimbabwean, he is a true Zimbabwean and the document is . . . not genuine. And so he served a couple of months (in prison) and then he was facing deportation and I don't know at the moment what happened to him . . . He was returned to Zimbabwe, that's what most of South African government does.* (KI, refugee, Leeds)

ALOs: The United Kingdom began posting ALOs abroad in 1983 and by August 2007 had thirty-four permanent representatives posted in thirty-one locations and had five additional officers they code named 'floaters' as well as regional ALOs. Deputy ALOs provided support in twelve locations. In all, the airport control network affected the movement of people from 126 countries. In 2003 alone 33,000 people were prevented from travelling to the United Kingdom from airports around the World where ALOs were stationed. As a result of their work the numbers of inadequately documented arrivals detected after arrival by air have fallen from 14,071 in 2003 to 6,831 in 2005.

Merchant Delivery Officers (MDOs). MDOs are British personnel tasked to assess the flow of refugees from conflict zones into Europe and the United Kingdom. They are usually placed in countries at the external borders of the European Union. Their job includes exerting pressure on countries near to external borders in the hope of controlling the flow of refugees and migrants into the European Union. In 2008, the United Kingdom had twenty MDOs posted to British Embassies in key locations overseas. These locations included Ethiopia, Kenya, DRC, Sri Lanka, Pakistan and Turkey. Their locations were chosen on the basis of internal intelligence, primarily concerning the flow of immigrants, both regular and irregular in both directions. The evidence collected by the Refugee Council form the MDOs based in Sudan, South Africa, and Ethiopia suggest that their main purpose is to promote compliance with UK immigration law and identify sustainable arrangements for the return of foreign nationals from the United Kingdom. They look at issues relating to managed migration including trafficking routes and methods used for irregular migration, organised immigration crime and country of origin information reports. They are also involved in the analysis of the political and human rights situation within the host country, in cooperation with UNHCR. MDOs are responsible for negotiating with host country immigration authorities to influence their decision making with regard to migration policy and programmes, in order to promote the United Kingdom's management priorities. This will include memorandum of understanding on returns and visa requirements. MDOs also examine the availability and use of valid travel documents within their region, and review the United

Kingdom's processes for accepting such documents. MDOs are responsible for shifting responsibility to European Union's poorer neighbours by promoting its immigration management programme in transit countries, with no regard for the level of protection afforded within that country.

Juxtaposed Controls: The 1991 Sangatte Protocol established reciprocal arrangements between Britain and France under which each state was permitted to operate full immigration controls on the territory of the other. It initially only applied to persons travelling through the Channel Islands with motor vehicles and allowed for passengers to be arrested, detained, and conducted to the territory of the state whose controls were being enforced. Where persons were refused entry or decided not to proceed to the other state, the state of departure must take them back. In May 2000, an additional protocol gave permission for pre-boarding immigration controls at Eurostar stations in Britain and France. Article 4 of the Additional Protocol states that a request for asylum or other form of international protection should be examined by the state of departure where it is made, either at immigration control or otherwise before shutting the train doors. In 2001, juxtaposed controls were extended from the Channel Islands terminal at Coquelles to further locations in France and Belgium. In July 2002, the decision to close Sangatte centre was accompanied by an announcement to establish British immigration controls at Calais, and later that year, French authorities began using British equipment at Calais to check persons hidden in lorries. An agreement with France in 2003 provided for the creation of control zones in commercial ports from which there is sea travel between the two states. The French government has also promised an increase in the number of French undercover officers, targeting gangs, smuggling people into the United Kingdom. As a result of these changes, thousands of refugees who have found all the legal routes of claiming asylum closed have been caught attempting to enter United Kingdom each year. The House of Commons Select Committee found that some 9,652 refugees had been caught at Calais in 2005 and 3,174 in the first three months of 2006. (House of Commons:

Home Affairs Committee on Immigration Control: Fifth Report of Session 2005-6: Volume 1, 13 July 2006)

Other forms of Cooperation: There are plans to broaden the merit of ALOs and ILOs to cooperate more with other agencies, such as Frontex, to detect smugglers and ensure that they are prosecuted. The UK Border Agency (UKBA) hopes to extend its cooperation with ALO networks in Europe and beyond to exchange information develop common positions in dealing with commercial carriers and deliver joint training. Since 2001, Britain and Italy ILOs have worked together in south-eastern Europe to provide training to local officials and gather intelligence on trafficking and smuggling. UKBA also intends to explore the possibility of posting Sea Carriers Liaison Officers at major maritime post around the world.

Biometrics: The UK government started collecting biometrics in 1993 to 'fix' the identity of asylum applicants in order to reduce 'abuse' of the system. The Nationality, Immigration and Asylum Act 2002 allowed the UK government to require people to provide biometric information when applying to enter and remain in the United Kingdom. In February 2004, new provisions were introduced to extend the government's fingerprinting powers. The UK Borders Act 2007 introduced further changes to the Biometric Law, this time allowing for additional conditions to be imposed on those granted leave to enter or remain in the United Kingdom, bringing in new penalties for employers and further restrictions in relation to the provisions of deportation, making deportation almost inevitable for foreign offenders. e-Borders: The programme consists of a multi-agency unit, (e-Borders Operations Centre or eBOC), which brings together staff from UKBA, Revenue and Customs, Serious Organised Crime Agency (SOCA), and the police. It was established with the intention of creating a single pool of information provided by air, sea, and rail carriers, on suspect identities and risky individuals, including those who had committed immigration offences, to be assessed quickly and easily by authorised officers for the purpose of denying entry to unwanted migrants. Global collection of biometric data from visa applications was formally launched in 2006, covering 75 per cent of the world population. Biometric data from visa issuance points, along with electronic Advanced Passenger Information (API) data and Other Passenger Information (OPI) from carriers, is subjected to further electronic background checks so that the UK immigration control staff posted overseas can advise carriers not to board a suspect individual, even at the last minute. Not only are passengers electronically monitored as they enter the United Kingdom, but, in future, e-Borders will also record departure information so that future visa applications can be informed by past compliance with immigration requirements. When planned, the UK government hoped that e-Borders would cover the majority of passenger movements by 2009 and 95 per cent by 2011 (Refugee Council: Remote Controls: How UK Border controls are endangering the lives of refugees: By Sile Reynolds and Helen Muggeridge: December 2008).

These are the basic systems used to control entry of refugees into the United Kingdom. There are several other immigration laws, but most of them are on governing treatment of refugees after they have entered the country.

Carriers Sanctions: The Immigration (Carriers' Liability) Act 1987 was the first piece of legislation to impose administrative fines on airlines and ship owners that brought people into the United Kingdom without documents. A penalty was imposed on the owners or agents of ships and aircrafts for passengers brought into the United Kingdom without a valid passport or equivalent document or without a visa (if a visa was required). A civil penalty can be charged against various people (owners or hirers of vehicles, captains of ships, and so on) who can be made jointly or severally liable. All vehicles are covered, including rail freight vehicles, tractors, trains, and any other means used to travel to the United Kingdom. To try to ensure that penalties are levied successfully, the Secretary of State has powers to detain transporters until penalties are paid. The immigration officer can require the person to provide documents, information, or up-to-date medical reports in order to determine the person's entitlement to leave to enter. Under the Immigration and Asylum Act 1999 a carrier is liable to a compulsory penalty of up to £2000 where a passenger who arrives by air, land or sea requires leave to enter the United Kingdom but fails to produce a valid identity document and, where applicable, a visa. New detection technology including carbon dioxide detectors, x-ray scanners and heartbeat monitors, is used in conjunction with dog teams and manned searchers to intercept people hiding in lorries and other vehicles heading for the United Kingdom. In 2006 alone, detection technology enabled the Border and Immigration Agency as it was then called to intercept 17,000 immigrants attempting to cross into the United Kingdom irregularly. Each one of these earned the Home Office £2000 from the carriers.

Consequences of external controls

(1) Preventing Refugees from Leaving Countries They are Persecuted: By preventing immigrants from leaving their country of origin, the United Kingdom exposes refugees to the very authorities from whom they are attempting to escape. Such action also disregards Article 13.2 of the Universal Declaration of Human Rights which state that 'Everyone has the right to leave any country, including his own, and to return to his country.' As border controls have become more sophisticated and more widespread, legal and safe routes to protection in Europe have been cut off. Routes have become more dangerous, more circuitous, and more crowded, as refugees are driven to more desperate means to reach safety in another country. People will not remain where their lives are in danger. *It's not a matter of choice, of going to which country you go, but actually it's a matter of survival . . .* (DF. RCO representative, London).

(2) Non-refoulement: Non-refoulement is a principle in international law, especially refugee law, that concerns the protection of refugees from being returned to places where their lives or freedoms could be threatened. A state which intercepts a boat carrying refugees on the high

seas and which returns them directly to their country of origin violates the principle. Equally, an intercepting state which disembarks refugees and asylum seekers in a country which it knows or reasonably experts will refoul them becomes party to that act. It adds or assists in the commission of the prohibited conduct. Moreover, no state can avoid its obligation by outsourcing or subcontracting out its obligations, either to another state, to an international organisation, or to a private agent such as a carrier. Interception activities conducted by the United Kingdom's out-posted immigration officers and private carriers contain no safeguards for persons who may need international protection, and could even lead to refoulement. Research has shown that out-posted UK immigration officers, as well as the government and private actors the government relies on to implement UK immigration controls, are not tasked with or trained in refugee protection. Immigration and airline officials have no knowledge of systematic procedures to follow in order to identify refugees and ensure that they are protected. There is no monitoring or publicly available information, as to who is stopped, whether they are refugees in need of protection or what happens to them after they are intercepted. Private carriers, who are forced to operate migration controls, are not trained in refugee protection and are not sufficiently accountable for actions which may lead to refoulement. There is lack of transparency surrounding private carriers' immigration control activities. Stronger borders mean that refugees have to take greater risks to find safety. NGOs and UNHCR are denied access to border and transit areas where refugees are intercepted, sometimes resulting in refoulement. Often refugees who have to wait years in countries of transit will search for their own durable solutions. They therefore end up using the same routes, employ the services of the same smugglers, obtain fraudulent travel documents from the same suppliers, and encounter the same border controls as non-refugees. *This process of returning an individual to a place where his/her life or freedom would be threatened for a reason outlined in the 1951 Refugee Convention is known as refoulement and is prohibited by the 1951 Convention relating to the State of Refugees to which the UK is a signatory* (Refugee Council: UK Border Control, Dec 2008, p. 15). Refugees have been returned to countries known to have records human right abuses and lack of respect for the principle of non-refoulement. The European Commission says this about allowing refugees to flee persecution: *Legitimate measures introduced to curb irregular migration and protect external borders should avoid preventing refugees' access to protection in the EU while ensuring a respect for fundamental rights of all migrants* (European Convention: 2008, p. 3). The UNHCR also noticed that rich nations of the North were tightening external controls and using them as a means to dump refugees on the poorer nations of the South.

Internal Immigration Controls

(3) Destitution

UK internal immigration control (and indeed that of most of the EU countries) can be divided into two clear sections: the first section 1905 to 1985 and second section 1985 to the present, 2010. In the first section, the United Kingdom, despite signing the 1951 Refugee Convention, did not have an asylum policy as such; it had a refugee policy and the policy centred on bringing to the UK victims of World War II and of the Cold War struggles in eastern Europe and the Far East into the United Kingdom on specific rescue programmes often agreed on with other European states and the United States. There were cases of people given asylum, but these were few in number. Policy allowed them to stay and work often as illegal or informal workers for wages agreed on by their employers, usually below the minimum wage. But after 1985, British policy became based on the principal of denying responsibility through (a)denying asylum seekers legal channels to enter the United Kingdom; (b)denying

the responsibility to provide asylum seekers with adequate
financial and material support; (c) denying them freedom to
live normal lives, through keeping them in detention for as long
as possible and making the asylum claim process very long and
painful; and (d) denying the human dignity by labelling them
criminals; destitute; terrorists. The overall intention is to make
the United Kingdom look very unattractive to asylum seekers,
thus undermine the principles of the 1951 Refugee Convention
and 1967 Protocol. Although the United Kingdom signed the
1951 Convention relating to the status of refugees in 1954 and
the Protocol in 1968, it took them up to 1993 to change the
system that managed refugee's issues in the United Kingdom.
Refugee issues remained under the general immigration law,
and they only made the 1993 changes because they wanted to
introduce restrictions which would allow them to 'override' some
of the conditions of the convention and protocol. In the United
Kingdom today, there is an overriding principle of refusing to
accept most the responsibilities that come with being a host to
asylum seekers. But instead of asking the UN institutions that
deal with refugee issues to assist them, the British government
has chosen to create legislation, which make it impossible for
asylum seekers to enter United Kingdom legally and then to
arrest asylum seekers that enter without passports or visas,
and for asylum seekers already in the United Kingdom, the UK
government has chosen wide-ranging legal measures to make it
very difficult to get refugee status or other forms of protection.
D. Flynn summarised what the UK asylum legislation has done
to the inflow of refugees into the United Kingdom and to the
failed asylum seekers in the following words:

*Since its election the (Labour) Government has taken draconian
action to restrict for people coming to the UK as asylum seekers.
For most practical purposes there are now no legal routes to
Britain for people fleeing persecution in their own countries.
Those who manage to clear the obstacles placed in the way
of entry to claim rights provided in the Geneva Convention
on Human Rights are then subjected to procedures which
effectively classify them as criminals, liable to be detained or
subject to serious penalties further infraction of the rules until*

such time as their applications for asylum are finally resolved
(D. Flynn . . .)

Why is this? It is because the United Kingdom has not, throughout its history, looked at asylum outside immigration. Asylum seekers have been welcome in the United Kingdom when there is need for labour, foreign cheap labour, and have not been welcome when there is shortage of labour. This analysis may look unfair to the UK government until you look how they have treated asylum seekers from the beginning of the 20th century. We have already seen that legally, there was no such thing as asylum law until after 1985 and that asylum were looked at under and treated as part of the general migrant community. So the legislation we will look at before 1985 will be on post-war rehabilitation of war victims and not necessarily people being persecuted for their political opinion.

The 1905 Aliens ACT and Jewish Refugees

The very first immigration legislation, the Aliens Act, made it possible for 'leave to land to be withheld if the immigrant was judged to be undesirable' by falling into one of four categories: if he could not show proof he could support himself and his dependants; if he was a 'lunatic or an idiot' or owing to any disease of infirmity liable to be a charge to the public . . . ; if he had been sentenced in a foreign country of a crime, not being an offence of a political nature; or if an expulsion order under this act had already been made. The act also legalised deportation of undesirable immigrants and also legislated prosecution of masters of 'immigration ships' defined as ships bringing more than twenty immigrants to a British port. (Aliens Act: Exploring twentieth Century London: Renaissance London Museums of Changing Lives). The 1905 Aliens Act had a section that specifically addressed the asylum seeker. It said, 'But in the case of an immigrant who proves that he is seeking admission to this country solely to avoid persecution or punishment on religious, or political grounds . . . leave to land shall not be refused on the grounds, merely of want of means or the probability of his becoming a charge on the rates.' The legislation legalised the entry of large number of Russian and Polish Jews who had arrived in the London's East End after fleeing persecution in tsarist Russia. These impoverished Jews arriving in London's East End became the first anti-Aliens Act victims. But as soon as they arrived, they were accused of taking British jobs and living on welfare. They were treated in a manner similar to that failed asylum seekers are treated today. Growing unemployment and particularly bad housing conditions in London's East End made newly arrived Jewish immigrants an easy scapegoat. Failure by politicians to provide employment and adequate housing were blamed on migrants. Statements such as this one, by the Liberal M. P. Cathcart Wilson, show how blame was transferred from government's maladministration of employment and housing to racism. He said, *What is the use of spending thousands of pounds on building beautiful workmen's dwellings if the places of our own workpeople, the backbone of the country, are to be taken over by the refuse scum of other nation?* (P. Foot: Immigration and Race in British Politics (Penguin, 1965) p. 85-91). *As with all subsequent immigration controls in Britain, the Aliens Act was thus designed primarily to create an easy target for an increasingly impoverished and unemployed working class and marks one of the first institutionalised attempts by the British ruling class to divide and rule the working population by means of overt racism. Of course, it was never clearly stated that the act was aimed only at Jews, but nobody was left in any doubt as who its intended target would be. Crucially the act was aimed only at keeping out working class Jews, those 'without visible means of support'* (Ruth Brown: Racism and immigration in Britain: Issue sixty-eight of International Socialism Journal, Published August 1955).

The first detention of foreign minority groups came after years of national dock strikes and national rail strikes. In 1914, the Aliens Restriction Act was passed and 32,000 non-British nationals were interned in prison camps, where they remained for the course of the war. So the culture of detaining foreigners did not start with failed asylum seekers. In fact, the Aliens Restriction

Act, combined with the Defence of the Realm Act, passed some weeks later, created for the first time a clear definition of British nationality law and laid down strict guidelines for local police and military authorities in their treatment of 'aliens'. The act also greatly restricted the employment of 'aliens' in Britain. The Aliens Restriction Act 1919 prevented aliens from landing in Britain, except at certain specified places, and made admission depend on the discretion of the Home Secretary exercised through Immigration Officers. Aliens were to register with the police and carried a pass if they were to stay longer than three months.

But following World War I, there was widespread unemployment. The British blamed immigrants, especially in the docks where they could be paid very limited wages unacceptable to the average British worker. Violence broke out against aliens throughout the British ports. In a book *Black 1919: Riots, Racism and Residence in Imperial Britain*, Jacqueline Jenkinson described police arrests in the following words: *Police arrested the Black victims of violence out of all proportion to their numbers, and relatively few white perpetrators. In nearly all cases white crowds numbering in the hundreds and sometimes thousands made up the aggressor sand Black men and their families the victims, yet nationally police arrested nearly twice as many Black men (155) as white men (80) and women (9).* The Aliens Restriction Act was amended by the 1920 Aliens Order, which required all aliens seeking employment or residence to register with the police. Further, under the order, the Home Secretary retained the power to deport any alien whose presence was considered detrimental to the public good. These additional immigration changes were used in the restriction of mainly Jews running away from the Nazis in Austria and Germany. Ruth Brown put it in the following words: *Even when Jewish refugees fleeing the rise of Nazis in Austria and Germany began to arrive in Britain during the 1930s, entry was granted to a tiny minority of those who promised that they intended to settle permanently elsewhere. MPs complained relentlessly about Jewish refugees 'scurrying' from Germany into Britain and regularly called for a regular tightening of controls. Many of those who managed to gain admission to Britain were deported within months of arrival, alongside thousands of 'enemy aliens'. Mass deportations continued throughout the Second World War even after a ship carrying a human cargo of mainly Germans, Italians and Austrians, most of whom had lived in Britain for more than twenty years, was torpedoed off the west coast of Ireland causing the death of nearly 700* (Ruth Brown, op. cit.). In 1941, the government reintroduced internment and included within its remit literally thousands of Jews who wanted to enlist in the war against Hitler. For those not interned, deportation—mainly to Canada and Australia—was usually their fate. Some put the number of Jewish refugees from the Holocaust who managed to get into Britain at a figure as low as 10,000 during the whole of the World War II. Some Jews were forced to stay in Germany, or to return there, because the doors of every major Western power were firmly closed in their faces. In this respect, the British government helped to play its part, alongside many European nations, in driving millions of Jews into Hitler's concentration camps during the course of the World War II.

Polish refugees (1939-1949)

From the times of the League of Nations to the formation of the United Nations, there was increasing concern about the welfare of the victims of World Wars I and II. Britain joined the movement in some Western nations to resettle some of the victims of war. As a result, between 1939 and 1949, nearly 36,000 Polish refugees arrived in the United Kingdom. The manner in which they were received and accommodated in the United Kingdom led to the formation of the British Council for Aid to Refugees (BCAR) at the request of the British Foreign and Commonwealth Office.

Aliens order (1953)

The Aliens Restriction Act 1914 imposed restrictions on the landing and embarkation of aliens in Britain and on their movements and residence in the country. It was a wartime act, so it was amended after the war. In 1920, an Aliens Order was introduced, and it remained in force until 1953. All these amendments did not really affect asylum seekers, as there were mainly refugees. The important aspect of the Aliens Order 1953 is that the order provided for admission of aliens in the United Kingdom for the purpose of work, provided that the permission of the Department of Works and Pensions was obtained. This created the crisis of housing and the use of improvised housing, which will be a main feature in the era of asylum seekers.

Hungarian programmed refugees (1956)

Hungarian refugee arrivals were programmed. Their immigration status was determined overseas. They were entitled to a resettlement programme comprising housing and social welfare support. Although many were assessed, some 21,451 Hungarian refugees eventually entered the United Kingdom. This figure included some 398 unaccompanied children. Despite the fact that from the times if the 1905 Aliens Act to the present-day Britain refuses to take asylum seekers with a criminal record of any form, Britain accepted Hungarians immediately released from prison: *A tragic characteristic of the Hungarian exodus was a high proportion of refugees with criminal records or experiencing British inmates took the opportunity to escape* (Mezey, 1960).

The BCAR, which had been formed in 1950 to help settle the Polish refugees that had arrived between 1939 and 1949, was once again asked to help find accommodation for refugees. BCAR was granted use of the army barracks as an initial reception hostels. These hostels were soon replaced by a large reception centre at Ridgeley in West Midlands. After the reception phase, the refugees were moved into second-line hostels, mostly in government buildings. Many of the refugees found work at this time, mainly in construction, mining, agriculture, or industries, experiencing a scarcity of labour. By the end of 1957, only 1,000 adult Hungarians were without work, although 6,172 of the original 21,000 arrivals had left the United Kingdom, for Hungary, or to live in Canada or Australia.

The 1950s were a time of acute housing shortages in the United Kingdom, and permanent housing could not be found for many of the refugees. It was for this reason, as well as the vulnerability of some Hungarian refugees, that the BCAR Housing Society was formed in the late 1957 with a grant of £200,000 from the Lord Mayor's fund. Within a year, it had supplied flats and houses to over 350 families (British Refugee Council, 1981).

The Czechoslovakia programme refugees (1968)

Following the Soviet invasion of Czechoslovakia in 1968, some 5,000 Czechoslovakians sought sanctuary in the United Kingdom. Initially, they were not recognised as refugees, but the Home Office decided to grant them temporary visas and permission to work. BCAR was invited to support those with social needs, and the BCAR Housing Society assisted them with their housing needs.

From the 1960s, Britain gave large numbers of their African and Asian colonies independence, and with that came the problem of many people in the colonies who had British passports and did not want to live in the newly independent states. So Britain was faced by large numbers of whites and Asians, especially from Africa, who wanted to migrate and live in the United Kingdom. Britain answered this with a set of laws against the members of the Commonwealth.

Commonwealth Immigration Laws

The first was the Commonwealth Immigrants Act 1962. The act made Commonwealth citizens, with certain (but few) exceptions subject to immigration control, meaning they would need visas to enter the United Kingdom. A few years later, the future of the large community of Asians in East Africa began to be in doubt as the new African leadership associated them with the previous colonial system since majority of them had British passports. The Jomo Kenyatta government of Kenya was the first to ask them to leave. About 23,000 Kenyan Asians left Africa for Britain between 1965 and 1967. East African Asians had relatives in the United Kingdom. The UK government panicked and rushed the Commonwealth Immigrants Act 1968 through parliament. The act made East African Asians subject to immigration control, despite the fact that they had British passport. To close remaining loopholes, the United Kingdom followed this with an immigration act.

The Immigration Act 1971

In the Immigration Act 1971, the United Kingdom created the concept of 'partiality', which made it difficult for East African Asians and many other people of the Commonwealth that had British passports to enter the United Kingdom. Many people with British passports were not partials and therefore had no right of admission to the country of their apparent nationality. 'Partials' were people with a parent or grandparent born, adapted, or naturalised in the United Kingdom. A surprise development was that there were many people with non-British passports who found themselves with the right to enter and live in Britain. For this study, what is important is that nearly all sub-Saharan African nationals were excluded unless they found a way to qualify to enter the United Kingdom. This law marked the beginning of a new era in the asylum and refugee story. The law also set out powers of the Secretary of State in respect of deportation, detention and bail, the issuing of entry clearance, and the issuing of leave to remain. The 1971

Immigration Act also described the machinery of immigration control for those with no right to live in the United Kingdom. It also described many other aspects of migration control.

Ugandan Asian (non-programme) refugees (1972)

But all these precautions did not help the crisis that was to develop just a year after the landmark 1971 Immigration Act. The United Kingdom found itself in an odd situation when the Ugandan President Idi Amin deported 80,000 Asians, majority of whom had UK passports. Efforts to resettle them in Asia and other parts of the world did not result in a total solution. So the United Kingdom was forced to accept 28,000 Asians and 400 stateless householders. Central government took a direct role in formulating and implementing settlement policy for the Ugandan Asian refugees. It founded a Uganda Settlement Board, which reported to the Home Office. The BCAR was not invited to assist, most likely because the Home Office did not want this particular scheme to be mixed or confused with the other schemes for which the BCAR was actively involved in. The BCAR Housing Society was not invited either. They assisted only in family reunion. The Home Office quickly put up some sixteen 'settlement camps', where refugees were received before being transferred to own homes. However, government could only find 2,000 places in private homes. After further advertising, the figure rose to 5,000. There was overwhelming negative approval of the scheme. 1,400 people demonstrated against what they called invasion of Britain by Ugandan Asians. There were many cases of abuse of the new arrivals in the communities they were placed. Then the government decided to spread their settlement throughout the country, except for areas they designated as 'Red' or 'no go areas'—usually cities with high proportions of minority ethnic groups and areas of high unemployment. Such a restrictive housing policy was new. It has, however, close similarities with the current policy of dispersing asylum seekers away from London and the south-east. But the new arrivals faced many problems, which forced them to move away from the designated homes in search for safer areas and communities where they could find employment. Some 62 per cent of them ended up living in the no-go areas. Racial harassment, the desire to be near compatriots, employment opportunities, and housing shortages in some 'green' areas all led to resettlement in the no-go areas (Community Relations Commissioner, 1974). The East African Asian programme could be regarded as one of the worst schemes of such schemes. There had to be three other groups before the asylum era 'ended'. The Cypriot refugees (1974 and 1975), the Chilean refugees (1974 and 1977), and the Vietnamese refugees (1979-1992).

Cypriot and Chilean programmed refugees groups (1974-1977)

Refugees from Cyprus, numbering around 10,000, escaping inter-communal violence, arrived in the United Kingdom between 1963 and 1964 and between 1974 and 1975. Some 3,000 Chileans arrived in the United Kingdom between 1974 and 1975, following the deposition of the Chilean socialist dictator, Salvador Allende. The UK government subcontracted BCAR and the World University Service (WUS) to assist them. The two bodies formed the Joint Working Group for Refugees from Chile in Britain to settle these people in houses. The government granted them full refugee status.

Vietnamese refugees

Britain closed to 24,000 Vietnamese refugees who came in three phases—1979, 1983, and 1989. These were accommodated mainly in the north. They had problems getting employment. About 40 per cent of them were employed in the hotel and catering industry. But the Vietnamese programme was important in that it marked the beginning of the compulsory dispersal programmes with refugees being sent to various locations around the United Kingdom to spread the financial and human cost of resettlement. The dispersal programme was many sub-Saharan Africans into many small towns, where NASS would not find them proper accommodation and where people whose asylum applications had been turned down would find difficult to travel to Croydon or Liverpool to appeal their cases and faced difficult lives as destitute people.

Arrival of refugees from former colonies

The instability created by the sudden departure of the former colonial masters and the collapse of the Soviet empire left the newly created governments in Africa and Asia with no one to turn to for support when internal conflicts became civil wars. The dictatorships that replaced governments from the 1970s forced many Africans and some Asians stranded because, in Africa, for example, there was virtually no country that was not involved in a civil or regional war. From the 1980s, we see asylum seekers from Iran, Sri Lanka, the Tamils, Iraq, Turkey, Ethiopia, Ghana, Poland, Uganda, and Eritrea. A greater proportion of Somali asylum seekers arriving in the United Kingdom were women and children running away from the total collapse of government system in Somalia and making the country the greatest failed state in the world. However, the largest national group of African asylum seekers came from the Democratic Republic of the Congo where several million people had become IDPs, and close to a million had reached Europe majority of them into the United Kingdom (RAL: Researching Asylum in London, 2006).

The Tamil refugees

The arrival of the Tamil asylum seekers in 1985 marked the beginning of the arrival of refugees, whom the United Kingdom and the rest of western Europe 'sought to restrict' (RAL: Researching Asylum in London, 2006). These asylum seekers were not programme refugees. They were not white. Majority of them were from Africa and Asia. And they were likely to cause political tension. The Tamils caused the introduction of the Carriers Liability Act in 1987, which imposed a £1,000 fine (raised to £2,000) on any airline or shipping company that gave passage to passengers without the correct travel documents. The act was introduced after the well-established case of fifty-eight Tamils who were ordered to be deported on the ground of taking part in an organised attempt to secure admission by fraudulent means, thus rendering their application for asylum unfounded. On 17 February 1987, the fifty-eight Tamils protested on the tarmac at Heathrow Airport by stripping to their underwear. On the same day, the High Court that their deportation be halted, and a week later, they won the right to a judicial review. The Home Office announced that it would challenge the ruling, but it baked down. Some of the fifty-eight proceeded to secure refugee status, and some were later deported.

The Asylum and Immigration Appeals Act 1993

Until 1993, the UK immigration law had not yet incorporated the 1951 Refugee Convention and the 1967 Protocol. This law not only incorporated the convention and protocol but also set about to exploit the loopholes in the convention and create laws that would in fact conflict with the basic principles of the convention and help the country begin to withdraw from the responsibilities of a host country. The law gave immigration authorities the power to detain asylum seekers while the outcome of their claim was pending. Detention should be for criminals and not asylum seekers, but the UK government equated asylum seekers to criminals by detaining them before deportation and the UN organisations that deal with asylum and refugee issues did nothing about it.

The 1993 Act also set strict time limits within which appeals against asylum decisions had to be made. The use of the word *deportation* was replaced by removal. The UK government legally adopted the 'third safe country' removal process which saw thousands of asylum seekers returned to countries mainly in southern Europe, where they had escaped extreme forms of social exclusion. The law also brought restrictions on those who could apply for asylum in the United Kingdom. But its most negative contribution was in the area of housing. Significantly, it amended housing entitlement for asylum seekers. Destitute asylum seekers could no longer claim to be homeless if they slept in a building, however the condition and however temporary. 'If you tell the immigration officer you are homeless, he will ask you where you slept the previous night, if it is in a building, then you have a home!' (From Refugee to Citizen: Standing on my own two feet: A research report on integration, Britishness and Citizenship: Jill Rutter et al: 2007).

In addition, while an asylum case was being determined, no asylum-seeking household could be offered accommodation. Instead, they could only be offered temporary housing. Research on the effect of temporary housing on refugee children has highlighted problems in securing school places, difficulties in building social relationships within schools, and achieving continuity of education and care. Other pupils too can be affected by high pupil mobility as teacher time is spent settling in new students. Through the disruption of social networks, housing mobility also prevents children and their carers developing attachments to their localities and an accompanying sense of belonging (Jill Rutter et al: op. cit. p. 20).

Immigration rules: Statutory instruments attached to immigration law that determine in practice how a person can enter or stay in the United Kingdom were also amended. The changes widened the criteria for refusal of an asylum application. For example, an asylum seeker who could reasonably live in another part of their home country would be refused asylum in the United Kingdom. Part of the arguments for the Zimbabwe Country Guidance Case: EM and Ors: Zimbabwe CG (2011) UKUT 0098 is based on this argument and is being used to send many Zimbabwean asylum seekers to places where they are likely to face persecution against the very principles of 1951 Refugee Convention. From 1993, there has been a large increase in the proportion of asylum seekers refused asylum, from 27 per cent in 1993 to 74 per cent in 1994 (Jill Rutter et al: op. cit. p. 20).

The Asylum and Immigration Act 1996

This act was passed to tighten gaps created as a result of asylum seekers being able to cross from Europe and being able to work illegally in the United Kingdom. The act introduced sanctions on employers who gave work to unauthorised asylum seekers. After original severe forms of benefit cuts were challenged in courts, the government ended up bringing back the National Assistance Act 1948 and the Child Act 1989. These made local authorities responsible for supporting asylum seekers who had been denied benefits. In England and Wales, adult asylum seekers were given supermarket vouchers and housed in hostels or other forms of temporary housing by local authorities. Families with children were given cash allowance and temporary accommodation. However, there was insufficient hostel and temporary accommodation in London, where most asylum seekers lived. By 1997, significant numbers of asylum seekers were moved by local authorities to accommodation outside the capital, often poor quality hostels in seaside towns. The 1996 Asylum and Immigration Act introduced severe restrictions on welfare entitlements and placed a requirement on employers to check the immigration status of potential employees, introducing other internal immigration controls such as immigration checks at the point of accessing services and other benefits. This presented a major shift from a culture of service to a culture of suspicion by service providers, benefit agencies, social services, employers, and other agencies. It was at this time that the phrase 'culture of disbelief' became shorthand to describe the relationship between the Home Office and refugees. The new social category of asylum seeker from the mid-1990s was the summation of the twentieth-century legislation, with recent subcategories of 'undeserving', 'bogus' asylum seeker or 'economic migrant', a continuation of the process of recasting the image of asylum seekers (Dispersal and Social Exclusion of Asylum Seekers by Patricia Hynes,

2011, p. 13). The act introduced a 'white list' of safe countries. Asylum claims made by those from such countries were treated by the Home Office as having no substance to them. Some of the so-called safe countries were far from safe. The list keeps changing, but countries like Zimbabwe, Rwanda, Nigeria, and Uganda have appeared on the safe countries' list. A country like Zimbabwe has been divided into safe and unsafe zones. But the problem is not whether there are safe zones in a country but if the refugees will be given the basic requirements need to protect them. But the United Kingdom is more interested in denying people entry into the United Kingdom. Those individuals who travelled through a 'safe third country' before arriving in the United Kingdom, and who failed to claim asylum while in that country, could only bring an out-of-country appeal against a decision refusing them asylum in the United Kingdom. Asylum seekers were only allowed to take up employment if their claim for asylum had not been determined in six months. (In practice, they were never allowed to work, because for one to work under these circumstances, one would have to first apply to the Home Office to be allowed to work. Usually, the answer would be negative, or the government will send a reply which stated that they were working on the case.) An employer who took on an asylum seeker with false permits or no documentation at all could face criminal sanctions if the employer had done so knowingly. (In practice, it would be difficult to employ an asylum seeker unknowingly because the asylum seekers' identity document would have the inscription—Employment Prohibited—Officially asylum seekers' right to work was withdrawn in 2002.)

The 1999 Immigration and Asylum Act

The Immigration and Asylum Act 1999 created the National Asylum Support Service (NASS) and implementation of the dispersal for 'destitute' asylum seekers; introduced the voucher system; imposed duties on registrars to report 'suspicious' marriages; strengthened powers of immigration officers; one-stop appeals; replaced Immigration (Carriers' Liability) Act of 1987; and extended liability to the carriage of clandestine entrants in any vehicle, ship, or aircraft. First, the Home Office took action to speed up the time taken to reach a decision. On the average, about 20 per cent of applicants got a positive decision. The Home Office did not positive plans to support failed asylum seekers. So the population of the destitute in the United Kingdom rose steeply.

The act also made major changes housing conditions. It removed existing housing and all types of benefits. It set up a new housing and sustenance scheme for asylum seekers, administered by the NASS, now a part of the UKBA. Homeless asylum seekers were housed in specially commissioned emergency accommodation when they first arrived in the United Kingdom. After this, they had the option to apply for a 'subsistence only' package or for subsistence and accommodation. (Until April 2002, subsistence entitled a cash allowance of £10 per person per week plus vouchers exchangeable at designated retail outlets. Vouchers were abolished in April 2002 and replaced by a cash allowance). The Home Office commissioned housing for asylum seekers. This was provided by private landlords, local authorities, and, in some cases, registered social landlords such as Refugee Support who began to work with asylum seekers in South Yorkshire and the East Midlands. But some accommodation provided by private landlords was not good quality. Some accommodation was provided in deprived outer-city estates, and significant number of asylum seekers requested to be moved as a result of racially aggravated attacks. Housing quality for those opting for subsistence only supported, and living with family and friends remained an issue of concern. It remained inevitably of a temporary nature and overcrowded.

The act also introduced a voucher system. But because there was chaos in the accommodation arrangements, some vouchers did not reach the asylum seekers. Not all shops accepted the vouchers. The Home Office has since replaced the vouchers with cash, but adult asylum seekers are given cash. But support is lower than the income support offered to mainstream claimants.

Under a Section 4 of the act, failed asylum seekers who have become destitute but indicated they are willing to be returned to their home countries are given temporary accommodation. They are not given cash but an Azure Card worth £35.39, which they use at certain shops that have pre-arrangements with the UKBA to exchange the card with groceries. Where a failed asylum seeker is unable to use all the money on the card, the shop keeps the difference. This was a very unpopular arrangement because most shops refused to accept the card. Most asylum seekers preferred to remain living as destitute than offer themselves to be deported to the politically unstable countries they had suffered persecution. But as the table below shows, destitution forced a rising number of failed asylum seekers to come forward and offer to be returned home despite the levels of insecurity.

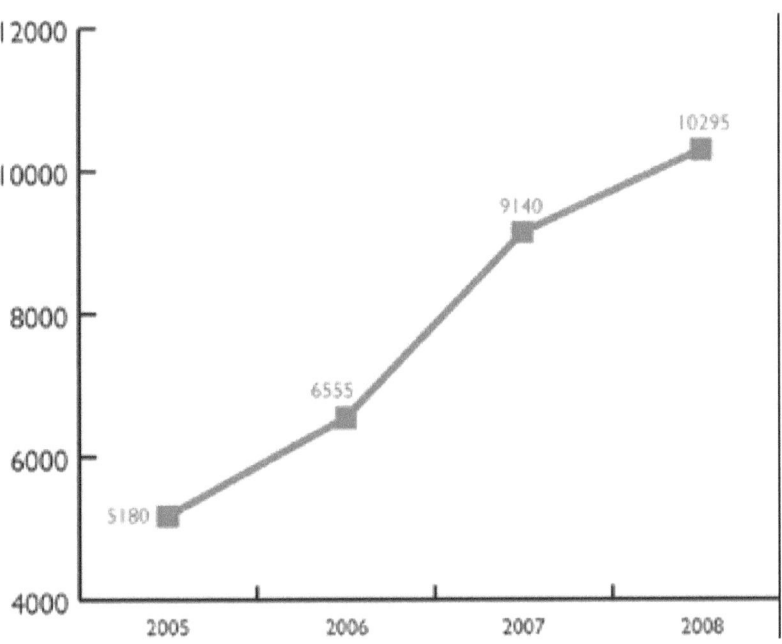

Number of refused asylum seekers on Section 4 support,
2005-2008

Source: Home Office

Nationality, Immigration, and Asylum Act (2002)

The aspects of the act were withdrawal of 'in-country' support; plans for induction, accommodation, reporting, and removal (previously deportation) centres; introduction of the Gateway Resettlement Programme for quota refugees; and introduction of Application Registration Cards (ARC)

With photograph, details and fingerprint of individual; repealed provision for automatic bail hearing; extended statutory provision for voluntary assisted return programme; required employers to ensure that employees are entitled to work; criminalised those who arranged facilitated trafficking into the United Kingdom for prostitution.

These many legal changes were a reaction to the sharp increase in the numbers of asylum applications made at the Home Office from 1997 as the graph below shows. A greater number of these arrivals were from the DRC, Iraq, Sierra Leone, Somalia, and Zimbabwe.

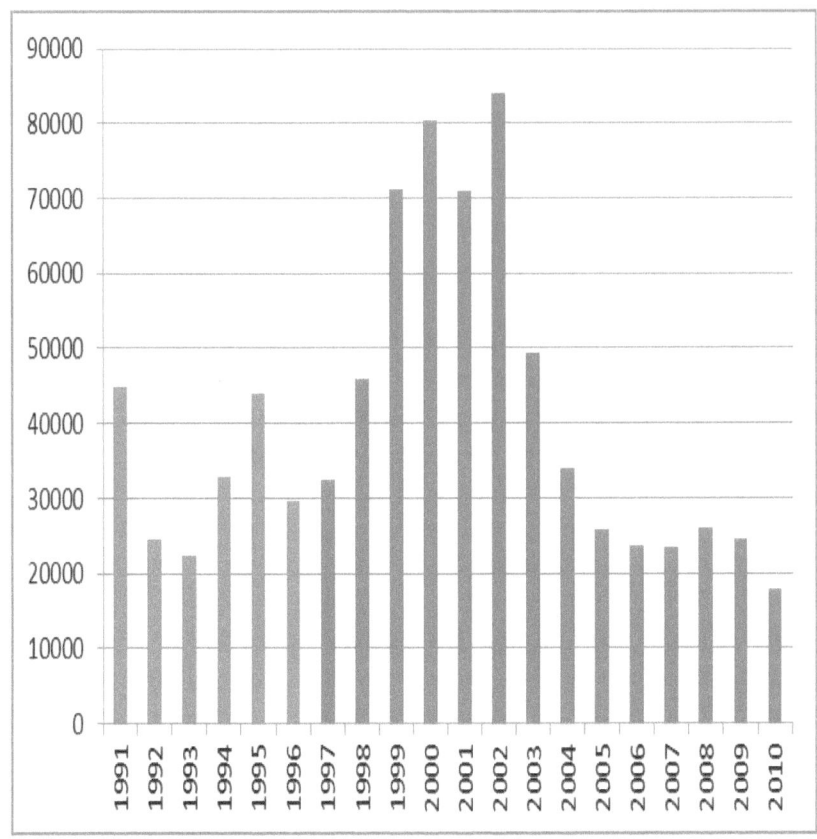

(Source: Home Office answer to Parliamentary Question 54493.)

The UK government began to look at a system of Quarters rather existing patterns of asylum arrivals. They felt they needed to go back to the programme refugees they used in the post-war era. The UNHCR proposed identifying asylum seekers, bringing them to the United Kingdom and offering a package of support to local authorities and refugee organisations. The UK government envisaged about 500 persons would be brought into the United Kingdom each year as part of this programme. A programme named the Gateway Protection Programme had already brought in a few refugees from Liberia, Sudan, Burma, and the DRC who had been settled in different parts of the country.

The act reduced the asylum seekers right to appeal a decision and gave the Home Secretary the power to withhold support from some asylum seekers, such as those who cannot provide a clear and coherent account of how they came to the United Kingdom.

In January 2003, the government enacted Section 55 of the Nationality, Immigration and Asylum Act, rendering asylum applicants who failed to lodge an application within a three-day period ineligible for NASS support. Hundreds of people were left destitute, and more were forced to work illegally. After an extensive campaign, the courts reversed this decision in June 2004 under Article 3 of the European Convention of Human Rights (Court of Appeal: SSHD vs Limbela, 21 May 2004).

In July 2002, all asylum seekers lost the right to work.

In April 2003, the Home Secretary ended the granting of Exceptional Leave to Remain, a form of temporary protection that was granted to many asylum seekers. (Some civil servants had argued that ELR was a pull factor for asylum seekers. It was replaced by the New Status of Humanitarian protection and Discretionary Leave.)

Asylum and Immigration (Treatment of Claimants and so on) Act (2004)

Summary of main issues: Arrival in the United Kingdom without a passport or valid identity document made a criminal offence; tightening of credibility of boundaries; withdrawal of basic support for families if voluntary return to country of origin not taken; community activity for 'hard cases'; 'local connection' to local authority area required if housing required; withdrawal of backdating of benefits and replaced by integration loan; unification of appeal system; 'safe third country' list extended; criminal offence not to cooperate with deportation procedure; electronic monitoring.

In April, the original intention was to simplify immigration law; strengthen border controls; extend time to 2004. Government introduced a limit to the amount of legal aid that could be claimed for an initial asylum application. From this time, legal aid costs were limited to five hours' work, unless special permission was granted from the Legal Services Commission. A number of eminent firms stopped undertaking asylum cases.

In the same year 2004, the right to free non-emergency secondary healthcare was removed from 'failed' asylum seekers.

The Housing Act of 1996 was amended by the Immigration and Asylum (Treatment of Claimants and so on) by stipulating that dispersed asylum seekers needed to have a local connection with the local authority in which their accommodation was located as an attempt to prevent secondary migration of refugees within the United Kingdom.

The act also created another class of person ineligible for support: a 'failed' asylum seeker with family, also known as Section 9 Case. Asylum seeking families that had exhausted the appeals process would lose their support if they failed 'without reasonable excuse' to leave the United Kingdom.

The act introduced the Controlling Our Borders concept. It introduced an overhaul of the asylum application process with the introduction of a new application process—the New Asylum Model—where asylum cases are dealt with by named immigration officers.

The act also introduced the move to limit the period of settlement of those granted UN Convention Refugee Status to a period of five years, revocable at any time during this period. This suggests a clear expectation that those with refugee status would return if conditions improved in their home countries.

Immigration, Asylum and Nationality Act (2006)

The act replaced the Asylum and Immigration Act 1996. It ended the granting of the Indefinite Leave to Remain (ILR) to recognised refugees, strengthened border controls, and introduced an integrated loan to replace grants for recognised refugees.

UK Borders Act 2007

The act extended the powers of the UKBA. There were provisions on the powers of immigration officers; immigration offences; biometric identity cards; conditions of; limited leave to remain; exchange of information between UKBA and other agencies; amended laws on trafficking to extend the extraterritorial reach so that acts outside the United Kingdom could be criminalised regardless of original nationality.

Borders, Citizenship and Immigration Act 2009

Gain citizenship in the United Kingdom; full access to social housing and benefits reversed for citizens and permanent residents; concept of earned citizenship introduced; integration of customs function with the UKBA; new UKBA duty to ensure safeguarding, and promotion of the welfare of children in immigration, asylum, nationality, and custom functions.☐

From the 1913 onwards, we see a pattern. There is clear policy to deny responsibility that come with looking after the destitute from other parts of the world. While they deported thousands of Jews and other refugees, they brought in more than 60,000 Irish men and women to work in the country. They also brought in a number of Caribbean and Indians. The message is the same; Britain has a tradition of refusing to accept the responsibility that comes with refugees. Instead of providing refugees with the basic provisions requested under the Refugee Conventions, they choose to prevent the refugees from reaching the country or making it extremely difficult for them to live in the United Kingdom. Britain's treatment of displaced persons and refugees after the World War II was so disgraceful that even the United Nations accused Britain of subjecting its newly arrived workers to 'an official policy of discrimination' (C. Homes: John Bull's Island: Immigration and British Society, 1871-1971, p. 20).

The problems of family reunion and the restrictions on them were there before Britain signed the 1951 Refugee Convention. As observed earlier, Britain encouraged immigration when the economy was growing, and there was labour shortage. Often they encouraged skilled persons by attaching packages to job offers. But the government was reluctant to accept dependences, especially family members, unable to work due to age or health. Family reunion also meant that there was a likelihood that the family would settle in the host country, thereby creating new demands for the provision of facilities and resources. As early as 1947, the British government abandoned any pretence of concern for the plight of refugees who had been separated from their families by war and effectively banned the entry of dependants by forcing prospective migrants to sign a form stating that they were single, unattached, and had no dependent relatives (C. Homes, op. cit., p. 214). This one single act effectively marked the beginning of a pattern of government legislation, which has dominated not only Britain but most of the advanced Western economies since the 1950s. Legislation controlled the level and nature of migration. In times of need, refugees were accepted and given working papers and even permission to settle. When there was unemployment, refugees were restricted. It has never been the need to meet the conditions of the 1951 Refugee Convention. It has always been the need to satisfy the labour needs of the West. This is why it has been difficult to accept the families of refugees. Refugees are accepted as 'ready made' workers. And by prohibiting the entry of the family dependents of the refugee workers, the host state ensures that it bears little, if any, of the cost of reproducing migrant labour. Moreover, most of the migrant labour which served the older industries of western Europe during the post-war boom was drawn from countries on the economic periphery of Europe like Greece, Spain, Turkey, Yugoslavia, Morocco, and Tunisia but also from colonial and ex-colonial countries of the major European powers. These were invariably societies whose economies had been ruined by decades of colonial domination. Poverty and unemployment drove many to emigrate. After the 1960 and 1970s, when most of the newly African independent national governments collapsed and there were civil wars across sub-Saharan Africa, refugees had no place to run. Many attempted to join relatives and friends that had migrated to Europe in the post-war boom years; others just came to Europe because Europeans that stayed in Africa had never stopped talking of how rich, how peaceful, how civilised Britain was. But the few that reached Europe found the countries already closing their doors, through numerous legislations, detentions, and deportations. The thirteen years of the Labour Government (1997 to 2010) passed the largest number of asylum laws than any government in the entire British immigration history. D. Flynn summarised what the Labour Asylum Legislation has done to the inflow of refugees into the United Kingdom and to the failed asylum seekers in the following words: *Since its election the (Labour) Government has taken draconian action to restrict people coming to the UK as asylum seekers. For most practical purposes there are now no legal routes to Britain for people fleeing persecution in their own countries. Those who manage to clear the obstacles placed in the way of entry to claim rights provided in the Geneva Convention on Human Rights are then subjected to procedures which effectively classify them as criminals, liable to be detained or subject to serious penalties further infraction of the rules until such time as their applications for asylum are finally resolved.* But the labour government only formalised what had been the general attitude of the British people towards foreigners that came into the country as asylum seekers.

Principle of Asylum Destitution: The second policy is one of denying asylum seekers dignity by refusing them permission to work; then deny them access to money; make the British people believe asylum seekers have caused shortages of employment, housing and welfare benefits; say, they abuse the benefit system; and that they are terrorists. In other words, instead of telling the nation that asylum seekers are vulnerable people that need the protection of the British, the government has painted the picture that British society is now unsafe because of the arrival of asylum seekers in their communities. To deny asylum seekers' dignity, make them be looked down upon by the British public. The government then argue that because the asylum seekers are destitute, destitution enable the government to reach them easily to help them with basic necessities, to help them accept repatriation schemes offered by the government or deport them. Because asylum seekers are associated with these two words, they can be labelled by the public as people without homes, beggars, prostitutes, and dangerous to society. Their asylum applications are labelled bogus and/or illegal. One source describes an asylum seeker as *the threatening outcast, the fearsome stranger, the excluded and the embittered—asylum seekers and refugees are depicted as maliciously exploiting Britain and British citizen's benevolence and routinely taking advantage of our generosity.* The same source described the British citizens as *kind, caring and innocent whose benevolence is abused thus casting us as victims in a deviant act* (The Criminalisation of Asylum Seekers and Asylum Policy: James Banks, 2008).

People (asylum seekers) have complained to Amnesty International of being treated harshly, disrespectfully, in humiliating ways, including by being taunted on account of their race or religion and being treated in other discriminatory ways. Almost all of those who were interviewed by the organisation for this report, whose stories are recounted earlier, have made similar complaints (United Kingdom: Seeking Asylum is not a crime: detention of people who have sought asylum: Amnesty International: 20 June 2005:47).

In 2006, Amnesty Internal also wrote this about the thousands of asylum seekers denied refugee status, refused to work, and denied the means to reach another country to seek asylum: *For the foreseeable future, thousands of rejected asylum seekers in the UK are condemned to live in abject poverty, stripped of their dignity and relying on others to subsist. Sometimes they go hungry and sleep in the streets. All avenues to a normal life are blocked. There is little incentive to remain in touch with the Home Office at this stage and therefore the whereabouts of many rejected asylum seekers is unknown.* (Down and out in London: The Road to destitution for rejected asylum seekers: Amnesty International, November 2006). There are hundreds of refugees who could be contributing positively to the British economy today but have been denied the dignity of living normal lives in the United Kingdom and have been reduced to destitution. No asylum seeker was allowed to work. They were forced to carry a plastic card, with details of their identity and large words printed at the bottom 'Employment Prohibited'. Those whose asylum applications had failed would receive no support at all from official sources. Those whose applications were being processed would receive a weekly voucher support, which was three-quarters of minimum wage. So asylum seekers would wear used clothes, survive on donations from well-wishers, and became the talk of the society—poor are discussed in homes, in churches, schools, the local press, and almost everywhere. Even doctors, nurses, teachers, and many whose qualifications would have benefited the economy were refused permission to work. Asylum seekers find themselves with problems of food. All the people interviewed by Amnesty International in 2006 were living from hand to mouth, surviving on charity from others, their dignity stripped away by this existence. Some had lost their will to live (Amnesty International, op. cit., 2006). A survey conducted in Glasgow for a snapshot month (between 30 January and 26 February) revealed that at least 154 asylum seekers, refugees, and their dependents were destitute, this number including twenty-five destitute children under the age of eighteen. The investigator indicated that these numbers are likely to significantly under represent the actual number of destitute people because of the method used and the problems associated with reaching a hidden population. Approximately half of the sample (47 per cent) had been destitute for longer than six months and around a fifth (22 per cent) for less than two months. Three-quarters (77 per cent) were destitute because they were refused asylum seekers, 9 per cent because of an administrative error, and 7 per cent because they had recently received asylum status and had yet to access mainstream support. The research estimated that the destitute figure among asylum seekers may be as high as 20,000 households. Investigators found that 44 per cent (1,524 of the 3,466 cases) of the people using the services of refugee agencies were destitute; 27 per cent were people pursuing claims for asylum and so were likely to be legally entitled to support but not receiving it because of procedural errors. London Housing Foundation found that one-fifth of bed-space in direct access hostels undertaking a one-night count were occupied by refugees and asylum seekers, the result indicating that destitution was a significant problem in London. Refugee Media Action Group reported widespread complaints regarding the condition of accommodation and the attitude of housing staff. *Problems range from poor furnishing, heating and cooking facilities to leaking ceilings, damp, infestation and lack of privacy* (Refugee Media Action Group, 2006:4). The report also highlighted that accommodation was often inappropriate for people with disabilities. Mixed sex accommodation was of particular concern to females, many of whom were victims of torture and rape. A female asylum seeker was raped and sexually assaulted three times before she was moved away from the area. In an investigation on destitution in Birmingham, Malfait and Scott-Flynn (2005) collected information about the number of destitute asylum seekers living within Birmingham and the West Midlands from a range of service providers and other stakeholders. They concluded from the information that 1,000 to 2,000 destitute asylum seekers were living in the area but with less than fifty destitute asylum seekers and refugees presenting in need of accommodation each week. Between January and February 2005, Refugee Action conducted a survey in Leicester and found 168 destitute asylum seekers, making about 77 per cent of the refugee population in the area. The Leeds Destitution Steering Group said that the figures of destitute asylum seekers were often significant underestimates. In the same Leeds area, The Joseph Rowntree Charitable Trust commissioned surveys which found high levels of destitution. They found in the Leeds area 273 destitute clients, including eleven adult dependents and thirty children. More than a third of these individuals had been destitute for one year or more. Destitution was linked to country of origin, two-thirds of those surveyed coming from just four countries—Zimbabwe, Iran, Eritrea, and Iraq—where it is impossible to arrange safe return. Further research undertaken in Leeds reported many asylum seekers in the city were often denied benefits and accommodation because of constraints applied through Section 55 (Dwyer, 2007). Dwyer and colleagues undertook a year-long project examining the basic needs and coping strategies of twenty-three refugees and asylum seekers from nine countries and interviewing eleven people involved in the delivery of special services. Commenting on aspects specific to accommodation, the researchers concluded, *Contrary to the image portrayed in some section of the media, the findings reveal an overall picture where many forced migrants live in poverty and others experience poor housing and harassment from neighbours. One respondent described the leaking lavatories, collapsing ceiling and dangerous wiring in the home of a single woman asylum seeker with two babies. Another whose application had been refused said, 'There is no way I can find money. In this country, I am not allowed to beg and I am not allowed to work. I don't even have accommodation to live in.'* In Manchester, over seventy people are supported each week by a food parcel supplied by Mustard Tree Christian Organisation, and British Red Cross Society reported to the Joint Committee that between January and June 2006, nearly 3500 asylum seekers approached them in need of emergency support (Joint Committee, 2007a).

While the position is that, there is no law preventing GPs from treating refused asylum seekers, and GPs have the discretion whether or not to register refused asylum seekers; many refused asylum seekers are not receiving treatment from GPs because of (1) the difficulties experienced in registering with a GP (the burden of documentation required to prove addresses and/or identity, including lack of address for rough sleepers or those in very temporary accommodation). (2) Unwillingness by the GPs to register asylum seekers for time or resources reasons. (3) Eligibility mistakes made by receptionists and others in GP surgeries. (4) A shortfall in the availability of interpreting services. One of the consequences of these difficulties is an increased reliance on accident and emergency services as a substitute. But people who are completely undocumented (that is, people who have never presented themselves to the immigration authorities or made any application for leave to remain) are not entitled to NHS treatment under this ruling. There is no health care service under Section 4 and Section 95. There is an estimated 7,600 failed asylum seekers under Section 95 support and an estimated 9,600 applicants under Section 4. The number of pregnant women under Sections 4 and 95 and who have been refused asylum and have not applied for support under the two sections and those that have not applied for asylum in the first place is not known. However, research studies and specialist datasets provide some information, and there does now appear to be robust evidence that pregnant asylum seekers are experiencing barriers to accessing maternity services, even when they are eligible for such services (Medact, 2007b). This may be particularly difficult for failed asylum seekers worsened by the confusion among healthcare professionals about eligibility. A number of reaches carried our across the United Kingdom show poor antenatal and pregnancy outcomes among refugees and asylum seekers. Studies of Somali women suggest unequal access to maternity services because of inadequate interpreting services, stereotyping and racism from health service staff, and a lack of understanding among staff of cultural differences. (Davis and Bath 2002. Bulman and McCourt 2003). With respect to outcomes, a Confidential Enquiry into Maternal and Child Health Studies (2004) reported that women from ethnic minority groups were, on average, three times more likely to die (a direct or indirect maternal death). Black African women, especially including asylum seekers and newly arrived refugees, had a mortality rate seven times higher than white women. It found that they had major problems in accessing maternal healthcare (Refugees and Asylum Seekers: A review from an equality and human rights perspective: Peter Aspinall and Charles Watters. University of Kent, 2010, p. 27). Vulnerable groups of asylum seekers and refugees are particularly likely to experience mental health problems as the high rate of Post Traumatic Stress Disorder among children from war zones suggest, *I feel lonely and uncertain about the future. I am frightened of being arrested and beaten. I have flashbacks of what happened to me in my country. I feel hopeless and helpless. When I was at home I was a happy person.* (Seventeen-year-old girl from Ethiopia: Refugee Action, 2006, p. 82)

There appears to be no urgency when it comes to solving asylum issues. The Parliamentary Ombudsman said this in 2010 about the UKBA: *Most of the complaints we receive are from people in this country who are facing long delays awaiting a decision on their application to the Agency. Delays by the Agency in deciding such applications means that people who should be given permission to stay are often left unable to support themselves and uncertain of their future; and those who should be removed remain here, with their chances of eventually being allowed to stay increasing because of the Agency's delay* (Fast and Fair?: A report by the Parliamentary Ombudsman on the UK Border Agency, 2010, p. 5). The Agency's biggest problem is the huge backlog of old asylum applications which has built up over a number of years, leaving hundreds of thousands of applicants waiting for years for a final decision on their application. In July 2006, the Home Secretary announced that the Immigration and Nationality Directorate of the Home Office had a 'legacy' of between 400,000 and 450,000 electronic and paper records relating to unresolved asylum cases, and that and that they would aim to clear those cases in five years or less. But by the end of September 2009, the agency had concluded 220,000 cases (Fast and Fair, op. cit., p. 9). Waiting is part of life for all asylum seekers. One waits for a letter that never comes, for a decision from the Home Office, for someone else to arrive, for a permit to work, for a place to stay, or for a call from the loved ones who disappeared without a trace. Waiting becomes a way of life as these three quotations show:

Life is very difficult because it's been about seven years since I don't know anything about my husband. And it is difficult because when you understand that somebody died, after two or three years you do like a compromise, but when you lost someone and you don't know what is happening, then all your life you are waiting.

There is no sense of belonging now. Also the children, they don't have a sense of belonging at all here. You are like someone in a desert, you don't know where you are, you don't know your next move, you don't know which direction you are heading, you are just there, waiting.

Sometimes I feel sad and angry; I think that there is no solution. But sometimes I am happy with people. And I pray, nobody can help more that God.

(Full Report: positive contributions: Being a Refugee in Britain. Written by Nando Sigona and Andrew Torre, 2005)

Principle of classifying asylum-seeker terrorists until proven otherwise

The fear or mistrust of foreign people is natural, hence when the 1951 Convention on Refugees mentioned and excluded terrorists from people seeking asylum. The convention explicitly stated that its provisions should not apply to any person who has committed a crime against peace, a war crime, or a crime against humanity. It explicitly enabled governments—subject to the oversight of the courts—to exclude individuals who, even though they may be facing persecution in their country, have been involved in serious crime or terrorist activities. The convention even allows a person with refugee status to be returned to his country if he or she has been convicted for a particularly serious crime and represents a danger to the community.

But since September 11, both the United States and Europe came up with legislation on terrorism. European policymakers viewed asylum as a liability in the fight against international terrorism and believed that more safeguards were needed to prevent the use of international refugee protection as a safe haven by those who had committed terrorist activities elsewhere. (Nils Coleman: From Gulf War to Gulf War: Martinus Nijhoff Publishers, 2007). On 27 December, just after Christmas, the Council of the European Union adopted four Acts by 'written procedure' (the measures were simply circulated to EU governments and adopted unless any objections are raised) on terrorism. None of the measures were subjected to democratic scrutiny.

The first, the Council Common Position on combating terrorism, which was passed on September 28 in the immediate aftermath of the 11 September, had significant differences with the Security Council Resolution. Point 2(a) of the Security Council Resolution says that 'states' are obliged to refrain from supporting 'entities or persons involved in terrorist acts'. Article 4 of the European Union Common Position is instead worded to require Member States to prevent 'the public' from offering 'any form of support, active or passive' to such persons or entities. The change of meaning by the EU fails to distinguish between individuals who consciously assist those individuals in terrorist acts and those who simply share the same goals as the 'terrorists' but who do not pursue these goals by violent means or knowingly assist with the preparation of violent acts. The EU definition does not distinguish between support for 'terrorist' groups and liberation movements—as does the statement attached to the proposed EU Framework Decision of harmonising national laws on terrorism agreed by the Justice and Home Affairs Council on 6-7 December (this has yet to be formally adopted).

The last seven points on the European Union's Common Position, Articles 11 to 17, clearly criminalise refugees and asylum seekers. They are not binding in the UN Security Council Resolution. Article 16 says, *Appropriate measures shall be taken in accordance with the relevant provisions of national and international law, including international standards on human rights before granting refugees status, for the purposes of ensuring that the asylum seeker has not planned, facilitated or participated in the commission of terrorist acts. The Council notes the Commission's intention to put forward proposals in this area, where appropriate (my emphasis).* Under EU law, this Common Position is binding on all Member States and will mean as follows:

(1) All asylum seekers are subject to vetting by the police and security services before their status can be granted.

In the United Kingdom, upon arrival, all asylum seekers are photographed, fingerprinted, security checked, and made to surrender all travel documents in exchange for a plastic ID card. They are then either detained while their case is being processed, or while waiting for deportation arrangements, or are given temporary admission subject to the arrangement that they report at fixed, or regular intervals to police stations or immigration screening centres while their application is considered. If they are considered a risk to national security or are suspected of having committed a crime a crime, asylum seekers can be detained until all investigations are completed. Following the introduction of the UK Anti-Terrorism, Crime and Security Act, they would never know what 'intelligence' or suspicions have recorded against them.

(2) The vetting by police and security services, when taken in conjunction with Article 4 of the EU Common Position covering 'any form of support, active or inactive' for terrorist activities could mean that a person who had helped raise funds for humanitarian needs for, say PKK prisoners in Turkish jails, could be refused refugee status.

The adoption of the two Common Positions by the Council of European Union (the fifteen EU governments) by 'written procedure' were made under Article 15 of the Treaty on European Union, which gives a very general power simply to 'adopt common position' and 'Member States shall ensure that their national policies conform to the common position.'

Common Positions are binding on all EU Member States but do not have to be submitted to national or European parliaments for scrutiny; they are simply adopted. In these two instances, the measures cover both Common Foreign and Security Policy. They cover 'third pillar' issues on police and criminal cooperation and the European Community's migration and asylum policy. By choosing to adopt these measures as Common Positions, the council has not only bypassed the European Parliament, but it also means that their validity cannot be challenged before the court of justice.

(4) Detention

Detention is an extreme sanction for people who have not committed a criminal offence. It violets one of the most fundamental human rights protected by international law, the right to liberty. In addition, some people will have been detained without charge or trial in their own country, and /or have been subjected to torture, only to be further detained at some stage of the asylum process (Amnesty International, op. cit., 2007:6)

Detention outside buildings: Detention is used both at the beginning and end of the asylum process. From the day you claim asylum you become a detainee. You are detained at the airport, border post, and every entry point until you are taken to a place where you are interviewed for as long as a continuous three hours. If your asylum story is not believed by the UKBA, your detention continues until you are deported. If your story is believable, you are given temporary admission, meaning you may go to live with relatives or if you are a destitute you are taken into a destitute home for a few days before you are taken back for detailed questioning. If your case remains believable, then the Home Office will take some months to dig into your life and prove you really an asylum seeker. For most of the asylum seekers therefore, life in the United Kingdom during the time their asylum claim is being processed is a form of detention since they are forced to live at a given and known address and to report to the police or the nearest Home Office station periodically, some as often as on a daily basis, treated more or less like criminals that await sentencing. Asylum seekers that have to report at these UKBA centres are being treated like prisoners on parole. Some are forced to travel very long distances to report regularly, but they are not assisted with transport. In theory, there is a provision to ask for assisted transport, but most asylum seekers do not know this, and there is no effort from the state structures to help them with this information.

Detention inside buildings: This is form of detention which takes place at what the UKBA call Immigration Removal Centres (IRCs). The detention there is officially called administrative detention, which is the arrest and detention of individuals by the state without trial, usually for security reasons. These detentions emphasise the fact that people that get to detentions are likely to be removed even though their detention may be administrative. In fact, the Home Office is very clear why it detains asylum seeker. The detainees are persons who are liable to removal under Section 10 Immigration and Asylum Act 1999 or Section 47 of the Immigration, Asylum and Nationality Act 2006. This is done on persons who have overstayed; breached conditions of leave to enter or remain; sought or obtain leave to remain by deception; indefinite leave revoked because they have ceased to be a refugee; families members of the above; had a decision to refuse to vary or to curtail leave, and a decision a decision is being made to administratively remove during statutorily extended leave.

The detention of persons subject to immigration controls was first introduced with the 1920 Aliens Act and expanded further with the 1971 Immigration Act. The decision to detain people who have been refused leave to enter or remain in the United Kingdom, or who are required to submit for further examination at ports of entry was hence forty regarded as 'act of administrative discretion' and those people are now liable to be detained for an indefinite period. The Nationality, Immigration and Asylum Act 2002 further extended the powers of Home Office caseworkers to authorise and prolong detention. Asylum seekers and other migrants, including dependents can now be detained at any stage of their application to enter or remain in the United Kingdom: on arrival, with outstanding appeal or prior to removal.

The United Kingdom is one of the few countries in Europe that has yet to impose limits on the length of time a person can spend in immigration detention. Despite the policy changes announced by the Deputy Prime Minister in December 2010, the government, as of early 2011, continued to detain some minors in a refurbished section of the Tinsley House Detention Centre. This centre serves as a high security detention facility to accommodate families deemed too 'disruptive' for non-custodial pre-departure accommodations. The minors were not freed from detention as such. They were transferred to a semi-secure 'family friendly' pre-departure accommodation facility opened in 2010 in Pease Pottage. Although this facility was partly run by the children's charity, Bamardo's, the firm responsible for security at the centre, is G4S. This is the private company contracted to run three detention centres; transport detainees to court and to the airport. The company is said to run prisons in countries on mainland Europe and in Australia.

The argument that asylum seekers should be detained because they will run away does not make sense when we consider what they had to go through to get to the United Kingdom. Yet in 2008, asylum seekers accounted for 75 per cent of the immigration detainee population even as they represent less than a quarter of the total number of people removed from the United Kingdom annually. Further, according to Bail for Immigration Detainees (BID), 42 per cent of asylum seekers detained in the United Kingdom go on to be released, their detention having served no purpose other than wasting human lives and taxpayers money (BID, 2009, p. 9).

The UKBA has acknowledged that most African countries are unsafe for asylum seekers to be returned there. These are the only sub-Saharan countries listed as safe: South Africa, Ghana (men only), Gambia (men only), Kenya (men only), Liberia (men only), Malawi (men only), Mali (men only), Nigeria (men only), and Sierra Leone (men only). The rest are regarded as unsafe, but you still find the UKBA deporting people to these unsafe countries. Another anomaly is with the newly institutionalised Fast Track Programme. Detention Action reported that 99 per cent of asylum seekers processed through Detained Fast Track are refused (Detention Action, 2011, p. 4).

A study by BID found that one third of all fast track detainees were still detained sixty days after their appeal hearing (Clayton, 2008, p. 421). BID found that 77 per cent of fast track detainees did not have access to publicly funded legal representation at their appeal hearing, and that they did not have sufficient time to prepare and may not understand the process. Limited availability of legal aid and funds with movement between detention centres can make high quality legal advice nearly inaccessible for many detainees (BID, 2009, p. 39).

BID was able to talk to a number of detainees who raised the following concerns: that there was lack of information about the system of detention; there was limited access to professional legal assistance; Detainees found that the bail courts were hostile; they also felt that their refusal was decided in advance; many bitterly complained about the introduction in 2008 of the use of video link in bail hearings, allowing detainees to remain at the detention centre and attending their hearing remotely (BID, 2005a). A study by the civic group campaign to close Campsfield revealed that 114 bail hearings observed, thirty-five detainees were present in person, seventy-three appeared by video link, and six were not present at all (Campaign to close Campsfield, 2011, p. 23).

A study by the London Detainee Support Group (LDSG) found that in only 18 per cent of cases it observed did detention lead to deportation during the course of a twenty-month study, with 57 per cent of the survey group remaining in detention and 25 per cent being released. Those who were deported spent an average of two years and two months in detention (London Detainee Support Group, 2009, p. 12).

Indefinite stay in detention: Detainees may remain in detention because removal to their home countries is impossible due to risk of refoulement. Detainees with countries of origin, such as Somalia, may only be returned to certain areas of their homeland, and are often reluctant to accept voluntary return given the significant safety concerns. Many of these detainees remain in detention indefinitely. Some detainees face problems with documentation because their embassies are slow to return documentation or demand evidence of documents such as birth certificates, which detainees may not have access to. The LDSG notes that these difficulties render these detainees effectively 'stateless', and although they may be willing to accept voluntary return, it is impossible for them to do so.

Private companies: Today, seven of the countries' eleven long-term immigration detention centres are managed by one of four private contractors: G4S, Serco, Mitie PLC, or Geo Group. The three remaining facilities are operated by HM Prison Service. Private contractors are provided with a fee per inmate per day, rendering immigration detention a lucrative business (Bacon, 2005, p. 6). They also operate prisons in other countries. Despite government standards, the performance of privately-run immigration detention centres has continued to be the subject of intense criticism, including from official bodies. G4S runs Brook House Detention Centre, where in 2009 there were reports of serious cases of bullying and violence. There were also serious reports of abuse of drugs. In other private company-run detention centres, there have been official and media reports regarding the assault and beating of detainees by private security guards during the detention and removal process. The death of an Angolan deportee, Jimmy Mubenga, in October 2010, led to rumours that Scotland Yard was considering filing corporate manslaughter charges against G4S guards, leading to allegations of excessive force (Coles et al, 2010). Three guards were initially arrested for the death on manslaughter charges but were later released on bail (Taylor, 2011). In 2008, a coalition of NGOs detailed some 300 cases of alleged assaults that took place between 2004 and 2008. Allegations came from detainees from more than forty-one countries, with the majority being made by African inmates. The report raised concerns about the complaints procedure within the centres, stating that the current procedure was largely ineffective.

Detention Centres or Immigration Removal Centres (IRC): There are eleven such centres with a total of 3,341 detention places. They are Brook House (London Gatwick Airport); Tinsley House (Gatwick Airport); Campsfield House (Kidlington, Oxon); Colnbrook IRC (Harmondsworth, West Drayton); Harmondsworth IRC (Harmondsworth, West Drayton); Dover IRC (Western Heights, Dover Kent); Dungavel IRC (Strathaven, South Lanarkshire); Haslar IRC (Gosport, Hampshire); Lindholme IRC (Hatfield, Woodhouse, South Yorkshire); Morton Hall (Lincolnshire); and Yarl's Wood IRC (Clapham, Bedfordshire).

Short-Term Holding Facilities (STHF): There are thirty-six short-term holding facilities throughout the United Kingdom, many of them located in or near airports or other points of transit. Three are residential short-term holding facilities, holding detainees for up to seven days. The others do not have residential facilities. There have been numerous complaints about conditions at the short-term holding facilities, which include lack of natural light; lights that cannot be turned off; poor ventilation; uncomfortable seating arrangements; and inadequate sleeping or washing facilities (HM Inspectorate of Prisons, 2011). Residential STHF that hold people up to five or seven days are Colnbrook STHF, Pennine House STHF, and Larne STHF. Prisons and police stations can also be used for immigration detention purposes (Global Detention Project: Programme for the Study of Global Migration, Geneva, 2011).

Most of the detention centres were built between 1990 and 2011. Although terms and conditions are clearly advertised on the UKBA web site and other media, it is very difficult to visit detainees. Visitors must bring with them photo identification (passport or drivers licence) and a utility bill with their name and address contained on it. Visitors must show security everything they want to bring the detainee. They are not allowed to bring him any food.

(5) Deportation

Very little had been published about deportations from the United Kingdom; very little was reported and is reported about asylum seekers hunting and capture at night and flown to mainland Europe to be deported as part of the joint deportations carried out either through inter-state arrangements or the Frontex flights. Information breakthrough came with the death of the Angolan national, Jimmy Mubenga (46) who despite shouting to the G4S security men that they had blocked his breathing system, the culture of disbelief typical of the Home Office immigration system made these people doubt him until he proved it by his death. The inhuman treatment which was witnessed by other detainees and Heathrow Airport staff could not be covered. So G4S lost its lucrative job of ferrying asylum seekers to the airport, and the three security persons that caused Mubenga's death were arrested but released on bail and have not yet been tried up to now. But G4S has been given other contracts to replace the loss. Researchers found that there was a lot of documented materials on deportations of UK detainees in Europe and vice versa and that Frontex had charter planes that removed asylum seekers from the whole of Europe. See Appendix 7 for the details of some of the schedules of some of the thirty-two flights that removed 1,622 persons in 2009. Majority of the deportees in these deportations were to sub-Saharan Africa and to Nigeria in particular. In 2010, Frontex coordinated thirty-eight flights from Europe and Britain, mainly to Burundi, Nigeria, and Cameroon. From January to March 2011, Frontex made seven flights to Congo, Nigeria, and other countries. On 28 April, Frontex rounded up sixty Congolese from different parts of Europe. And a week later, it reported that it had fifteen Congolese migrants trapped in closed detention centre in Belgium together with forty-five others from Great Britain, Ireland, the Netherlands, and Sweden. They were probably the sixty that had not yet been flown out (London *no Borders: Frontex* flights blocked by Activists in Belgium, 28

April 2011). On 5 May 2010, a Frontex charter flight deported between forty to fifty immigrants from Rotterdam Airport to Lagos or Nigeria and Cameroon. These were from Germany, Belgium, Netherlands, and the United Kingdom (Frontexplode: Frontex deportations charter, 5 May 2010).

We have seen that the rise in the number of detention centres came with the arrival of sub-Saharan asylum seekers, many of whom had become destitute by the time they reached the United Kingdom. We also see that deportations using charter planes began in 2001 when the United Kingdom began to deport sub-Saharan Africans. The UKBA Strategic Director David Wood said this about charter flights: 'The Government started using charter flights in 2001. It was a response to the fact that some of those being deported realised that if they made a big enough fuss at the airport—if they took off their clothes for instance or started biting and spitting-they would delay the process. We found that the pilots would then refuse to take the person on the grounds that other passengers would object. So although we still use scheduled flights for individuals who are difficult to remove and might cause trouble' (The Telegraph: Asylum airlines—your one-way flight to deportation by Alasdair Palmer, 23 May 2009).

The death of Jimmy Mubenga made Birnberg Peirce and Partners, Medical Justice and the National Coalition of Anti-Deportation Campaigns want to know what was happening in the detention camps and what was happening when detainees are taken to court and are deported. They came up with shocking results on the abuse, torture, and assault of detainees in the detention centres, in *Outsourcing abuse: The use and misuse of state-sanctioned force during the detention and removal of asylum seekers* can never be adequately summarised because every point raised is unique and scary. The report starts by this: Since 2007, there had been reports that since the introduction of private security companies in the detention, deportation, and escort between detention centres and removal of asylum seekers, security guards employed by private companies have assaulted and beaten asylum seekers. It goes on to say that a 'dossier' of alleged 200 assault cases that had been made was shown to The Independent by campaigners. The Complaints Audit Committee then set out to monitor the Home Office's procedures for investigating complaints about the conduct of staff. It reported 190 complaints about alleged assaults in a period of twelve months. When the members of this committee carried out its investigations, it came out with hundreds of complaints of assault but could only publish 300 of them because they could not get the permission from all the victims. They reported that they felt that their report was just 'the tip of an iceberg'. They reported, *We have found an alarming and unacceptable number of injuries have been sustained by those subjected to forced removals. This dossier provides evidence of widespread and seemingly systematic abuse of one of the most vulnerable communities of people in our society, who have fled their own countries seeking safety and refuge. The alleged assaults took place between January 2004 and June 2008* (Outsourcing abuse, p. 2)

The report then gives details of the types of assaults. They said the following:

One asylum seeker ended up with his leg in a plaster cast and a woman was pushed through the airport in a wheelchair after having been allegedly assaulted. The most common form of injury recorded resulted from inappropriate use of handcuffing, including swelling and cuts to the wrist, sometimes leading to long-lasting nerve damage. Other injuries include d bruising and swelling to the face and fractures to the wrist, ribs or ankles. Often psychological consequences resulted, such as the onset or exacerbation of post-traumatic stress disorder (PTSD), panic attacks, suicidal feelings and depression.

The report then discusses where these assaults took place:

48 per cent of the assaults occurred at the airport before the detainee was placed on the plane and 12 per cent took place in the transport van on the way to the airport. 24 per cent of the alleged assaults took place in the aeroplane before takeoff and

3 per cent after take-off. 7 per cent took place in the van back to the detention centre after the removal had already failed and 6 per cent took place within the detention centres . . . Alleged assaults took place on scheduled airline flights, charter flights and military planes. Private jets have also been arranged to remove people from the UK.

Sub-Saharan Africans: Although there were removal of people from forty-one countries, the report states that majority of removals were sub-Saharan Africans. It adds that 'most common nationalities of those being removed were Ugandan, Nigerian, Cameroonian, Congolese (Democratic Republic of Congo) and Jamaica'. In addition, the report adds that as they removed these Africans, they made some racist remarks. It says, 'Many of those assaulted made allegations of racism against the escort; there are reported accounts of abusive language used such as "black bitch" and "black monkey, go back to your own country."'

The report also says a number of children were assaulted; that they avoided assaulting people where there were witnesses and that the victims that were allowed back into the British system are afraid to come out and speak because they fear reprisals.

But despite the report and the cosmetic changes brought in against G4S, the company that replaced G4S, Reliance Security Task Management, is alleged to be doing the same, assaulting asylum seekers and injuring them. The Guardian of Wednesday 12 October 2011 reported, 'Reliance Security Task Management has since won the government contract to escort people being deported, yet allegations of abuse and use of excessive force have continued. Medical Justice volunteer doctors continue to see deportation injuries.'

The government has not improved the healthcare provisions in detention centres as the *Guardian* report says, 'Sadly, the context is based on medical evidence from many hundreds of detainees that we have assessed, we have documented the disturbingly inadequate healthcare provision that detainees are subjected to in immigration removal centres.'

Culture of disbelief: One of the cornerstones of the UKBA is culture of disbelief. A person that claims asylum is grilled for three of more hours asked the same issues in different ways just to establish some irregularities. Once they are found, the asylum application becomes easy for the UKBA to refuse. So whatever story a deportee will come up with, he is unlikely to find a sympathiser from the UKBA or security removing personnel for that matter. So when detainees commit suicide and behave in all those irregular ways, the UKBA will paint the impression that the asylum seekers loves the United Kingdom so much he is prepared to die here rather than the fact that he is likely to face death at the place he escaped from and that the British system has betrayed his trust in British democracy. The *Guardian* ended the article with 'Mubanga said that he couldn't breathe but no one believed him until he died. UKBA habitually disbelieves asylum seekers', accusing them of fabricating accounts of persecution in their countries and declaring as fact that they are in danger if deported to that country. Yet some detainees choose death rather than deportation and take their own lives—as one man reportedly did in Campsfield detention centre near Oxfordshire in August 'I believe them'.

Of late, it appears they have even improved on their violent techniques because the Belfast Telegraph warned MPs on 26 January 2012 that potentially lethal force was being used to remove detainees from the United Kingdom. The paper said that 'unauthorised and potentially fatal control and restraint techniques, including holding the detainee's head down, may be used by staff on removal flights, despite bosses insisting such moves are never used' (Belfast Telegraph: MPs concerned at deportation restraint techniques: by Wesley Johnson: 26 January 2012).

Removals & departures, asylum & non-asylum, 1997-2010

Chart provided by www.migrationobservatory.ox.ac.uk

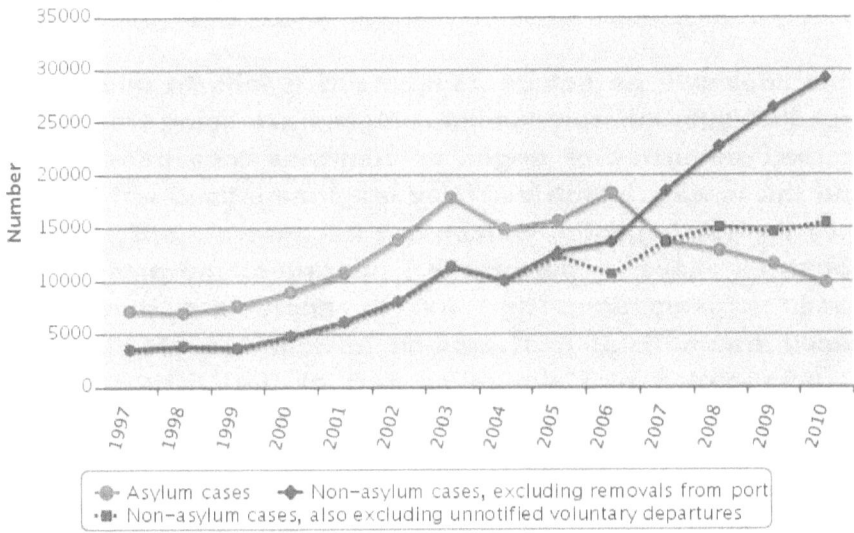

Source: Home Office, Control of Immigration Statistics UK, Q4 2010 Table 3.3, 2009 Table 3.1, 2007 Table 6.1

CHAPTER 9

Conclusion

This book will be not be complete if it fails to address the fact that sub-Saharan women refugees are being traumatised in their countries of origin, in countries they pass through and the in host countries. They are traumatised not because they are (biologically) women but because majority of these countries have governments, liberation movements and bandit organisations that fail to appreciate that gender based traumatisation of women asylum seekers is a form of persecution that should be part of the UNHCR Refugee Convention. One of the root causes of these attitudes is that the initial UNHCR 1951 Refugee Convention failed to define persecution on grounds sexual orientation. Gender based asylum claims were subordinated to the broad subheading "membership of a particular social group". Because of the inadequacy of the UN 1951 Refugee Convention, gender based persecution of especially women has been either dismissed as common societal violence expected in unstable third world countries, and did not qualify to be cited as reason for asylum protection; or they have been re-defined and placed under the nearest alternative often eroding the severity of the trauma in the process. Yet there is serious gender based torture affecting asylum seekers all the time.

Majority of such persecution of women often take the form of sexual assault. The methods of torture can consist of rape, the use of electric current upon the sexual organs; mechanical stimulation of the erogenous zones; manual stimulation of the erogenous zones; the insertion of objects into the body-openings (with objects made of metal or other materials to which an electrical current is later connected); the forced witnessing of "unnatural" sexual relations; forced masturbation or to be masturbated by others; fellation and oral coitus; and finally, a general atmosphere of sexual aggression and threats of the loss of the ability to reproduce and enjoyment of sexual relations in future [*Guidelines on the Protection of Refugee Women: by the Office of the UNHCR, Geneva. July 1991*]

There are numerous other forms of gender violence that should be used as forms of persecution when women claim asylum. Female genital mutilation, forced abortion and sterilisation and denial of access to contraception can be forms of persecution that justify refugee status depending on how they were enforced. Each asylum application based on gender violence needs to be considered in detail but in depth. Linked to political and other forms of injustices they can constitute grounds for asylum consideration. Domestic slavery, trafficking and violence within the family may be linked to political violence. Most of them take place in political volatile environment.

RAPE

But rape remains the most commonly used form of assault. The world knows that women are being raped and gang raped for reasons of their race, religion, nationality, membership of a particular social group and political opinion. Women are being sexually assaulted and killed because they belong to political movements or because they do not belong to one. Up to 500 000 women were raped in Rwanda because of their race during the genocide. [*The experiences of Refugee Women in the UK: Refugee Council Briefing: March 2012*]. According to UNHCR figures, the number of women sexually violated in the first six months of 2009 in eastern DRC was 3500. "Some were raped like animals, one after the other, others were forced to be slave of armed groups and raped every day for six months. The women are of all ages, from eight years to the very old." *[UNHCR: The Congolese rape victims a UNHCR officer will never forget: Telling the Human Story. 3 September 2009].*

The Egyptian Institute for Personal Rights says that hundreds of African asylum seekers cross into Israel every month from Egypt with the help of "International human trafficking rings. Rights groups say around 200 of these asylum seekers, mostly from Eritrea, are held in the Sinai desert and face torture and rape from their captors. The captors demand ransom money before they are allowed into Israel. The organisations say the African hostages are beaten, burned and lashed with electric cables, while their captors communicate with their relatives to pressure them to pay ransom. Women are separated from the men and repeatedly gang raped by their captors—Between January and November 2010, 1303 women were referred for gynaecological treatment(in Israel), a large percentage as a result of the trauma endured in Sinai, according to PHR-Israel. *[Egypt: Abuse of Asylum—Seekers in Sinai must stop, say activists: UNHCR Integrated Regional Information Network (IRIN), Egypt 6 January 2011].* In the Ugandan forest region, women may be kidnapped in the morning, raped all day and then let go at night; other times they are kept and held as porters, informers or sex slaves; the tactics of the LRA are always changing. Despite all these risks women still go out to collect firewood because they have no choice; firewood is required for survival, so women are obliged to travel very far. *[Women's Refugee Commission—We have no choice. W.F.P. 28 March to 10 April 2011].*For any host country to fail to classify rape with form of persecution deserving protection is to seriously miss the point because before rape women are often assaulted, enslaved, tortured and/or threatened with death. After rape some are either killed or physically injured. Some are made pregnant. Some are infected with HIV or other STDs. Why would the gays and lesbians be given asylum when women that suffer so severely are not?

ASYLUM STATISTICS

If we look at statistics (or even estimate figures from many sub-Saharan countries); if we analyse the gender proportions of men and women refugees as they leave their home countries, we notice that the overwhelming majority of people that leave the sub-continent are women(little girls, teen-age girls, mothers and grandmothers-thousands upon thousands of women). The average woman will be carrying a baby and often watching over two or three others. But statistics of arrivals in North Africa, Europe and the UK show that the majority of asylum seekers (excluding those that fly in) are not women but men, often young men. These are the only people able to survive the trauma of crossing the forests infested with bandit groups, entering and surviving in the mainly Muslim communities of the surrounding the Sahara desert; crossing the Sahara, surviving in the North African states; crossing the mighty Mediterranean Ocean in makeshift boats; surviving in the southern European countries and travelling without documents from Greece, Italy, Malta and other southern states to reach northern Europe. These are the people that can ride between the wheels of vehicles or in windowless containers. The average woman will either be captured and enslaved by bandit groups, or sold into sex slavery by Muslim traders or die in a makeshift boat—generally she will fail to reach Europe. A study made by *Asylum Aid: Issue 107: December 2011 to January 2012* show that since 2003 women arrivals constituted just one third of all main asylum applicants. In 2010 only 5329 women claimed asylum in their own right compared to 12571 men *[Home Office: Immigration Statistics, April to June 2011: Asylum Table AS. 03: Asylum Applications from main applicants by age, sex and country of nationality]*. Even the most generous of sources show that there is no time in recent history when women arrivals went above 40%. The question is—Where do the rest of the women that escape dictatorships of countries like Zimbabwe and civil wars in countries like Nigeria, DRC, Rwanda, Uganda, Somalia, Mali, to name a few, go? Where do these tens of thousands of women disappear to? If you ask the surviving arrivals, the staff of the UKBA and those of corresponding offices in the EU countries, you will learn that many of these women and children die along the way. The experiences of travelling from country of origin through countries with different types of oppressive regimes to countries of preferred asylum are too traumatic for girls, mothers and grandmothers. Why then are women with such stories of persecution to support their application claims often fail to get asylum? One of the answers lies in the UNHCR's inability to find a machinery to either persuade or force host countries to accept these stories as grounds strong enough for granting people asylum. The other reason is that the host countries may not be adopting all the conditions in the UNHCR resolutions they sign. Many host countries argue that asylum applicants either fabricate of exaggerate gender based persecution but cases coming up in courts and being told by NGOs demonstrate that there is gender based persecution deserving to be used as reason for granting asylum protection.

PRESSURE FROM NGO COMMUNITY

In recent years however there has been much debate on gender based persecution. The UNHCR admitted the weaknesses of the UN1951 Refugee Convention. This followed years of debate by NGOs, Universities and courts in which it became obvious that gender based persecutions were not being given appropriate consideration in asylum decision-making. As a result the UNHCR came improvements in a document called: *Sexual Violence Against Refugees: Guidelines on Prevention and Response, Geneva 1995*.The document provides a primer on when and how sexual violence can occur in the refugee context and the physical, psychological and social effects it can have on those exposed. The document highlights the fact that many, and perhaps most, incidents of sexual violence remain unreported for reasons including shame, social stigma and fear of reprisal or the case going to trial. It addresses ways to combat the occurrence of sexual violence and how to respond when incidents occur; emphasises the need for education, training and information campaigns and the need for refugees, and in particular refugee women, to receive legal awareness training, leadership and skills training and education. Then after further debate the UNHCR came up with guidelines that provide legal interpretative guidance on assessing claims which assert that a claimant has well-founded fear of being persecuted for reasons of his or membership of a particular social group. The UNHCR found that while "membership of a particular social group" is one of the five grounds enumerated in Article 1A (2) of the 1951 Convention relating to the Status of Refugees, it was the ground with least clarity. Since states had recognised that the term membership of a particular social group included women, families, tribes, occupational groups and homosexuals as constituting a particular social group for the purposes of the 1951 Convention the UNHCR came up with legal *Guidelines on International Protection within the Context of Article 1A (2) of the 1951 Convention and/or its 1967Protocol relating to the status of Refugees, 7 May 2002.* More debate followed and the UNHCR continued to make improvements on the gender issues of asylum applicants. They kept on publishing guidance notes. One such guidance document was *Guidance Notes on Refugee Claims relating to Sexual Orientation and gender Identity, 21 November, 2008.* These were legal guidelines of the UNHCR to host countries in response to the growing number of asylum claims made by lesbians, gays, bisexuals and transgender individuals. As the debate on how to understand and improve the complicated aspects of gender based persecution intensifies, the UNHCR continues to issue guidance notes on how to help asylum seekers.

Due to the fact that courts and international organisations have begun to implement many of these recent decisions, European governments have been forced to adopt some of the changes into their immigration policy decisions. The UK government was one of the first to respond. The Home Office sent out instructions to its immigration staff which read: *"There are international and national legal instruments which impose positive duties on the UK to eliminate discrimination and gender based violence: UN Convention on the Elimination of All forms of Discrimination against women [CEDAW] ratified by the UK in 1986; the ECHR as implemented by the Human Rights Act 1998; and Gender*

Equality Duty introduced by the Equality Act, 2006." The UK government then adopted the European Council Directive [2004/83/EC] of 29 April 2004. Article 9(f) of this directive is on act of gender—specific or child—related nature and part 2.2 defines most forms of gender-related persecution. The UK became one of first EU member states to have adopted gender guidelines for initial decision-making. Its instructions to its staff analysed to a great detail gender issues as they are discussed on the international fora. The Home Office gave instructions to the immigration staff to consider them in decision making. But in doing so the Government also reminded them of the traditional culture of disbelief. Government went to some lengths to show that many issues now regarded as gender violence by UNHCR and other NGOs existed in third world and were "accepted" and could not have forced people to leave their home countries. So, asylum seekers that brought gender based arguments on their own must not be readily believed. Government emphasised that each case must be viewed individually and that staff must use their discretion. As a result the UK staff still relegate gender issues to the UN 1951 Convention description of "membership of a social group" classification. The UK could not sign Article 60(3) of the Council of Europe Convention on Persecution and Combating Violence against Women and Domestic Violence which European countries discussed for two years and the UK had the opportunity to make its amendments. The UK said it had "difficulties with several articles" [*Home Office: Ending violence against women and girls: Action Plan progress Review: 24 November 2011p. 27]* The UK also announced its intention not to be bound by all recast Directives to be adopted under the Second Phase of the Common Asylum System. Consequently the UK will continue to be bound by the initial Directives which have been criticised for establishing minimum standards. This basically means the UK will continue to base decisions on the UN1951 Convention although they will take post 1951 Directives into consideration. The question is why have they so elaborately discussed the modern views of the gender related forms of persecution.

Because of Government failure to implement the UNHCR adjustments, the UK still turn down asylum applications of pregnant women; mentally ill women; cancer patients and children. Failed asylum seekers who are not allowed to work are asked to pay for treatments; to pay travel expenses to hospitals.

The UKBA still make it very difficult for asylum seekers to give evidence in support of their claims for asylum. The Asylum Screening Unit (ASU) in Croydon is extremely difficult to access. Because the Home Office is reluctant to change with the EU on some basic gender issues, they need to interview applicants extensively to arrive at conclusions. But there are the usual problems where applicants cannot speak English, are afraid of relatives, the effect the interview will affect relatives that remained at home and other factors. It is natural to be concerned about how victims of trafficking for example who do not speak English and are probably severely traumatised are expected to arrange this by themselves without legal representation.

Assuming one manages to get an appointment with ASU, there are concerns about women's ability to travel safely to and from south London, often without financial support, to attend their appointment or arrive early enough, to be seen on the day and not be turned away.

The environment under which ASU interviews asylum seekers does not respect their privacy and confidentiality. Nyasha from Zimbabwe was placed in a terrible position by the lack of privacy at the ASU in 2010. She wasn't comfortable speaking in public about her HIV—positive status, and she was deeply distressed at the prospect of doing so in the presence of so many people. The conditions at ASU were so bad that Nyasha asked for paper on which to write down her medical condition, rather than discuss in front of strangers.

Emiola who was a victim of trafficking from Nigeria was asked how many men she had slept with and whether she liked working as a prostitute. Most of the women interviewed explained that interviewing officers asked them the same questions on numerous occasions in what they felt was an attempt to confuse and trip them up. They mentioned the difficulties they had faced disclosing information that was relevant to their case and how this had impacted negatively on the outcome of their asylum case. *[Asylum Aid: Issue 107: December 2011 to January 2012]*

CULTURE OF DISBELIEF

Overally, Europe as a whole has not yet risen above the culture of disbelief. In countries like the UK, no matter how obvious it is that you were persecuted in Africa, you have to prove that it really happened. Many asylum seekers are turned down simply because they do not come from countries that the UK has classified as politically unstable. The consequences of disbelieving tortured victims of gender violence are that they are forced to suffer further in countries they had believed would sympathise with their plight. Victims of rape and health problems resulting from it are being denied appropriate health services. Pregnant asylum seeking women; pregnant women living rough; and people with cancer resulting from gender related trauma continue to be denied health care in developed countries. Women with abdominal pains and bleeding after being sexually traumatised have been asked to pay for health services when governments know asylum seekers are not allowed to work. People with terminal illnesses and survivors of sexual violence have all been denied medical services in Western Europe.

Black African women who are asylum seekers are estimated to have a mortality rate seven times higher than white women, partly due to problems in accessing maternal health care[Aspinall P and Watters C. (2010): Refugee and Asylum seekers: A review from an equality and human rights perspective. Research report 52 Manchester: Equality and Human Rights Commission]

Midwives have identified the poverty and destitution experienced by pregnant asylum seeking women as significant barriers to providing effective care, citing that appointments are missed because the women do not have money for transport.

The 2008 Joseph Rowntree Charity Trust study says that 75 percent of destitute asylum seekers were from Zimbabwe, Sudan, DRC, Somalia and Eritrea.

The UN1951 Refugee Convention remains the basis for gender based applications and resolutions in most European countries despite all the debate and resolutions made by the NGO community. One of the reasons why countries like the UK can turn down 80% of asylum applications is that they still base most decisions on the 1951Refugee Convention and we know that many of the words that make the Convention may mean one thing to one immigration officer and quite another to the next. Words like race, religion, nationality and membership of a particular social group have been used and continue to be used as tools to deny asylum to deserving persons.

The traumatic experiences of sub-Saharan Africans will not be known to the World unless the people that suffered tell their stories. The World is waiting to hear from us before it comes to our assistance. Let us come forward and tell the World how the different communities we asked for food water and accommodation responded to our request. The World is waiting.

Appendix 1

Pro ASYL Bundesweite Arbeitsgemeinschaft für Flüchtlinge e.V.

Postfach: 16 06 24

Telefon: 069/23 06 88

Internet: http://www.proasyl.de

60069 Frankfurt/Main Telefax: 069/230650 email: proasyl@ proasyl.de

Press release: 29 October 2007

The truth may be bitter, but it must be told.

Greece: Pro ASYL and Greek Group of Lawyers reveals systematic human rights abuses in the Aegean

Call on EU to react

On two fact-finding missions in July or August and in October 2007, representatives of Pro ASYL and the Greek Group of Lawyers for the Rights of Refugees and Migrants examined the situation at the EU external border in the Aegean.

The research findings are shocking. Serious human rights violations are taking place:

- The Greek coastguard systematically maltreats newly arrived refugees. It tries to block their boats and force them out of Greek territorial waters. Regardless of whether they survive or not, passengers are cast ashore on uninhabited islands or left to their fate on the open sea.
- In one reported case on the Chios Island, the degree of maltreatment amounted to torture (serious beating, mock execution, electric shocks, pushing a refugee's head into a bucketful of water).
- The police detain all refugees and migrants on their arrival on the islands, including minors. This is in contravention of international law. Without exception, all new arrivals are placed under a deportation order, also in breach of international law. The detainees are left without any information about their rights and without legal counsel.

- **All three of the detention camps visited by the delegation offer unacceptable living conditions.**

The circumstances of detention amount to degrading and inhuman treatment.

Today Pro ASYL and the Greek Group of Lawyers for the Rights of Refugees and Migrants issued an extensive documentation under the heading *The truth may be bitter, but it must be told* in Athens and Brussels.

It is the publishers' view that these critical findings have to be placed within a European context. The border which we visited is one of the external borders of the European Union. The European Union bears responsibility for what is happening there. Otherwise, Europe is jeopardising its achievements in human rights development—of which it is rightly proud—at its very own borders.

Pro ASYL and the Group of Lawyer for the Rights of Refugees and Migrants call upon European institutions to take immediate action in view of the blatant abuses and human rights violations in Greece. The European Commission, the European Parliament, the Council of Europe Commissioner for Human Rights, its Committee for the Prevention of Torture (CPT) and also the national governments of the EU member states cannot accept the gross violation of international law by one of breach of the European Convention on Human Rights, the Geneva Convention on the Protection of Refugees and European Directives. As long as the systematic practice of violating human rights is not halted and Greece has not introduced an appropriate system for receiving refugees, it is irresponsible to return refugees to Greece in the framework of the Dublin II Regulation, establishing the competence for asylum procedures within the European Union.

Karl Kopp—Director for European affairs (Pro ASYL), board member of the European Council for Refugees and Exiles (ECRE)

Annex

Excerpts from interviews with refugees on the East Aegean islands:

'We had nearly reached the Greek island of Lesbos, which lay in front of us. Suddenly a boat from the Greek coastguard appeared. The officials beat us. Then they drove us back into open water. We had to take off our belts and shoes, and were made to disembark on an uninhabited island, without food or water.'

'The Greek coastguard forced us back into the rubber dinghy on high seas. Before we got back on they made small cuts in it with knives. Ever group only got one oar. Our shoes were thrown into the water. It was very difficult for us to reach the shore in the damaged boat and with only one oar.'

'They stopped our dinghy and forced us to enter their boat. The beating started right away. They took my mobile phone and looked in my mouth, even in private orifices. They took all the money I had on me. Before my eyes they threw the Holy Book (note: the Koran) into the sea. Then they set course for Turkey and left us on an island.'

'I had been in Mitilini for three hours. Then other police came. I had to get into a car and we drove off through the mountains to another coast. From there I was taken back to Turkey on a small boat.'

'We were a group of twenty-two. We were in the middle of the sea when the Greek coastguard arrived.

'Then they pulled us out of the water and they began beat us and shoot . . . they beat me up and broke my rib. We had to lie flat on the floor and they stood on us. All this took place on coast guard's boat.'

Chios-Case: Torture during interrogation

'I had to kneel down. One policeman stood behind me while two stood in front of me. The one behind me hit me with a stick on the head, deliberately and hard. He hit me on the crown of my head repeatedly with the stick. I tried to protect myself with my arms. Then he hit my arms. I tried to look behind me, and he started hitting me again. The two policemen in front of me were armed and showed me their weapons while I was being beaten. They looked at me very seriously. They said, "We are going to kill you." The expression on their faces was terrifying. I was very scared. The other policeman—a fat one—came up to me and said into my ear, "Tell the truth. These two policemen are very dangerous. They will kill you."

'Then they brought a plastic bucketful of water. I was kneeling the whole time. "Do you see the water?" My arms were pressed together behind my back, held by one of the policemen. The other policeman put his hand on the nape of my neck and pushed my head down into the water. I couldn't breathe anymore. I was only pulled up after some time. "Do you now know the colour and name of the boat?" I said no. He punched me twice in the face. The policeman behind me grabbed my arms again. I wanted to take a deep breath of air. The policeman in front of me asked, "Do you remember now or not?" I said no again. He grabbed my head and pushed it into the water. I was absolutely terrified. I thought I would not survive. When I came up again, the policeman again asked, "So you don't remember?" I repeated that I did not.

'So then the policeman took a plastic bag and put it over my head. With one hand he tightened the bag around my neck. I couldn't breathe anymore. They repeated the process of the plastic bag three times—every time they asked the same question. Then a policeman signalled with his hand that's enough.'

Quotation to be used to support treatment of DRC asylum seekers in Angola:

According to the information received, since January 2009, collective deportations and expulsion of nationals of the DRC have taken place, reaching a peak in late August 2009. Overall, approximately 18,800 DRC nationals have been allegedly expelled from Angola; approximately 16,000 of them since late August 2009. The following are two instances that illustrate the human rights violations that often take place during these expulsions.

In May 2009, in the Ngazi settlement in Lunda Norte Province, refugees, asylum seekers and irregular migrant workers were subjected to ill-treatment, including gender-based violence, and deprived of their belongings. These violations were mostly perpetrated by Angolan security forces and intended to force them to return to the DRC.

Whereas most of the DRC nationals were expelled from the provinces of Lunda Norte and Lunda Sul, expulsions have also reportedly occurred in the territories of Soyo and Cabinda since early October 2009. Citizens of the DRC were detained and kept in very poor conditions prior to their expulsion. It appears that the administrative detention of asylum seekers is not subject to independent monitoring, and takes place without prior authorization from a judicial body. The detainees are most often denied access to legal counsel. In the context of the expulsions, many of them were subject to sexual violence at the risk of HIV transmission, body searches without minimum hygienic standards and theft.

In this respect, we note the initiative to create a commission in late November 2009 to discuss this concern with the DRC authorities and the issuance on 13 October 2009 of a joint communiqué announcing the concerted cessation of expulsions and the political will to find sustainable solutions to the issue. In spite of these commitments, we received reports that expulsions have continued to occur, albeit at a lesser scale.

Appendix 2

UNHCR Statistical Yearbook 2010: Refugees in African Countries

UNHCR Statistics Yearbook 2010			
Country	Total Refugees	Country	Total Refugees
Angola	136,076	Niger	332
Burkina Faso	1,650	Nigeria	1,0562
Burundi	253,508	Rwanda	66,594
Cameroon	17,065	Senegal	8,573
DRC	2,718,550	Somalia	1,489,862
Eritrea	236,059	South Africa	229,601
Ghana	14,578	Sudan	1,958,524
UN	57,428	Uganda	585,253
Guinea Bissau	8,009	Zambia	48,182
Kenya	61,327	Zimbabwe	5,031
Malawi	15,102	Ethiopia	117,736
Mali	15,261	Liberia	27,926
Mauritania	28,349	Morocco	1,072
Mozambique	9,996	Egypt	8,501
Namibia	8,704	Tunisia	112

Appendix 3

UNHCR Statistical Yearbook 2010: Refugees in Selected EU Countries

UNHCR	Statistics	Yearbook 2010	
France	250,394	Malta	7,431
Germany	670,462	Netherlands	90,075
Greece	57,428	Poland	18,444
Italy	61,327	Portugal	487
Spain	6,566	United Kingdom	253,235
Europe		4,064,530	

Appendix 4

UNHCR: Country of Origin and Country of Asylum for Sub-Saharan Refugees in 2010 (Annex 5, UNHCR Yearbook 2010)

Country of Origin	Country of Asylum	Total
1. Angola	1. DRC	84,374
	2. Namibia	5,924
	3. South Africa	5,758
	4. Zambia	25,329
2. Burundi	1. DRC	17,585
	2. Tanzania	53,823
3. Central African Republic	1. Cameroon	85,824
	2. Chad	71,015
4. Chad	1. Cameroon	8,342
	2. Sudan	41,140
5. Congo (Brazzaville)	1. Gabon	7,523
6. Côte d'Ivoire	1. Liberia	6,414
7. DRC	1. Angola	13,364
	2. Burundi	24,614
	3. CAR	20,899
	4. Congo (B)	103,213
	5. France	10,841
	6. Germany	6,093
	7. Rwanda	53,647
	8. South Africa	11,708
	9. Sudan	19,709
	10. Uganda	73,175
	11. Tanzania	63,275
	12. Zambia	21,965
8. Eritrea	1. Ethiopia	36,164
	2. Israel	11,852
	3. Italy	10,377
	4. Sudan	113,528
	5. Switzerland	3,944
	6. United Kingdom	8,829
9. Ethiopia	1. Kenya	17,103
	2. Sudan	9,170
	3. United States	12,238

10. Ghana	1. Togo	8,073
11. Liberia	1. Côte d'Ivoire	24,038
	2. Ghana	11,476
	3. Guinea	11,120
	4. Nigeria	5,261
	5. Sierra Leone	9,030
12. Rwanda	1. Congo	7,121
	2. DRC	80,525
	3. Uganda	15,717
	4. Zambia	5,145
	5. Gambia	7,546
	6. Guinea Bissau	7,492
13. Somalia	1. Djibouti	11,198
	2. Egypt	6,096
	3. Ethiopia	58,980
	4. Italy	7,747
	5. Kenya	310,280
	6. Netherlands	11,068
	7. Norway	7,064
	8. South Africa	9,718
	9. Sweden	10,636
	10. Uganda	8,172
	11. United Kingdom	32,299
	12. Yemen	161,468
14. Sudan	1. Chad	262,194
	2. Egypt	9,818
	3. Ethiopia	23,516
	4. Israel	5,502
	5. Kenya	20,315
	6. Uganda	20,836
15. Togo	1. Benin	5,921
16. Zimbabwe	1. United Kingdom	14,119

Appendix 5

Internally Displaced Persons (IPDS) Protected and Assisted By UNHCR 2010

Country	Population (of IDPs) End of 2010
Burundi	157,200
CAR	192,500
Chad	131,000
Côte d'Ivoire	3,672,100
DRC	1,721,400
Kenya	300,000
Somalia	1,463,800
Sudan	1,548,000
Uganda	125,600

Appendix 6

Asylum Applications in Europe 2005-2009						
	2005	2006	2007	2008	2009	Total
Belgium	15,960	11,590	11,120	12,250	17190	68110
Cyprus	7,750	4,550	6,790	3,920	3200	26210
Denmark	2,260	1,920	1,850	2,360	3,750	12,140
France	49,730	30,750	29,390	35,400	41,980	187,250
Germany	28,920	21,030	19,100	22,090	27,650	118,840
Greece	9,050	12,270	25,110	19,880	15,930	82,240
Hungary	1,610	2,120	3,430	3,120	4,670	14,950
Ireland	4,320	4,310	3,990	3,870	2,690	19,180
Italy	9,550	10,350	14050	30,320	17,600	81,870
Malta	1,170	1,270	1380	2,610	2,390	8,820
Netherlands	12,350	14,470	7100	13,400	14,910	62,230
Poland	6,860	4,430	7,210	7,200	10,590	36,290
Portugal	110	130	220	160	140	760
Spain	5,250	5,300	7,660	4,520	3,000	25,730
Sweden	17,530	24,320	36,370	24,350	24,190	126,760
Switzerland	10,800	11,170	10,840	16,610	14,490	63,910
Turkey	3,920	4,550	7,650	12,980	7,830	36,930
U. K.	30,840	28,320	28,300	31,320	29,840	148,620
Western Europe (19)	229,030	197,540	215,540	248,390	253,170	1,143,670

Sothern Europe (8)	36,830	38,440	62,890	74,400	50,090	262,650
Total Europe	261,740	222,410	249,630	283,690	286,680	1,304,150

Southern European states: Albania; Cyprus; Greece; Italy; Portugal; Spain and Turkey.

Appendix 7

Joint Return Flights coordinated by Frontex January/December 2009

Frontex in a nutshell, see end of page

There were 32 flights removing 1,622 persons, main destination was Nigeria 17 flights involving 849 persons approximate

Average cost of each Frontex Flight last year £183,643

11 Flights originated from Austria

Destination	Organizing country	Countries returning persons	Number removed
Nigeria	IE and UK	IE, UK, DE, CH	86
Ecuador and Columbia	Spain	ES, FR, IT	98
Nigeria	Italy	IT, ES, MT, FR, PL, CY	51
Nigeria	Austria	AT, BE, DE, LV, SE, CH	38
Georgia	Austria	AT, UK, IE	8
Mongolia	Sweden	SE, AT, CZ	61
Nigeria and Cameroon	Netherlands	NL, DE, PL, SE, BE, FR, ES, AT	52

Kosovo and Albania	France	FR, AT, IS, SE, NO	47
Côte d'Ivoire and Togo	Switzerland	CH, DE	6
Nigeria	Ireland	IE, UK, MT, LU, ES, SK	62
Kosovo and Albania	Austria	AT, FR, NL	32
Nigeria	Italy	IT, FR, GR, ES	40
Nigeria	Switzerland	CH, FR, IE, PL	29
Nigeria	Austria	AT, RO, CY, NL, PL, FI, DE, NO, SE	35
Vietnam	Germany	DE, PL	112
Georgia and Armenia	Austria	AT, SE, ES, FR, IE, PL	42
Nigeria	United Kingdom	UK, IE, CZ, NO, PL	96
Nigeria	Netherlands	NL, DE, FR, UK, ES, PL, IT, AT	50
Georgia and Armenia	Austria	AT, DE, PL, ES	14
Nigeria	Austria	AT, DE, FI, CZ, PL, IE, CH, FR	50
Kosovo and Albania	Austria	AT, FR, SE, LU	50
Columbia and Ecuador	Spain	ES, FR, IT	85

Nigeria	Italy	IT, AT, DE, FR, NL, CY, GR	50
Georgia	Switzerland	CH, FR, PL	30
Nigeria and Gambia	Austria	AT, DE, NO, SE	30
Nigeria	Ireland	IE, NO, HU, SI	58
Mongolia	Sweden	SE, AT	63
Nigeria	Italy	IT, FR, DE, HU, NL, NO, ES	47
Nigeria	Austria	AT, GR	23
Georgia	France	FR, ES, AT, GR, PL	51
Kosovo and Albania	Austria	AT, IS, FR, DE, HU	74
Nigeria	Ireland	IE, AT	52

Totall number removed 1,622

Appendix 8

Copyright Red Cross Blogs

Blogs highlighting the work of staff and volunteers within the British Red Cross, part of the largest humanitarian organisation movement in the world.

Bottom of Form

Asylum seekers: popular myths debunked

Alia's story: Building a new life

©Info

After fleeing torture and persecution in Eritrea, refugee Alia is building a new life in the UK with the help of the Red Cross.

Following a sustained campaign of religious persecution and abuse, Alia* was forced to flee from Eritrea seven months ago. Upon arriving in the UK, she was relocated to Newport, South Wales where she was granted refugee status and put in touch with the Red Cross' refugee service.

As she was imprisoned and tortured in her home country, the housing association in Newport made Alia a priority and offered her a council flat. However, the new arrival was completely alone in an unfamiliar country and desperately needed support during her first few months in the city.

A new home

Help soon arrived in the form of Theresa, a Red Cross service co-ordinator. She said, 'I went with Alia to view the flat she had been offered, which was in a terrible state and also quite far from other people in Alia's community.

'At first she wasn't sure about the flat but I reassured her that, with the money she would receive from her community grant application, she could soon make it feel like home.

'Four weeks later, the flat looked fantastic. Friends helped Alia to redecorate and we bought furniture from a second-hand furniture project. By now she was receiving her benefits, so we also helped her to get connected to the gas and electricity supply.'

Grateful

Safely settled and comfortable in her new home, Alia could also rely on the Red Cross with help in other areas of her life. Theresa remembered: 'Alia mentioned that her feet had been really painful for a while and she'd like me to go with her to see her GP. Following our visit, she has now been booked in for an x-ray and is awaiting her first podiatry appointment.'

Looking back on a busy few weeks, Alia said, 'I'm so happy that I've been able to settle into my new home—I've even got an interview for a job with a local bakery. I'm so grateful for all the help the Red Cross has given me to help me settle into Newport.'

Theresa added, 'When she left Eritrea, Alia had to leave behind her eleven-year-old son. I've now put her in touch with the Red Cross' international tracing and message service so that hopefully, in time, he can join her in her new home.'

*Name has been changed to protect identity

The asylum seekers who survive on £10 a week

They can't work, they can't claim benefits, and they have nowhere to live. And their only means of survival is one £10 food voucher a week. Four failed asylum seekers tell their desperate stories.

This failed asylum seeker has been living rough on the streets of Birmingham for the last five years. Photograph: Fabio De Paola

Since this era of financial austerity began, newspapers and magazines have hurried to publish advice on how to get by on a straitened budget. So here is one to beat all others. Today we offer a guide to surviving on under £10 a week. Without a roof over your head! Without a bed to lie on! With no support from family or friends!

It's quite possible, and here's how. These helpful tips come from four failed asylum seekers in Birmingham, who remain in this country, preparing to appeal the Home Office decision, sleeping meanwhile in hedges, doorways, old garages, and staircases.

Abdi, 34 (Somalia)

It would be wrong to describe Abdi as poor because this suggests he doesn't have enough money to survive on, which would be to put a rather optimistic spin on his situation. He isn't poor, he just doesn't have any money at all, and hasn't done for the last six months since his asylum claim was rejected in December.

He is pragmatic and uncomplaining as he explains how he manages to subsist beyond the fringes of society, hand to mouth, on meals of bread and tuna bought with Red Cross food vouchers. He has noticed, however, that the longer he lives like this, the heavier the toll on his health.

The Red Cross today publishes an uncharacteristically hard-hitting report attacking the 'shameful' way the British immigration system treats those whose claims for asylum have been denied, and who have yet to return home. Once an application is turned down, the asylum seeker loses all eligibility for accommodation and financial support. Estimates suggest that there are about 200,000 asylum seekers who receive no state support, of whom perhaps 20,000 are surviving on food provided by the Red Cross or other charities. The organisation compares this emergency aid distribution to the work it does in Sudan, and is calling for the government to adopt a more 'humane' approach.

Once you lose your home and financial support, the priority is to find somewhere safe to sleep. Abdi has three places he sleeps regularly, and he rotates them according to weather conditions. The first is in a mosque in a suburb of Birmingham, particularly useful when there was heavy snow. To stay there, you need to go to last prayers, join the worshippers for a while and then slip away and shut yourself in a toilet cubicle. Shortly afterwards the lights are switched off and the building locked up, and there is a secure place for the night.

Anxious to avoid suspicion, he doesn't risk staying there too often. So he has also been sleeping intermittently on a flattened cardboard box at the top of a concrete stairway to a block of flats nearby. This place is sheltered from the rain, and it has the added advantage of a light bulb that can be left on or unscrewed when he wants darkness, but the neighbours are not tremendously welcoming, and he tries not to get there until he calculates they will all be asleep. When they see him, they are generally abusive and threaten to call the police. Someone has scratched 'Your Dead' into the side of his cardboard container, which he has left leaning against the wall.

'They're just joking with me,' he says amiably.

The third place is in a narrow alleyway between park railings and a row of back yards, a few streets away. He has hidden his sleeping bag (marked 'Don't take it. Please. Homeless') underneath a heap of discarded building materials, wooden planks with protruding nails, and broken mirrored glass. The adjoining section of park is a place where teenagers hang out to take drugs in the evening, so most people prefer to avoid the area, which means he is mostly left undisturbed.

For food he goes to the Red Cross every Tuesday, where he queues up for £10 worth of Morrison's vouchers, usually alongside up to 100 other failed asylum seekers. Volunteers here used to distribute emergency handouts of £15, but funding shortages forced them to reduce this to £10. The recipients did not protest, says Joseph Nibizi, manager at the destitution clinic; they are desperately grateful for whatever help they can get.

'People say "Go home" or "Get a job". I can't do either.'

Although Birmingham has a large number of destitute asylum seekers they are not very visible. They do not sit at train stations or by cashpoints; instead they linger in the shadows, afraid of attracting attention from officials.

Abdi cultivates invisibility. He spends his day pacing from one spot to another, afraid to loiter too long, worried that people will think he is a criminal. He doesn't approve of begging. He is prohibited from working, and does not want to try working illegally—washing cars at the traffic lights—for fear of jeopardising the fresh claim for asylum he is preparing.

Existing without any money naturally causes logistical problems. Tomorrow he has to travel to Solihull on the outskirts of Birmingham for his monthly registration with the Home Office, and the bus fare will cost £3.50. He visits Morrison's to see if he can get change from his vouchers, but he knows from previous visits that the cashiers are not very well disposed to asylum seekers, and will only give change if at least half the value of the voucher is spent. It seems a trifling point, but since the change from the Morrison's voucher represents the only coins that pass through his hands during the week, it is of critical importance.

As he walks through the 14 aisles of the vast supermarket, he waves towards the shelves full of food and says: 'I pass everything by because of my budget.' He buys some discounted sliced bread, four tins of tuna chunks, four small tins of baked beans, and a litre of milk. He doesn't own a tin opener, but a nearby cafe owner usually agrees to lend him one, and he eats whatever he buys cold.

(At the till, there seems to be some inconsistency about the policy on giving change from tokens. A cashier is happy to give me £4.50 change when I give her one of the £5 tokens to buy the 50p loaf of bread. A manager I check with smiles and says

I can spend as much or as little of the £5 gift token as I like. When Abdi asks another cashier, he is told he must spend at least £2.50.)

Abdi pours out stories from his existence on the streets; they are not very cheerful, but he tells them with a sense of humour, outlining the absurdity of his situation. He has a story about a young woman who befriended him on a bench; after several days of sympathetic visits from her, it transpired that she was merely attempting to recruit him to deal drugs in the park. He has another story, told equally cheerfully, about a family who set their dogs loose on him in the alleyway where he was sleeping.

It is a bleak existence, but he is not inclined to return to Somalia. He won't say much about what prompted him to flee through Africa and then Europe hidden in cars and lorries, commenting only: 'If you understand that it is a choice between living here in this way and going back to be slaughtered, then you understand that there is no choice.'

His original asylum claim was refused by a judge who described it as 'not credible'. Campaigners point out that the asylum system is not wholly reliable, characterised by a 'culture of disbelief', the onus being on asylum seekers to prove that they are not lying. Last year, 28 per cent of people who appealed against refused asylum cases were granted leave to remain, a figure that campaigners say reflects serious flaws in the initial decision-making process. Besides, whether or not someone's claim is legitimate is not relevant to the question of whether they should be forced to live on the streets, campaigners argue.

The Red Cross is responding to the humanitarian needs of people who have nothing and nowhere to live, and staff members do not attempt to judge whether their clients' claims are solid or not. 'We are a humanitarian organisation, and we believe that people run away from persecution. It is for the government to decide whether they have good cases or bad cases,' Nibizi says.

Abdi has a meeting with a Home Office official later this month to go through his appeal submission. It is increasingly hard to find a solicitor, especially if you have no money. The UK's leading asylum charity, Refugee and Migrant Justice, announced yesterday that it was going into administration because of funding shortages, due to government delays in the payment of legal aid. If he submits an appeal, and it is accepted by the Home Office as potentially viable, then he will be eligible for hardship support payments and housing, but it is difficult to secure that status. Until then, he exists in limbo.

It is a confusing situation to understand. Abdi is not here illegally, since he is going through all the correct legal hoops, registering his presence with the Home Office every month, and until he gets served a removal notice he is not breaking the law by staying. He is at pains to do everything correctly, abiding by the stipulation not to work, determined not to break the law, even if that means surviving in a gutter on ad hoc charity handouts.

'Criminals in your prisons still get their basic needs. What about people who come here searching for safety?' he asks. 'If they deny these things, do they want us to die? Or do they want us to break the law? When people see me sleeping in the stairway, they say "Go home" or "Get a job". I can't do either.'

Abdi is careful not to express any hostility towards the government for its policy, but Nibizi is angry. 'You can remove people back to their home country, or you can keep them here. But you have to give people food. It is inhumane not to give people food. You cannot starve people out of the country,' he says.

'Nowhere else is providing the kind of support (the Red Cross does). Ten pounds is not enough to live on, but it can sustain them until someone else can help them. Our service is meant to be an emergency response, but the government is not dealing with them. We can't leave them to die outside.'

Haile, 32 (Ethiopia)

These attitudes towards asylum seekers are on display among a group of 40 or so homeless people sheltering from the rain on the ground floor of a multi-storey car park in the city centre, waiting for soup and sandwiches to be distributed by volunteers from a Baptist church.

One tall, white man in his 40s is expressing loud anger about the decline of the country. A few years ago, he remarks, there would have been no foreigners queuing up at these soup kitchens. 'It was just the English,' he laments, adding that the outsiders should be sent home. 'If they try to come back, their passports should be taken away and they should be sent to prison.'

Haile, who has been living homeless in central Birmingham for five years, since being released from an immigration detention centre, does not respond. 'He's always like that. He says, "English first for food." I don't pay any attention to him. He drinks,' Haile says. On the whole, he avoids telling people about his background. 'If they knew I was an asylum seeker,' he says, gesturing to the group, made up mainly of local drug addicts, alcoholics and the mentally ill, 'and that I don't have papers to be in this country, I think I would be dead now. I don't make friendships with anyone; I don't know who is good or bad.'

He lives alone, in conditions similar to those we see in news reports highlighting the plight of survivors whose lives have been torn up by faraway natural disasters before the major aid agencies have arrived—no electricity, no shelter from the elements, no sanitation, no water, no food, no mattress etc.

For over a year now, he has been living in a fenced-off doorway, at the back of an expensive hotel in the city centre, by the entrance to a now defunct car park. Local authorities have tried to block the way in, erecting a sheet of chipboard marked 'Trespassers will be prosecuted' over the gap he used to squeeze through. Now he has to climb a ten feet metal fence with flattened prongs at the top, and slide down on the other side, where there is a space in the old doorway, covered from the rain.

It has been raining a lot, so it is difficult to get over the fence which (since he is a little short) is over twice his height. He puts his trainers on two black-painted railings, legs apart, and tries pull himself up. There is a slipping noise of wet rubber from his shoes and he fails to get over. He slips down the railings and tries again. It is painful to watch.

'This is my sleeping bag, my table, bed, blanket,' he says through the fence, once he has made it to the other side. 'My toilet,' he says, pointing to a dank corner. 'My clothes,' he adds, nodding towards a heap of crumpled clothes and shoes. Piles of rubbish have been thrown through the railings by passersby—McDonald's yellow polystyrene containers, Sprite and Quavers packets, KFC and Red Bull, cigarette packets.

Haile says he has rat problems and fox problems, but is upbeat about the place he has found. The difficulty of getting in gives him a sense of security once he is inside.

'Sometimes I look and think it's like a prison, it's like a cage. But no one can throw stones at me here,' he says. 'This is my mansion. I'm a rich man. I own this hotel. If you want a room, I'll rent it to you cheap, cheap.'

The strain of living in these conditions has taken a toll and Haile is clearly struggling to cope with life. Immigration letters in brown envelopes (delivered to the Red Cross and passed on to him) lie strewn in between the clothes. Taken by his parents from Ethiopia to Tanzania as a baby, he came here as a stowaway on a boat in 2000. Several asylum applications have been refused, and he is under instructions to return to

Tanzania. But he is not clear whether he would be accepted there, since it is not his original home. He has no capacity to get himself there, and one attempt to deport him forcibly was cancelled at the last moment several years ago, since when he has been left to forage for survival in central Birmingham.

'My life is wasted. My parents died. I don't have parents. I don't have a country. I don't feel like a human any more,' he says.

A large proportion of failed asylum seekers have some kind of mental health problem, charities say, the result of the stress through which they are living. Haile probably needs some kind of medical help, but in his limbo status it is hard to access. 'They live on paracetamol,' Nibizi says. Last year, Haile broke an index finger but, alarmed by the questions he was asked when he went to casualty, left the hospital without getting it treated; the bone has mended but the finger no longer bends, and juts out at an awkward angle.

Mimi, 33 (Ethiopia)

The worldly possessions of one asylum seeker living rough in Birmingham. Photograph: Fabio De Paola

Sleeping on the streets, as Mimi puts it, is 'not easy for ladies', so she has been sleeping on the floor of three Ethiopian families, two days here, two days there, for the last two months, since her asylum claim was refused. The families help her because they know she would otherwise be on the streets, but she can see she is a burden they cannot afford. Each morning she wakes up, dresses and gets ready to leave the house before she gets in the way, pausing at the doorway to see whether they will invite her to sleep another night.

'It's not easy living like this. It makes you go mad. It makes you want to kill yourself,' she says.

She uses the £10 vouchers from the Red Cross to help contribute to the food supplies of the families that she visits; she has lost her own appetite, she says.

There are no night shelters that failed asylum seekers can go to in Birmingham (the Salvation Army hostel is not allowed to accept them), but the Red Cross has told her about a place in Coventry, 20 miles away, which offers emergency shelter to destitute migrants. She calls but there are only men staying at the centre, and the woman who runs the centre suggests it might be not be ideal for her. Mimi will continue sleeping on sofas.

The majority of destitute asylum seekers live in similar conditions, sharing rooms with other asylum seekers who are still receiving state support—housing and a basic weekly allowance—as their first asylum claim goes through. Because there are no accurate sources of data, it is impossible to know how many people are sleeping rough and how many on sofas.

'It is a hidden problem,' says Penny Walker, who runs the night shelter in Coventry as part of a housing co-operative. 'As a rule, they don't beg, they don't commit crime. These people try to remain invisible all day. They don't want to be loitering; they don't want anyone to see them and wonder whether they are about to rob them. There is this huge emptiness, huge uncertainty.'

She regrets not being able to offer Mimi a space to sleep, but the living space at the housing co-operative she runs with fellow environmental and peace activists is already full. Between 14 and 16 destitute migrants arrive each night at 9 p.m., receive a hot meal and sleep together in one room, on camp beds lined up, side-by-side, about a foot between each bed. The atmosphere tonight is cheerful, but it isn't always. A few years ago, a failed asylum seeker gave up and hanged himself from a tree in the garden.

'They come here exhausted once they have run out of friends on whose floors they can sleep. Often they've been sleeping in friends' cars. They wouldn't come here unless they were desperate,' says Walker.

'People think we should give asylum only to those who have a genuine need, not to those who have a so-called bogus claim,' she says. 'But what people don't understand is that the system is not fair. People don't flee their country unless they have a very good reason for doing so, and it is difficult to prove what happened to you unless you have scars from torture up your arms. The fact that you failed in your asylum claim does not mean that you are not a genuine asylum seeker.'

Walker argues that their determination to remain in these conditions is a reflection of the seriousness of their difficulties at home.

'Who would choose this sort of life?' she asks. 'Nobody.'

Muhammad, 27 (Somalia)

Muhammad is unsmiling and guarded, very troubled by the eighteen months he has been sleeping in Birmingham's parks. He came here in 2008, helped by an uncle who bought him a plane ticket to Heathrow, where he was immediately arrested. He claimed asylum, giving details of the murder of both his parents in 2006, shot dead by al-Shabab militants as they were minding their vegetable stall in the village market. The gunmen were raiding the stalls; when his parents tried to protect their stock of bananas and tomatoes, they were killed. His claim for asylum was refused eighteen months ago. Shortly afterwards, he had to hand over the keys to the hostel where he was staying; that was the last time he had a shower or slept in a bed. He hopes to appeal against the decision but has not yet managed to put together a new case.

Everything he owns he carries in his backpack—one shirt, one sheet, one T-shirt, one pair of shorts, two heavy files of documents relating to his case, letters, photographs. He sleeps with his head on the bag to be sure it is never stolen. He doesn't have a sleeping bag, so he relies instead on old cardboard boxes as protection against the wind.

He speaks almost no English, but explains through the translator that he has learned to understand 'Move' and 'Back home' from the refuse collectors who sometimes find him still asleep by the hedge or at the edge of the outdoors baseball court, where he usually spends the night. Sometimes some west Africans sleep there too, but he can't speak to them, because they have no common language. He admits he has become very lonely. Another Somalian whom he met occasionally at the Red Cross recently disappeared, leaving his cardboard boxes behind. Muhammad wonders if he was taken to a detention centre but is not sure.

With his Morrison's vouchers, he has bought a pot of Nutella (£1.21), a long baguette (60p) and a bottle of Highland Spring water (78p), because he has no access to a tap. He will cut the baguette into small sections, and that way it should last for three days, when he will return and spend the second £5 voucher.

'My ambition is to live in peace. My ambition is to get peace. I would like to work and contribute to the community where I live, which I cannot do now. There is no peace in Somalia.'

He is not optimistic that an appeal to the Home Office would succeed. 'The last letter they sent me, they said I should go back to Somalia. I will be killed in Somalia.'

All names have been changed.

•This article was amended on 16 June 2010. The word *straitened* was misspelt in the original. This has now been corrected.

Any of the other falsehoods which are mouthed about refugees and migrants.

The reality is that these people are caught in a perverse catch-22 and the rest of society would rather look away.

I was told by someone the other day that in Coventry there is one tower block where all the asylum seekers live (presumably this is before they become 'failed' asylum seekers and have support removed). Apparently, they only get to live somewhere for a short time before being moved somewhere else, the implication being that the authorities do not want them to develop any kind of community roots or relationships.

That is so wrong on so many different levels.

INDEX

The letter *t* following a page number denotes a table.